Ellis Island Nation

ELLIS ISLAND NATION

Immigration Policy
and American Identity
in the Twentieth Century

ROBERT L. FLEEGLER

PENN

UNIVERSITY OF PENNSYLVANIA PRESS

PHILADELPHIA

A Haney Foundation Book

Published by
University of Pennsylvania Press
Philadelphia, Pennsylvania 19104-4112
www.upenn.edu/pennpress

Printed in the United States of America
on acid-free paper
10 9 8 7 6 5 4 3 2 1

Library of Congress Cataloging-in-Publication Data

Fleegler, Robert L.
   Ellis Island nation : immigration policy and American
identity in the twentieth century / Robert L. Fleegler. —
1st ed.
       p.   cm. — (Haney Foundation series)
   Includes bibliographical references and index.
   ISBN 978-0-8122-4509-7 (hardcover : alk. paper)
   1. United States—Emigration and immigration.—
Government policy—20th century.   2. United States—
Emigration and immigration—20th century.   3. Immigrants
—United States—History—20th century.   4. Acculturation
—United States—History—20th century.   5. Multicultural-
ism—United States—History—20th century.   I. Title.
II. Series: Haney Foundation series.
JV6455.F59   2013
325.73—dc23   2012031343

Contents

Introduction

In the first decade of the twenty-first century, Americans across the political spectrum have fiercely debated the costs and benefits of immigration. Lou Dobbs, Pat Buchanan, and others have declared that the recent wave of "new" migrants from Latin America and Asia are not assimilating into American culture. By contrast, they praise the eastern and southern European immigrants who came through Ellis Island in the early twentieth century, suggesting that those newcomers eagerly embraced American traditions. Indeed, politicians and intellectuals of all ideological stripes now routinely refer to the United States as a "nation of immigrants," which includes Jews, Italians, and others who arrived at the turn of the century. In 1998, for instance, President Bill Clinton discussed the value of immigration in a commencement address at Portland State University: "More than any other nation on Earth, America has constantly drawn strength and spirit from wave after wave of immigrants. In each generation, they have proved to be the most restless, the most adventurous, the most innovative, the most industrious of people." He added, "Bearing different memories, honoring different heritages, they have strengthened our economy, enriched our culture, renewed our promise of freedom and opportunity for all."[1] Such proclamations are repeated so often and so frequently by politicians from both sides of the aisle that they have almost become banal.

It was not always this way. In the first quarter of the twentieth century, the country was similarly divided by debates over the costs and benefits of that era's "new" immigration. Between the 1880s and early 1920s, America's immigrant population shifted from so-called "old" immigrant stock of northern and western Europeans to predominantly Jewish and Catholic arrivals from southern and eastern Europe. At the time, many insisted that these groups weakened the country and could not be assimilated into American culture. To stem the rising tides of undesirables entering the country, Congress passed the Immigration Act of 1924, which placed strict quotas on immigrants, particularly those from southern and eastern Europe.

By 1965, when the next major immigration law was passed, these very same immigrants and their descendants had become accepted as part of the "nation of immigrants." The Immigration Act of 1965 abandoned national quotas and replaced them with limits on each hemisphere, welcoming newcomers on a first-come, first-serve basis with family ties and, to a lesser extent, job skills as the primary criteria. This dramatic change in attitudes toward southern and eastern European immigrants between 1924 and 1965 reflected policymakers' and intellectuals' changed understanding of the role these newcomers played in American culture, politics, and the economy. This new ideology, which I call "contributionism," shaped Americans' beliefs about both immigration and the contours of American national identity. Contributionism emphasized that the United States was enhanced by the ideas and skills brought by eastern and southern European immigrants and expanded the definition of American identity to include this generation of former undesirables.

The contributionist ideology suggested that recent immigrants brought important cultural and economic benefits to the country and strengthened the nation. Those expressing this view repeatedly suggested that the U.S. was enhanced by the presence of the Ellis Island immigrants. They did not demand that immigrants completely abandon their traditional cultures, as nativists did in the period before 1924. They also did not suggest that immigrants maintain their native culture, as a few progressive thinkers recommended throughout this period. Instead, they stressed that the varied cultural and economic assets brought by the immigrants enhanced American culture and paved the way for its economic growth. They viewed immigrants as supplementing the existing culture as well as influencing it in a beneficial direction. Finally, they believed that the newcomers must adopt certain American norms.

It took time for the contributionist vision to gain acceptance between 1924 and 1965. Resistance to the "new" immigrants remained strong in the 1920s and 1930s, as some nativists never changed their view of the recent migrants. Even among those sympathetic to the new arrivals, disputes raged over how to encourage their acceptance into American society. In the World War II-era, many thought that discussing the separate contributions of these groups only reinforced ethnic difference, which threatened the unity necessary to defeat Germany and Japan. As a result, some intellectuals and policymakers sought to diminish the differences between groups and accentuate what they had in common. They debated the contributions—as well as the potential dangers—of newcomers in a variety of forums, ranging from wartime propaganda, political debates, public celebrations, school textbooks, and Hollywood films.

It was during the 1950s and 1960s that the contributionist view gained widespread approval. The imperatives of the Cold War accelerated this process as many contrasted the ethnic and religious diversity of the United States with the uniformity of the Soviet Union. By the passage of comprehensive immigration reform in 1965, eastern and southern Europeans had been incorporated to a broader definition of American identity and were considered an integral part of the "nation of immigrants."

Of course, this broader definition of American nationhood did not encompass all ethnic and racial groups. As eastern and southern European immigrants entered the American mainstream, nativists increasingly focused on Asian and Latino immigrants as the major threat. By the 1950s and 1960s, restrictionist politicians became more and more concerned about these groups and their presumed inability to assimilate into American culture. Asians and Latinos, as well as African Americans, remained outside the "nation of immigrants" when reform was passed in 1965.

∽

Contributionism has deep roots in American history. Well before the immigration wave of 1882–1924, various thinkers discussed the shape of American nationality and how immigrants benefitted the national polity. In 1782, the French observer Hector St. John de Crevecoeur provided one of the earliest versions of the "nation of immigrants" paradigm. Various European nationalities, he wrote, were merging to form a new race of men in America: "They are a mixture of English, Scotch, Irish, French, Dutch, Germans, and Swedes. From this promiscuous breed that race now called Americans have arisen."[2] Crevecoeur added, "He is an American, who, leaving behind him all his old prejudices and manners, receives new ones from the new mode of life he has embraced, the new government he obeys, and the new rank he holds."[3]

This idea had great currency among American intellectuals during the nineteenth century. Herman Melville wrote of America, "Settled by the people of nations, all nations may claim her for their own. You can not spill a drop of American blood without spilling the blood of the whole world. . . . No: our blood is as the flood of the Amazon, made up of a thousand noble currents all pouring into one."[4] Ralph Waldo Emerson and Walt Whitman made similar comments, noted John Higham, a leading historian of American immigration, who added, "Out of such assumptions, Americans fashioned an image of themselves as an inclusive nationality, at once diverse and homogeneous, ever improving as it assimilated many types of men into a unified, superior people."[5] While a few states tried to regulate immigration in the nineteenth century, the federal government specified no restrictions on immigration during this time, despite a burst of nativist sentiment against Irish and German immigrants in the 1850s.

Starting in 1882, American policy broke with this general trend.[6] During the 1870s and 1880s, Irish immigrants in California, motivated by a combination of racism and economic fears, led the resistance to a growing Chinese presence on the West Coast. Chinese workers, they claimed, were often willing to accept very low wages and were undercutting their living standards. In response to this working-class anger, Congress passed the Chinese Exclusion Act in 1882. This act barred the immigration of Chinese laborers for ten years and was the first major piece of legislation restricting immigration.[7] Congress renewed the law on a regular basis until the 1940s. In addition, President Theodore Roosevelt negotiated the Gentlemen's Agreement of 1907–8, in which the U.S. and Japanese governments worked out a deal to bar Japanese immigration. These measures foreshadowed how Asian immigrants would remain outside the "nation of immigrants" throughout much of the twentieth century.

In the late nineteenth century, the nature of American immigration changed considerably. Increasingly, arrivals came from southern and eastern Europe, a shift from the earlier "old" immigrants from northwestern Europe. Economic modernization in southeastern Europe, which displaced farmers and workers from their traditional modes of production, along with the political repression of some groups, particularly Jews in the Russian Empire, precipitated this wave. Indeed, the total immigration from eastern and southern Europe grew from 900,000 in the 1880s to 1.9 million in the 1890s to 8 million in the first decade of the twentieth century.[8] The foreign-born share of the population doubled, from 7 percent in 1880 to 14 percent by 1920.[9] Many characteristics of the immigration between the 1880s and the passage of restrictive legislation in 1924 were different from the old. These "new" immigrants, as they came to be called, tended to be

Catholic or Jewish rather than Protestant, and many congregated in tightly knit urban ghettos such as the Lower East Side of New York City. By 1910, three-fourths of the population of major midwestern and eastern cities, including New York, Detroit, and Cleveland, were immigrants and their children.[10]

During this time, foes of large-scale immigration from southern and eastern Europe became increasingly vocal and organized. These restriction-ists largely rejected contributionism, declaring that the new immigrants weakened the nation, both economically and culturally. Some advocates for restriction relied on old American prejudices, such as anti-Catholicism, anti-Semitism, and anti-radicalism. Working-class supporters cited tradi-tional concerns about loss of employment and lower wages. Still others offered new notions of Anglo-Saxon racial superiority to make the case for narrowing the gates.[11]

American anti-Catholicism was deeply rooted in rivalries from Europe that could be traced back to the Reformation and the religious wars of the sixteenth and seventeenth centuries. Brought by early American colonists from the Old World, these ideas reemerged from time to time, most notably following the Irish Catholic migration during the 1840s and 1850s. The Catholic Church's support for monarchical and authoritarian regimes fur-ther disturbed Americans who saw their country as a beacon of liberty and democracy for the world. Many feared that Catholic immigrants were completely loyal to the pope's political agenda, endangering American lib-erties. Tom Watson, a prominent Georgia politician and former Populist leader, summed up the nativist case in 1914: "There is a foreign foe at our gates and that foe is confidently expecting the spies within to unlock the portals," adding that the "domestic traitors" included the "Roman Catholic priesthood."[12]

Anti-Semitism had equally deep roots in the Old World. The charge of deicide, namely, that the Jews were responsible for the death of Jesus Christ, haunted European Jewry, resulting in anti-Jewish acts ranging from bans against the ownership of land in some nations to pogroms in others. With the arrival of industrial capitalism in central and eastern Europe in the nineteenth century, Jews frequently became scapegoats for the difficulties of economic modernization. Though these prejudices existed in the United States, the American version of anti-Semitism tended to be weaker than the European strain, and usually manifested itself in social and employment discrimination. A minister in Baltimore in 1893 offered an extreme version of some anti-Semitic stereotypes, calling Jews "greedy, merciless, tricky, vengeful," adding that the Jew is "A veritable Shylock who loses every sentiment of humanity in his greed."[13]

Anti-radical sentiments could be dated to the French Revolution's descent into the Jacobin terror of the 1790s. At that time, many people feared that France and its American sympathizers would bring their ideology to the United States. President John Adams signed the Alien and Sedition Acts in 1798 to silence what he perceived to be the pro-French feeling in the Republican Party. Similar fears of radicalism emerged when German refugees from the Revolution of 1848 came to America. During the late nineteenth century, socialist and anarchist ideologies were becoming increasingly fashionable in Europe, arousing alarm that radical immigrants would disrupt the American way of life. Observing the frequent strikes that marked American life in the late nineteenth century, Reverend Theodore Munger expressed his dismay at "anarchism, lawlessness," declaring that "This horrible tyranny is wholly of foreign origin,—the plain and simple fruit of ignorance of American institutions."[14]

Believing that immigration lowered the living standards of union members, organized labor actively supported restriction. In 1909, Samuel Gompers, head of the largest umbrella of unions, the American Federation of Labor (AFL), outlined his rationale for limiting immigration, saying it subjected workers to "the ruinous competition of an unending stream of men freshly arriving from foreign lands who are accustomed to so low a grade of living of that they can underbid the wage earners established in this country and still save money." Gompers added that "Whole communities, in fact whole regions, have witnessed a rapid deterioration in the mode of living of their working classes consequent on the incoming of the swarms of lifelong poverty stricken aliens."[15]

In the late nineteenth and early twentieth centuries, scientific racism became yet another element in the restrictionist argument. Applying the theories of Charles Darwin, new scientific ideas provided intellectual respectability to the concept that a racial hierarchy existed, with native-stock, Anglo-Saxon Protestants at the top of the order, southern and eastern Europeans below them, and Asian Americans and African Americans on the bottom. Popular books such as Madison Grant's *The Passing of the Great Race* (1916) and Lothrop Stoddard's *The Rising Tide of Color* (1920) gave these views a wide airing. Grant and Stoddard believed biological differences were immutable and rejected the idea that environment was responsible for variations in the intellectual and physical prowess of different groups. Denouncing the supporters of immigration, Grant declared, "If the melting pot is allowed to boil without control . . . the type of native American of colonial descent will become as extinct as the Athenians of the age of Pericles, and the Vikings of the days of Rollo."[16]

Others fought against these theories. Born in Germany in 1858, Franz Boas became one of the leading anthropologists of the twentieth century. Once ensconced at Columbia University, he led efforts to discredit the racial theories that buttressed discrimination against minority groups. Motivated by his research and his own Jewish background, Boas fervently attacked this consensus throughout his professional career, contending that environment rather than genetics determined the intellectual achievements of the "new" immigrants. Boas's theories, however, would not gain widespread acceptance until the late 1930s.[17]

Using the arguments of Grant, Stoppard, and others, old-line Protestant organizations such as the American Protective Association and the Immigration Restriction League formed to lobby for immigration restriction between the 1890s and the outset of World War I. Labor unions, led by Gompers and the AFL, were also instrumental in such efforts. These groups faced significant obstacles to implementing their agenda before World War I. Opposition from American business, which sought a continuous supply of cheap labor, and from immigrant groups was politically powerful enough to stop these campaigns. For example, many restrictionists backed efforts to test whether new arrivals could read in their native language. They hoped a literacy test would significantly reduce the number of newcomers entering the country, particularly from southern and eastern Europe. Though Congress passed legislation that would have established a literacy test on several occasions, presidents Grover Cleveland, William Howard Taft, and Woodrow Wilson vetoed the legislation.

During this era of increased nativism, even those supportive of liberal immigration policies believed newcomers needed to abandon their Old World traditions and conform to Anglo-American ways in order to become truly "American." Theodore Roosevelt wrote that an immigrant "must revere only our flag; not only must it come first, but no other flag should even come second. He must learn to celebrate Washington's birthday rather than that of the queen or kaiser, and the Fourth of July instead of St. Patrick's Day."[18] In a speech at a naturalization ceremony in May 1915, Woodrow Wilson told new citizens that he "certainly would not be one even to

suggest that a man cease to love the country of his origin . . . but it is one
thing to love the place where you were born and it is another thing to
dedicate yourselves to the place to which you go." The president elaborated,
"You cannot dedicate yourself to America unless you become in every
respect and with every purpose of your will thorough Americans."[19]

Echoing a theme that was common in the first quarter of the twentieth
century, Wilson and TR both rejected any social or political organizing
along ethnic lines. The Rough Rider exclaimed, "We have no room in any
healthy American community for a German-American vote or an Irish-
American vote, and it is contemptible demagogy to put planks into any
party platform with the purpose of catching such a vote. We have no room
for any people who do not act and vote simply as Americans."[20] Concur-
ring, Wilson admonished newcomers that "America does not consist of
groups. A man who thinks of himself as belonging to a particular national
group has not yet become an American."[21] Wilson, however, did invoke
some aspects of the contributionist tradition, observing, "This country is
constantly drinking strength out of new sources by the voluntary association with it of great bodies of strong men and forward-looking women out
of other lands."[22]

To accomplish the ends sought by Wilson, TR, and others, proponents
of Americanization programs demanded that immigrants adopt American
norms.[23] These Americanization advocates came from various backgrounds
in business, academia, and conservative groups such as the Daughters of
the American Revolution (DAR). As World War I threatened to engulf the
U.S., the movement gained momentum as several states created Americanization programs that mandated teaching the English language and American history in public schools, as well as various other patriotic exercises.[24]
Business leaders such as Henry Ford often took part in these efforts because
they wanted employees schooled in American mores.[25] Ford created an
English school where his foreign-born workers learned their new language
as well as other American traditions. "Our great aim," a Ford spokesman
stated, "is to impress these men that they are, or should be, Americans, and
that former racial, national, and linguistic differences are to be forgotten."[26]

Contesting these trends, some intellectuals continued to welcome new
arrivals and held to more cosmopolitan ideas similar to those of Crevecoeur
and Melville. In his play The Melting Pot (1908), Israel Zangwill outlined
his vision of contributionism. The main story of the play is the relationship
between the Jewish protagonist, David, and his love interest, a Russian

Christian woman whose father had been responsible for the death of David's family in a pogrom in 1903. In the end, love conquers Old World rivalries and the two are married.

David, a musician, presents Zangwill's view of America as a fusion of races and nationalities that produce a new nation:

> Here you stand, good folk, think I, when I see them at Ellis Island, here you stand, in your fifty groups, with your fifty languages and histories, and your fifty blood hatreds and rivalries. But you won't be long like that, brothers for these are the fires of God you've come to— these are the fires of God. A fig for your feuds and vendettas! Germans and Frenchmen, Irishmen and Englishmen, Jews and Russians— into the crucible with you all! God is making the American.[27]

In Zangwill's world, much like Crèvecoeur's and Melville's, immigrants to America formed a new race that was the sum of their cultural contributions. David says at the end of the play, "Yes, East and West, and North and South, the palm and the pine, the pole and the equator, the crescent and the cross—how the great Alchemist melts and fuses them with his purging flame."[28]

The Melting Pot drew diverse reactions at the time. To many immigrants, the melting pot demanded they discard any traces of their native culture. Jewish groups were disturbed that the play celebrated intermarriage, a dramatic break with tradition. *The Melting Pot* also offended nativists, many of whom believed that assimilation was impossible and immigration needed to be sharply curtailed.[29] Zangwill, however, departed from more extreme forms of assimilation by suggesting that the immigrants' contributions would merge to form a new culture. He did not suggest that immigrants completely dispose of their traditions to adapt to Anglo norms.[30]

Americans debated the meaning of the "melting pot" over the following decades. To some, it would be a synonym for complete assimilation to white Protestant norms. Students at Henry Ford's English school displayed this version of the melting pot when one group wearing traditional garb entered the pot and another group exited wearing identical American clothes.[31] Others believed that the melting pot suggested an image of American identity where immigrants fused to create a new people that was a melding of different traditions. Historian David Hollinger later described how a contributionist interpretation of the melting pot changed over time: "As it was first construed in the early twentieth century, the melting pot . . . served to transform not only the immigrants, but everyone, including Mayflower descendants, who were to be improved through a dynamic mixing of immigrants." He added, "This notion of 'melting' was consistent with the ideas Crevecoeur, Emerson, and Melville had articulated much earlier. Yet in Zangwill's time this figure of speech had become associated with an antithetical, conformist impulse to melt down the peculiarities of immigrants."[32]

Randolph Bourne, a young radical, broke with the melting pot ideology in his 1916 essay, "Trans-National America." Instead, he stressed the immigrant origins of all Americans. "We are all foreign-born or the descendants of foreign-born," he insisted, "and if distinctions are to be made between us they should rightly be on some other ground than indigenousness." Emphasizing that the early American colonists had come to the New World for a variety of reasons, he argued that they did not intend "to be assimilated in an American melting pot. They did not come to adopt the culture of the American Indian."[33] He believed the diverse cultures of the new immigrants strengthened the nation, declaring, "What we emphatically do not want is that these distinctive qualities should be washed out into a tasteless, colorless fluid of uniformity." The least-developed part of the country, the South, he observed, was the region with the fewest immigrants. Indeed, Bourne feared that immigrants would assimilate and adopt Anglo-Saxon norms: "It is not the Jew who sticks proudly to the faith of his fathers and boasts of that venerable culture of his who is dangerous to America, but the Jew who has lost the Jewish fire and become an elementary, grasping animal."[34]

Bourne's vision of contributionism led him to a conception of American nationality that differed from Zangwill's. Like Zangwill, he believed the many ethnic and religious groups that made up America were a cultural asset. But he did not think these groups should merge to form a new culture. Rather, he said, "it is apparently our lot rather to be a federation of cultures." He urged Americans to accept the idea of dual citizenship and the continual movement of immigrants between the United States and their native lands. "America is coming to be, not a nationality, but a transnationality," declared Bourne, "a weaving back and forth, with the other lands, of many threads and colors."[35]

Horace Kallen, a German Jewish professor at the University of Wisconsin, also viewed Zangwill's melting pot as a conformist ideology and offered his own vision of "cultural pluralism." In a famous essay in *The Nation* in 1915, "Democracy vs. the Melting Pot," Kallen criticized nativists who believed immigrants weakened America by maintaining their traditional ways. On the contrary, Kallen said cultural heterogeneity and diversity were sources of national strength. Discussing the cultural attributes of the Polish American community, he declared, "Their aspiration, impersonal, and disinterested, as it must be in America, to free Poland, to conserve the Polish spirit, is the most hopeful and American thing about them."[36] He added, "The same thing is true for the Bohemians, 17,000 of them workingmen in Chicago, paying a proportion of their wage to maintain schools in the Bohemian tongue and free thought; the same is true of many other groups."

In Kallen's mind, the melting pot meant the destruction of immigrant culture. Instead, he wanted America to become "a great republic consisting of a federation or commonwealth of nationalities," where different groups would preserve their traditions. In Kallen's vision of contributionism, the proper analogy was not the melting pot but an orchestra, where "every type of instrument has its specific timbre and tonality, founded in its substance and form; as every type has its appropriate theme and melody in the whole symphony so in society each ethnic group is the natural instrument," adding that "its spirit and culture are its theme and melody, and the harmony and dissonances and discords of them all make the symphony of civilization."[37]

American entrance into World War I pushed the general climate of opinion toward restriction and away from the melting pot, as well as from the identity politics of Bourne and Kallen. The hyperpatriotic atmosphere generated by the conflict caused many Americans to doubt the loyalties of the country's foreign-born citizens. In particular, German Americans faced intense hostility. Government and private groups accelerated their Americanization initiatives, promoting measures to insure that immigrants learned English so they could work in factories and serve in the army. The head of the U.S. Bureau of Education, which was extremely active in this effort, observed, "Since the beginning of the war, the increasing importance of Americanization as a war measure has been more and more brought to the front. Anti-American influences are working upon the vast un-Americanized population residing in this country."[38] Buoyed by this sentiment, restrictionists achieved their first major victory since the Chinese Exclusion Act of 1882, when Congress overrode Wilson's veto of the literacy test in 1917. The bill also created a "barred Asiatic zone" that excluded virtually all Asians.

Anti-immigration sentiment remained strong following the war. Patriotic societies such as the American Legion joined the fight for restriction. The Bolshevik Revolution in October 1917, the strike wave of 1919, and the ensuing First Red Scare reinforced the nation's fear of radical newcomers. Many Americans feared Europeans fleeing the chaos of the postwar world would flood the country. Reflecting this sentiment, Madison Grant exclaimed, "When the Bolshevists of Russia are overthrown, which is only a question of time, there will be a great massacre of Jews and I suppose we will get the overflow unless we can stop it."[39] The war also temporarily halted immigration from Europe and forced the business community to search for a new source of less-skilled labor. A large black migration to the North followed, reducing business dependence on immigrant labor and muting their traditional opposition to restriction.

In 1921, Congress enacted a measure that, for the first time in U.S. history, placed a limit on total immigration. Set to expire after three years, the bill created quotas for each country equal to 3 percent of its share of the U.S. population in the 1910 census, thereby reducing immigration from southern and eastern Europe. The temporary nature of the legislation set the stage for a historic battle over immigration restriction in 1924. The various bills, using a wide range of scientific and demographic arguments, were designed to reduce the number of "new" immigrants and prompted heated debates over the role of immigrants in American life.

༄

Starting with this debate, this book explores the fate of the arguments of Zangwill, Kallen, and Bourne by following the discussions of policymakers and intellectuals in congressional debates, public celebrations, films, and school textbooks. Contributionism, which had fallen out favor around the turn of the century, gradually gained strength between 1924 and 1965. While it featured elements of the early twentieth-century ideologies, it did not completely replicate any of them. Contributionism emphasized that the cultural and economic assets of immigrants enriched America by celebrating the unique benefits of immigrants' native cultures to American life. At the same time, however, contributionists frequently assumed that immigrants would lose some of the very distinctions that set them apart as their talents and skills were incorporated into the American nation.

The decades between 1924 and 1965 witnessed a significant improvement in attitudes toward these immigrants and a gradual push for immigration reforms that would benefit them. While I do not argue that the rise of contributionism was solely responsible for these changes, it was a crucial factor in fostering a greater tolerance toward these newcomers and their descendants. Understanding the emergence of contributionism in American culture and politics helps us better understand the change in America's policy toward immigrants and the greater inclusiveness of American national identity in the second half of the twentieth century.

The prevailing narrative of America's growing acceptance of southern and eastern European immigrants typically emphasizes the replacement of the nativism of the 1920s by cultural universalism during the World War II era.[40] That is, by the 1940s, the intellectual message diminished the differences between groups and emphasized that eastern and southern European immigrants were acceptable because they were little different from native-stock Americans. This ideology helped to bring these groups closer to the American mainstream, but did so by neglecting the varied cultures brought by ethnic groups. Postwar Hollywood films like *Gentlemen's Agreement* (1947) and *Crossfire* (1947), which addressed issues of religious and ethnic bigotry, reiterated that all Americans, regardless of background, remained fundamentally the same. In *Gentlemen's Agreement*, Gregory Peck's character, Phil Green, espoused this view while rejecting anti-Semitism: "There are lots of different churches. The people who go to that particular church are called Catholics. Then there are people who go to other churches and they're called Protestants. And there are others who go to still different churches and they're called Jews. Only they call their kind of churches synagogues or temples."[41]

Then, the story goes, the identity politics and ethnic particularism of the late 1960s and 1970s displaced this vision when the "white ethnic revival" stressed how different the cultural backgrounds of the European immigrants were from the country's Anglo-Saxon founders. In this time, many rejected the assimilationist ethos of the postwar era and emphasized the need to maintain their traditional, non-WASP culture. Michael Novak, one of the leading proponents of this philosophy, outlined this view in this book, *The Rise of the Unmeltable Ethnics* (1971). "Whereas the Anglo-Saxon model appears to be a system of atomic individuals and high mobility, our model has tended to stress communities of our own, attachment to family, stability, and roots," wrote Novak. He added, "The melting pot is a kind of a homogenized soup, and its mores only partly appeal to ethnics: to some, yes, to others, no."[42]

Recent scholarship has supplemented this discussion. Some have suggested that the roots of this change can be found in the interwar period, when various groups promoted the "cultural gifts" of the "new" immigrants or alternatively, emphasized their similarities.[43] Others stress how immigrants themselves shaped the process of Americanization during this time.[44] This book will show how the contributionist ideology replaced the universalism of the war years, laying the groundwork for the "nation of immigrants" paradigm which predominated during the post-1965 period.[45] Contributionism suggested that immigrants strengthened the American culture and economy while also adapting to a basic set of norms.[46] Furthermore, this philosophy stressed the unique cultural contributions of European immigrants without emphasizing difference in the same way as proponents of the "white ethnic revival" in the 1970s or advocates of multiculturalism in the 1980s and 1990s. This exchange between Eva Marie Saint and Paul Newman in *Exodus* (1960) illustrates the difference between traditional universalism and contributionism. Saint's character, sounding much like Gregory Peck's Phil Green in *Gentlemen's Agreement*, tells Newman, "All these differences between people are made up. People are the same no matter what they're called." Newman's character responds skeptically, "Don't ever believe it. People are different. They have a right to be different. They like to be different." Reflecting the growing prominence of contributionism, he concludes, "It's no good pretending that differences don't exist. They do. They have to be recognized and respected."[47]

Contributionism suggested that the varied heritages of immigrants strengthened the nation, breaking from the wartime message that recent immigrants were acceptable because they were little different than other Americans. It also departed from the identity politics of the 1970s and 1980s because it did not urge the wholesale retention of traditions.

Over the past few decades, historians have also spent a great deal of time analyzing how these immigrants become seen as "white" Americans. Matthew Jacobson, David Roediger, Matt Guterl, and other scholars of "whiteness" have thoroughly examined this process. In the late nineteenth and early twentieth centuries, these scholars argue, many native-stock Americans did not view the new immigrants as "white" because of the prevailing scientific racism of the period and its concomitant racial classifications. Over time, the decline of scientific racism, the black migration to the North, as well as a series of federal policies, allowed the immigrants to develop a truly "white" identity by the middle of the twentieth century. This inclusion, they argue, came in part because these groups distanced themselves from African Americans.[48]

This book seeks to answer a different—but related—question. How did a significant number of Americans begin to see the cultural and economic contributions of eastern and southern European immigrants as assets that strengthened the nation? Rather than focusing on the racial identification of new immigrants, I consider other factors that also allowed these immigrants to be considered integral to American national identity. While their acceptance in the mantle of whiteness was certainly important to their inclusion in the nation of immigrants, race was not the only issue. When Congress passed immigration restriction in 1924, eastern and southern European immigrants were largely outside the American mainstream. Most observers believed that they could not be culturally assimilated into the nation's culture and that they were a drain on the American economy. By the mid-1960s, views on these kinds of immigrants had shifted considerably. More and more Americans saw the eastern and southern European immigrants and their descendants as an essential part of the "nation of immigrants" and instrumental in creating the contemporary American economy and culture. This vision expanded the definition of American identity, while still excluding Latino and Asian Americans.

By analyzing textbooks, public celebrations, policy and political debates, popular culture, and the writings of a variety of public figures and intellectuals, I chart the gradual growth of contributionism between the 1924 and 1965 immigration acts. I show how the idea of the "nation of immigrants" became such a central aspect of American national identity, as well as the ways it continued to exclude Asians, Latinos, and African Americans. I begin by considering the initial successes of contributionism in the 1930s, which were spurred by the need to contrast the U.S. with totalitarian regimes. At this time, two approaches to handling issues of ethnic and religious diversity emerged. Some policymakers wanted to emphasize contributionism while others stressed that this message would only exacerbate ethnic divisions. They recommended that any programs promote a more universal message that stressed what different groups had in common as well as the need for greater tolerance toward religious and ethnic minorities.

Contributionism moved into the foreground during World War II and the immediate postwar period in favor of the tolerance message. At this time, policymakers believed an approach that delineated the gifts immigrants brought to the United States would weaken national unity during a time of war. While the war accelerated the acceptance of these groups, support for the national origins system remained strong. Contributionism slowly gained prominence during the 1950s as the Cold War became a major part of American life, and as restrictionists became more concerned about nonwhite immigration from Latin America and Asia. The triumph of contributionism came with the passage of the Hart-Celler Act in 1965, which eliminated the national origins system Congress put in place in 1924.

The passage of the Immigration Act of 1965 was relatively unheralded at the time, but it signified the emergence of a broader conception of American identity and a "nation of immigrants" that included southern and eastern Europeans. The grandchildren of the Ellis Island immigrants who were once so despised had achieved a new level of acceptance. There were important limits to the "nation of immigrants," as this more inclusive version of American identity did not encompass Asians and Latinos, who were about to start the third major wave of immigration to the United States.

Chapter 1

The Beginning of the Era of Restriction

During the debate over immigration restriction in 1924, Representative Samuel McReynolds (D) of Tennessee declared, "This country can no longer be the melting pot for foreign nations. There was a time when that could be done, when conditions were different, but this time has long since passed." Senator Arthur Capper (R) of Kansas, like many of McReynolds's colleagues, echoed this concern, saying, "the experience of the last quarter century warns us that the capacity of the 'melting pot' is sadly over taxed, and that the fusing has all but ceased."[1] These comments summarized congressional thinking concerning the nation's ability to assimilate immigrants from southern and eastern Europe in the 1920s. Believing that the newcomers who had arrived since the 1880s could not be integrated into American culture, many demanded that the open door to immigration be closed. Passage of the Johnson-Reed Act of 1924, which dramatically restricted immigration from southern and eastern Europe and Asia, demonstrated that this philosophy had become part of American law.

Only a few objected to the view outlined by restrictionists such as McReynolds and Capper. Even those who tried to "Americanize" the newcomers thought that the "new" immigrants needed virtually to abandon their native culture to assimilate. Some congressmen from the immigrant-heavy cities in the Northeast and Midwest, as well as a few intellectuals and ethnic organizations, dissented from the consensus and praised immigrants from southern and eastern Europe in contributionist terms, arguing that they strengthened the American economy and culture. At the same time, all sides used contributionist language with regard to the Irish and German Americans whose ancestors had arrived in the mid-nineteenth century. While the 1924 immigration law expanded the "nation of immigrants" to include Irish and German Americans, the Ellis Island immigrants remained

excluded throughout the 1920s. Asians and Latinos lay even farther outside
its boundaries.

∾

During and immediately after World War I, government and private
agencies supported efforts to "Americanize" recent immigrants. Various
organizations designed programs to ensure that immigrants learned English
and understood American traditions. Seeking to make English the de facto
official language of the country, the Department of the Interior, through
the Americanization section of its Bureau of Education, urged immigrants
to take night school classes and suggested employers teach the language
in their factories.[2] Summarizing the primary aims of the Americanizers,
Philander Claxton, commissioner of education, instructed immigrants to
"learn the English language and study about the United States. You should
study its geography and the location of its states and cities, its history and
lives of its great men, its industries and varied business activities, its institutions and the purposes for which they were created, and above all, its
government."[3]

Americanizers also sought to ensure loyalty among the recent arrivals.
Concerned about the ties immigrants maintained to their countries of
origin, a wide range of individuals, groups, and organizations expressed
grave concerns about potential subversion in immigrant communities
during World War I. These fears persisted following the conflict as the
Syracuse Americanization League declared its intention "to combat anti-
Americanization propaganda activities and schemes and to stamp out
sedition and disloyalty wherever found."[4]

Though the advocates of these programs broke with the most extreme
restrictionists by suggesting that recent newcomers could be assimilated,
they took a one-sided view of this transition. In their minds, immigrants
must abandon virtually all of their previous traditions to adapt to American
culture. Consequently, Americanization programs featured little discussion
of how immigrants benefited and reshaped the United States. According to
one pamphlet written by a Massachusetts group, Americanization meant
learning "a common language, common governmental, social and economic ideals and a common relationship of the aims of the United States
in and after the War."[5] Echoing this view, the Syracuse Americanization

League advocated the abolition of "racial prejudices, barriers, discrimina-
tions and immigrant colonies and sections which keep people in America
apart; to maintain an American standard of living through the proper use
of American foods."[6]

These efforts continued into the early 1920s and followed a similar narrow definition of assimilation. For example, the U.S. Army, under the aus-
pices of the American Legion, worked to incorporate foreign-born soldiers
into American society under a program called "Americans All." This initiative taught recent immigrants English, American history, and civics and
saw little place for contributionism. "In this school," program materials
noted, "racial distinctions disappear almost over night—they are all
Americans. . . . Every day, all day, the men live and work in an American
atmosphere"[7]

While most educational programs did not pay respect to immigrant
culture, one exception featured elements of contributionism. The Chicago
Citizens' Committee, which was composed of community leaders, wanted
to hold an "All-American Exposition" in 1919 to improve relations among
all citizens.[8] In particular, the organizers wanted "to win for foreign-born
citizens of the United States from their fellow-citizens of longer standing
recognition and appreciation of their service to this nation through their
great contribution to the upbuilding of this country and its institutions."[9]

To achieve this goal, the exposition displayed a number of exhibits that
would promote the accomplishments of different immigrants. Each ethnic
group would have its own day to display its cultural material, though only
naturalized citizens would be allowed to participate. The exposition would
include "exhibits of works of arts created by Americans of foreign birth and
of the arts and crafts that may be a part of our own culture by giving
protection and encouragement to those who have brought with them from
other lands the knowledge and skill to create these things."[10]

The organizers understood that the All-American Exposition represented a departure from previous efforts to incorporate immigrants.
According to the group's internal documents, "No work similar to this in
principle has been done hitherto; it constitutes a reversal of the customary
attitude toward the foreign-born."[11] Nevertheless, the Bureau of Education
approved of the exposition and considered using it as a model for the other
large cities. "Our own native born people must widen their sympathies if
they ever expect to assimilate these people," declared Fred Butler, head of
the Americanization Division, "They now form the great part of the labor

in all our great industries yet we have not considered it worthwhile to make Americans of them."[12]

Despite the more inclusive message, not every group appeared to be welcome, as controversy emerged regarding German American involvement in the exposition. Organizers planned to set aside a day for German Americans, just as they did for other ethnic groups. On this day, among a series of events, German American singers would perform "American" songs.[13]

Coming less than a year after the end of World War I, one participant balked, exclaiming, "German day? Count me out." In response, one of the organizers defended their involvement in the exposition, arguing that German Americans had made a vital contribution to the war effort. While this response seemed to suggest that wartime passions were fading, the planners officially changed German day to Army day, though German Americans were still allowed to perform the same songs.[14]

As a commercial enterprise, the All-American Exposition was unsuccessful. Local employers did not provide enough money to support the venture and native-born citizens did not attend in significant numbers. Some suggested that the end of the war had diminished interest in the program, which barely had enough money to complete its run as creditors demanded payment.[15] While bemoaning the failure of the event to stimulate interest, a representative of the Department of the Interior praised the spirit of the show, remarking that "the attempt to bring the foreign born and the native born citizens into closer touch, to bring about full public sympathy and understanding between the various peoples of Chicago, is worthy of the highest recommendation."[16]

While the All-American Exposition may not have been typical of post-World War I Americanization campaigns, its tactics would be emulated throughout the late 1930s and early 1940s. Government and private agencies would promote contributionism through a series of events using similar techniques, sponsoring festivals where each immigrant group displayed its culture in fairs, radio programs, and other forums.

∽

The same divisions could be observed during the 1924 congressional debate over immigration restriction, as the supporters of restriction espoused a conception of American identity that excluded eastern and southern European migrants. These representatives believed that these groups weakened the nation, both culturally and economically. Only a small minority disagreed and expressed the contributionist viewpoint.

Some congressmen espoused versions of the scientific racism of the time. "We have admitted the dregs of Europe until America has been orientalized, Europeanized, Africanized, and mongrelized," announced Representative John Tillman (D) of Arkansas, "to that insidious degree that our genius, stability, and greatness, and promise of advancement, and achievement are actually menaced." Representative Ira Hersey (R) of Maine concurred: "We have thrown open wide our gates and through them have come other alien races, of alien blood, from Asia and southern Europe, the Malay, the Mongolian, the oriental with their strange and pagan rites, their babble of tongues."[17]

Others invoked concepts of racial superiority in a slightly more subtle fashion, declaring that northern and western Europeans were solely responsible for the achievements of the United States. Representative William Vaile (R) of Colorado declared, "What we do claim is that the northern Europeans and particularly Anglo-Saxons, made this country." Earl Michener (R) of Michigan agreed: "The Nordic people laid the foundations of society in America. They have builded this Republic, and nothing would be more unfair to them and their descendants than to turn over this Government and this land to those who had so little part in making us what we are."[18]

Representative Charles Stengle (D) of New York reiterated the concerns of McReynolds and Capper: "The fire has apparently gone out under the melting pot and the original American stock is not absorbing these insoluble elements."[19] What evidence was there that the melting pot had failed? To the restrictionists, the mere existence of ethnic communities in the major eastern and midwestern cities was proof enough. To many congressmen, particularly those from the South and the West, any residue of an immigrant's native traditions proved they had not assimilated into American culture. Restrictionists often cited the proliferation of foreign language newspapers and magazines as evidence of the melting pot's failure. "One thousand four hundred foreign language newspapers, printed in 40 different languages," declared Capper, "foster the alien racial solidarity of these groups and set up barriers against Americanization by encouraging and perpetuating foreign customs and alien prejudices."[20]

Restrictionists also feared that the large concentration of "new" immigrants would eventually be able to outvote native-born citizens. Representative Jasper Tincher (R) of Kansas presented this argument in its most extreme form: "On the one side is beer, Bolshevism, unassimilating settlements, and perhaps many flags. On the other side is constitutional government; one flag, the Stars and Stripes; America, 'a government of, by, and for the people'; America, our country."[21] Immigrant political power particularly concerned the staunch restrictionists because they were convinced that the new arrivals were disloyal. Vaile even questioned the allegiances of his congressional colleagues: "Now of course the 9 percent of the population of crowded New York City which sent our friends, Mr. Sullivan and Mr. Dickstein, to Congress are Americans, and I am sure they are good Americans. But they have the interests of other countries in mind."[22]

To the restrictionist, any remaining affection on the part of immigrants for their compatriots or display of ethnic solidarity was simply evidence of a lack of patriotism. The restrictionists were particularly disturbed by the presence of ethnic organizations such as the Sons of Italy. Representative James Taylor (R) praised the willingness of the small number of immigrants in his native Tennessee to completely abandon Old World ties: "Our foreign born immediately and in good faith renounces his allegiance to the fatherland; he learns our language, adopts our customs, sends his children to our public schools."[23]

Outside Congress, some interest groups sympathized with the restrictionists. American Federation of Labor (AFL) president Samuel Gompers, like Taylor, questioned the patriotism of recent arrivals who opposed new limits, suggesting they were behaving "not as Americans, but as aliens, loyal only to the country of their birth." "The plain truth," the aging labor leader added, "is that the attitude of a large number of racial groups in the United States toward restrictive immigration furnishes the best and most complete reason for the absolute necessity for restrictive legislation." Gompers also expressed his concern that the continuing migration of relatively less-educated workers undermined the living standards of American workers. Certain employers, he alleged, wanted to hire people "at the lowest possible wages and who prefer a rapidly revolving labor supply at low wages to a regular supply of American wage earners at fair wages."[24]

Some in the African American community seemed to share Gompers's concerns about the economic impact of immigration. No blacks served in the Congress in 1924, but the *Chicago Defender*, the leading black newspaper of the period, with a circulation extending well beyond the Second City, endorsed restriction after its passage.[25] In an editorial titled "Immigration Law Is Help to Our Race," the *Defender* explained that a liberal immigration law policy "would result in the mills and factories of the North becoming flooded with foreign labor and the first person to suffer would be the Negro."[26] While some blacks were concerned about the scientific racism that underpinned restriction, W. E. B. Du Bois wrote that "despite the inhumanity of this [immigration law], American Negroes are silently elated at this policy," because "with the cutting down of foreign immigration the Negro becomes the best source of cheap labor for the industries of the white land."[27]

A small group of representatives from the Northeast and the Midwest, particularly from districts with large percentages of the new immigrants, responded to the various charges. Challenging the scientific notions of racial superiority, Representative Patrick O'Sullivan (D) of Connecticut explained that "in the background of this doctrine of the inferiority of the southern European a rather extraordinary fiction is built relating to a race known as the Nordic, which appears to have been quite overlooked by the anthropologists until recently." He listed the cultural accomplishments of Italians and Jews, two of the principal targets of the legislation. "Friends, let us not prate about racial superiority," remarked Representative Charles Mooney (D) of Cleveland, Ohio. "It is only the outgrowth of egotism. . . . It is a stupid and ungodly notion, this idea of superiority."[28]

These congressmen went to great lengths to convince their colleagues that immigrants made the country stronger, both economically and culturally. "These 'foreigners' and 'aliens' are the very people who have helped build America," declared Representative Ole Kvale (D) of Minnesota, "on farm, in shop and factory." Stanley Kunz (D) of Chicago, Illinois, observed, "Our most developed industrial States are those which have had the largest immigration. Our most backward States, industrially, are those which have had no immigration to speak of."[29]

Signifying their incorporation into the "nation of immigrants," the proposed legislation provided large quotas for emigrants from Ireland and, in spite of the tensions of the World War I period, Germany. In light of these provisions, opponents contended that an earlier generation of restrictionists had leveled similar charges against Irish and German newcomers, only to be disproved by experience. Representative Emanuel Celler (D) of New York City retorted, "Just so, in 1840, 1850, and 1860 you did not want the 'beery Germans' and the 'dirty Irish.' The Germans and Irish were mongrels, self-seekers, disreputable, and would not assimilate. We now know how good a citizenry they have become."[30]

Celler, the grandson of German Jewish immigrants, typified the kind of urban liberal legislator who opposed restriction in 1924. Representing a Brooklyn district with a large population of new arrivals, he played an important role as an outspoken freshman backbencher during the fight over Johnson-Reed. Over the next four decades, he would emerge as a central figure in every major debate over immigration, becoming the congressional leader in the battle for a more liberal immigration policy.

The foes of restriction rejected the charge that recent immigrants were disloyal. Representative Meyer Jacobstein (D) of Rochester, New York, cited their military service: "they fought loyally and valiantly in every war for the creation and the preservation of this Union. The splendid service of the foreign born in the recent World War established that beyond question." Adolph Sabath (D) of Chicago concurred, "Unfortunately, some of the Members are sometimes under the impression that because people who are born here have foreign names, that they are foreigners. That is not true."[31]

They also defended the institutions of immigrant life that the restrictionists detested. Speaking of the foreign language press, Nathan Perlman (R) of New York City declared, "Some gentlemen talked about foreign-language newspapers, and some said that it is a crime to publish foreign language papers. . . . The foreign language newspapers have contributed a great deal to Americanization work." They countered the accusation that it was unpatriotic for recent immigrants to oppose the immigration bill. Frank Oliver (D) of New York City elaborated, "They protest not because they are un-American but because they refuse to believe that the people of the United States, who have profited by their loyalty to America in peace and war, should now condemn them on the ground that they are inferior in quality and unfit for citizenship.[32]

While most restrictionists were concerned with limiting immigration from eastern and southern Europe, some Western congressman focused on Japanese immigration. They insisted on barring all Asians, inserting language that would ban any aliens from entering the country if they were ineligible for citizenship. Recent court decisions, most notably, *Ozawa v. United States* (1922) and *United States v. Thind* (1923) upheld the legal notion that Asians could not become American citizens, unless they had been born in the United States.[33]

Some congressmen resented the economic success of the Japanese in agriculture, fishing, and other industries along the West Coast. Representative James MacLafferty (R) of California declared, "Go into the State of California to-day and I will show you whole sections given over to the Japanese." Arthur Free (R) of California alleged that the Japanese men worked long hours that "would break down the health of any white person" and forced their wives and children into difficult employment to assist them. He added, "The people of the West contend that no more should be admitted, as, first, it is impossible for white people economically to compete with people of that sort."[34]

Racial concerns also emerged during the debate over the Japanese, and some restrictionists seemed more disturbed by the presence of Asians in America than that of eastern Europeans. Using language similar to the proponents of Jim Crow, Free alleged that intermarriage between whites and Asians posed a grave threat to the nation: "Marriage between the yellow and white races is impossible to consider, would tend to lower the standard of both races, and create a lot of poor individuals hated by the Japanese and not accepted by the people of the United States."[35]

Those congressmen who defended southern and eastern Europeans made little attempt to protect the Japanese. Only Fiorello LaGuardia (R), future mayor of New York City, seemed to apply the contributionist argument to the Japanese, suggesting to MacLafferty, "Is it not true that the agricultural development and the successful industrial development of the gentlemen's great State is due to the industry and frugality of the interests that we are seeking to bar?" MacLafferty responded by reiterating that the Japanese had been successful in displacing native-born whites from various industries in California. Following this exchange, Sabath, a leader of the opposition to restriction, expressed the consensus view: "I must say that all the committee are in favor of exclusion of the Japanese."[36]

The *Chicago Defender* dissented from congressmen who were generally pro-immigration but opposed to Japanese immigrants by suggesting that allowing a few Japanese into the country posed no threat to American ways. Like LaGuardia, the *Defender* praised the contributions of Japanese farmers, extolling them for having "taken so-called unproductive California lands and made them yield bumper crops." Nevertheless, the *Defender* also believed Japanese immigrants were simply unable to adapt to American culture. "They are less assimiliable [*sic*] than any other nationality," declared the paper. "Their manners, customs, and traditions are decidedly different. It matters not how long they may live in a foreign country they still swear allegiance to their mother country; in other words, once a Japanese always a Japanese."[37]

Congress also debated the fate of Latino immigrants. When the Senate passed the bill, it contained no restrictions on immigration from the Western Hemisphere. Some restrictionists supported an amendment creating a quota on migration from Latin America, believing it made little sense to limit immigration from Europe and Asia while leaving immigration from Central and South America uncontrolled. Senator Matthew Neely (D) of West Virginia declared, "Mr. President, having subjected immigration from European countries to the most rigid restrictions, we shall reach the height of folly, and prove ourselves the most illogical of legislators if we leave our southern border to the unobstructed invasion of the United States by the population of Mexico."[38]

Those supporting the amendment espoused several other reasons for restricting immigration from Latin America and, in particular, Mexico. Senator Frank Willis (R) of Ohio feared that more and more Mexicans who were "not at all qualified for present citizenship or for assimilation" were entering the country. Indeed, some favorably compared eastern and southern European immigrants to Mexicans. "The immigrants from many of the countries subject to the quota provisions of the bill before the Senate are much more desirable from every point of view," declared Neely, "than are those from Mexico."[39]

The senators opposing the amendment did not dwell on the contributions of Latino immigrants. Rather, they suggested that such a measure was unnecessary because immigration from Mexico and Latin America remained very low. "What is there in the present situation that calls for these drastic provisions?" asked Senator William King (D) of Utah. "There is scarcely any immigration from these Republics to the United States; a few thousand annually." Holm Bursum (R) of New Mexico added, "There is no danger of this country being overrun by Mexican migration and, so far as South America is concerned, it is a joke to talk about it, for there is practically no immigration from the countries of South and Central America."[40]

They emphasized that most Mexican immigrants arrived for brief periods to engage in seasonal work that most Americans would not undertake but was essential to the economic well being of the Southwest. Ensuring the continuing flow of low-wage labor was a key reason for the opposition to the quota, as agricultural interests in the Southwest relied heavily on temporary workers from south of the border. Senator John Kendrick (D) of Wyoming declared, "I want to say for the information of the Senate that I am satisfied that the majority of the 60,000 Mexicans who came last year were brought into the country in the regular way under the law and returned to Mexico in the fall." He elaborated, "They came for the purpose of cultivating and harvesting agricultural crops, and it is not too much to say that this kind of labor does not appeal to white people."[41]

Finally, in an early example of American foreign policy shaping immigration decisions, some senators stressed the need to maintain strong diplomatic ties between the United States and Latin America. Senator David Reed (R) of Pennsylvania explained, "So far as Central and South America go, the policy indicated by this amendment is obviously unwise if we intend to attach importance to the Pan-American idea . . . we ought to treat them differently in the measure now pending, because there is no occasion for singling them out and clapping a quota down upon them." King agreed, "I believe it would be most unwise to apply the terms of this bill to our neighbors upon the north or the south. It is important for the prosperity of the people of the United States that they develop larger markets upon the Western Hemisphere."[42]

The 1924 immigration debate featured two dramatically different views of the behavior necessary for assimilation into American society. The restrictionists, predominantly from the South and West, believed that virtually any remaining trace of immigrant culture was unacceptable. Furthermore, they suggested it was un-American for ethnic groups to join together for political purposes. The opponents of restriction, primarily congressmen from the northeastern cities, rejected these notions. They also believed that immigrants, at least those from southern and eastern Europe, had contributed to strengthening American culture and expanding the American economy and were an essential part of the "nation of immigrants." Both sides included Germans and Irish in their conception of American identity while leaving Latinos and Asians out.

The restrictionists won a resounding victory in 1924 as the final bill, known as the Johnson-Reed Act, passed the House by an overwhelming margin of 323 to 71 and the Senate by 62 to 6. The voting patterns mirrored the debate as restriction garnered virtually unanimous support from the

South and West. The minimal opposition to the legislation came from congressional districts with large populations of new immigrants: a majority of House members from the Northeast voted against Johnson-Reed, as did a small number from the Midwest.[43]

The bill placed a total limit on immigration, with the number of newcomers arriving from an individual nation determined by their percentage in the 1890 census. The bill mandated Congress to change the criteria in 1929 to make the national origins of the U.S. population in 1920 the basis for the quotas. Through a series of questionable calculations, social scientists estimated the origins of the population in 1920 and produced a new set of quotas that provoked another debate over the nature of American identity. The new quotas became controversial because they raised the number of English immigrants allowed entry at the expense of Irish, German, and Scandinavian newcomers.[44] Opposition from the disadvantaged groups made the immigration law an issue in the 1928 presidential election, as Republican candidate Herbert Hoover campaigned against the national origins criteria and for maintaining the 1890 census as the baseline for the quotas. The 1929 congressional debate repeated many of the themes from the 1924 fight but differed because some who supported the restriction of southern and eastern Europeans criticized the new criterion for providing fewer slots for Irish and German immigrants.

As with the first debate, the discussion firmly established the inclusion of Irish and German newcomers in the "nation of immigrants." "During the Civil War alone the Irish and Germans in the service outnumbered the whole army of the South," observed Representative John McCormack (D) of Boston, Massachusetts. Echoing this line of thought, Senator Gerald Nye (R) of North Dakota declared, "one can not go into any history of the Revolutionary War period and the make-up of the Continental Army without being convinced of the very material part played by people of Irish and by people of German extraction."[45]

Though the nation was only a decade removed from hostilities with Germany, some even went so far as to suggest that German immigrants were superior to those from northwestern Europe. Senator Otis Glenn (R) of Illinois observed that "the class of German immigrants we are getting now and have been getting in recent years is a class superior, generally, to some of these others." On the other hand, some remained divided as to which Irish immigrants had been most beneficial to the United States. Senator Thomas Heflin (D) of Alabama remarked that "some Senator stated that about half of those who served in the Revolutionary Army were Irish. Those troops came from northern Ireland and no Irishmen of any consequence came here from southern Ireland until about 1850." Nye responded, "I think the division was quite even . . . or that the greater number came from southern Ireland rather than from northern Ireland."[46]

Though there was disagreement on the exact numbers for particular countries, most continued to agree on the need to favor northwestern Europeans over southern and eastern Europeans. "We all know," Representative Thomas Jenkins (R) of Ohio declared, "the policy of restriction is aimed to restrict immigration from southern and eastern Europe." He added, "In the immigration from England, Scotland, North Ireland, and Wales were many of the real pioneers and builders of this Nation."[47]

As before, Latinos remained outside the boundaries of the "nation of immigrants," despite the lack of formal barriers as the pro-restriction, anti-national origin forces believed there should be a quota for the Western Hemisphere. Nye made his case: "We are discriminating, to a degree, or at least the German, the Irish, and the Scandinavian people are given reason to feel that there is discrimination against them under the national-origins clause." He continued, "Is it any wonder that they should feel that it is discriminatory, in view of the fact that while we are limiting the number who can come from their countries we are not raising our finger against the 50,000 or 60,000 people who are coming into our land each and every year from Mexico."[48]

With Asian exclusion firmly established, Congress did not discuss them much during the debate in 1929. Still, when the subject arose, the debate reaffirmed that Asians remained firmly outside the "nation of immigrants." When a colleague asked Senator Glenn if he would want any Chinese quota at all, he jocularly responded, "I would say I would about as soon as have the Chinese here as the Mexicans."[49]

The final bill allowed for roughly 154,000 immigrants to enter each year from the Eastern Hemisphere while prescribing no limits on immigrants from the Western Hemisphere. The law excluded nearly all Asians, with the notable exception of Filipinos.[50] The origins criterion provided very large quotas for immigrants from northwestern Europe and very small ones for southern and eastern Europe. Great Britain, for example, had the largest quota of 66,000, while Greece had a mere 310. Every European nation received a quota of at least 100, and 70 percent of the total quota spaces, roughly equivalent to 110,000, went to Germany, Ireland, and England.[51]

This favorable consideration firmly established Irish Americans and German Americans as part of the "nation of immigrants." Furthermore, the policy enshrined into law the restrictionists' belief that immigrants from southern and eastern Europe and their children weakened the country and that American identity was synonymous with being a northern or western European.[52]

At the same time, the quotas began the process of integrating the European immigrants into a broad "white" identity. With Asians barred, southern and eastern Europeans, despite their low quotas, occupied a higher place in the racial hierarchy constructed by Johnson-Reed. By the end of the 1920s, policymakers and intellectuals were starting to move away from viewing eastern and southern Europeans as members of different races. As Mae Ngai observed, "At one level, the new immigration law differentiated Europeans according to nationality and ranked them in a hierarchy of desirability. At another level, the law constructed a white American race, in which persons of European descent shared a common whiteness distinct from those deemed to be not white."[53]

Furthermore, the beginning of the Great Migration of African Americans from the South to the North started a gradual process by which differences between black and white Americans superseded the divide between the Ellis Island immigrants and native-stock Americans. Prominent nativists who had been concerned about the dangers of unfettered immigration turned their attention to the growing African American population in the major cities. By the close of the Roaring Twenties, recent immigrants were increasingly seen as part of "white" America.[54]

While Mexicans and other Hispanics faced no quotas, both supporters and opponents of Johnson-Reed saw them as outside the "nation of immigrants." Furthermore, the emergence of a system of restriction led to stronger enforcement of the southern border, leading to the emergence of the concept of the "illegal alien." Policymakers increasingly used a number of tools, such as the liable to become a "public charge" provision, to limit Hispanic migration. As a result, Latinos would often be seen as "illegals," even if they had entered the country legally.[55]

The racialization of Hispanics was clearly visible in congressional attempts to implement a Western Hemisphere quota toward the end of the 1920s. In a 1930 report, congressmen opposed to the nonquota status of Latin America compared the problem of rising Latino immigration to the growth of the slave population before the ban of the slave trade in 1808.

Submitted by Representative Albert Johnson (R) of Washington, one of the cosponsors of the 1924 law, the report declared, "During the last 10 years the racial problem has become acute in the Southwest. Here there have been established, as the demand for cheap labor increased, a great many Mexican immigrants who seem to be driving out the Americans." Elaborating on the racial dimension of the problem, the report continued, "The Mexican peon, of course, as we know him, is of mixed racial descent— principally Indian and Spanish, with occasionally a little mixture of black blood," concluding that, "The recent Mexican immigrants are making a reconquest of the Southwest."[56]

Though opposing a Western Hemisphere quota, Representative Samuel Dickstein (D) of New York City seemed to agree with Johnson in his minority report. "One can not say, for instance, that a Mexican alien readily becomes Americanized," wrote Dickstein, "or is of the same blood or language with us."[57] Repeating the arguments of 1924, he suggested Mexican immigration was not a problem because it was so low and recommended against a quota because it would harm relations with Latin America. He urged greater enforcement of the literacy test to restrain Mexican immigration.[58]

By the end of the 1920s, these changes could be seen in the evolution of the rhetoric of restrictionists. Lothrop Stoddard, who had been a driving force behind the Johnson-Reed law, remained concerned about southern and eastern European immigrants but observed in 1927 that "it is probable that most of them can eventually be absorbed into the nation's blood without such alteration of America's racial make-up as would endanger the stability and continuity of our national life." He was not so sanguine, however, regarding nonwhites, suggesting "what is true of European immigrants, most of whom belong to some branch of the white racial group, most emphatically does not apply to non-white immigrants, like the Chinese, Japanese, or Mexicans; neither does it apply to the large resident Negro element which has been a tragic anomaly from our earliest time."[59]

∽

The debate over immigration could be seen in a wide range of cultural and intellectual forums. For instance, intellectuals, ethnic groups, and conservative patriotic societies clashed over the portrayal of immigrants, as well as the benefits of immigration, in the academic and high school history textbooks of the period.[60] In particular, the high school books reveal what most Americans learned about immigration in a period when relatively few Americans attended college. In its first study of college enrollment in 1940, the Census Bureau revealed that only 10 percent of the population attended at least a year of college, with only 5 percent receiving a degree.[61] In all likelihood, the percentages were the same or lower during the 1920s. Those who attended high school in this period learned from textbooks that largely echoed the views of the restrictionists, suggesting that the immigrants largely weakened the country.[62]

Early academic histories of immigration largely discussed the reasons that the Ellis Island-era immigrants moved to the U.S., while offering little analysis of the benefits they brought. George Stephenson's *The History of American Immigration*, published in 1926, described the process by which southern and eastern Europeans, as well as Asians, came to the country but provided little about their life in the United States. Stephenson focused on the politics of immigration, commenting that battles over restriction revealed that "the heavy majority of the American people, irrespective of national origin, accepted the restriction of immigration as a social and political necessity," adding that "as long as this act remains in effect our population will largely be recruited almost entirely from northern and western Europe and from the non-quota countries of the Western Hemisphere."[63]

In his 1925 high school textbook, *History of the United States*, Charles Beard, one of the leading academic historians of the time, discussed the differences between the immigrants of the late nineteenth century vis-à-vis the earlier wave of migration: "By 1890, all the free land was gone. They [immigrants] could not, therefore be dispersed widely among the native Americans to assimilate quickly and unconsciously the habits and ideas of American life." Like the restrictionists, Beard disdained the culture of urban ethnic neighborhoods: "There they crowded—nay overcrowded—into colonies of their own where they preserved their language, their newspapers, and their old world customs and views." Beard featured no discussion of immigrant contributions and concluded by attacking American business for supporting a liberal immigration policy: "So eager were American business men to get an enormous labor supply that they asked few questions about this 'alien invasion' upon the old America inherited from their fathers. . . . As for the future, that was in the hands of Providence."[64]

Other textbooks were more generous than Beard, though they had relatively little positive to say with regard to southern and eastern Europeans. In *The American People and Nation* (1927), Rolla M. Tryon and Charles Lingley discussed the new immigrants matter-of-factly, writing, "*Before 1882* most of the immigrants were from Germany, the British Isles, and the Scandinavian peninsula. . . . *After 1882*, they began to come increasingly from Italy, Austria, and Russia; that is, they came from southern and eastern Europe."[65] Carl Fish said that some of the new arrivals had become good citizens, "But the majority have not become Americanized so quickly."[66] *A History of the United States* (1925) by Henry Bourne and Elbert Benton contained a condescending discussion of contributions: "They all seem to love painting, sculpture, and music. . . . Like the Germans and French, the Slavs, the Greeks, and the Italians have helped in spreading the love of music and other arts in the United States."[67]

Beard himself moved toward some discussion of immigrant contributions in *History of the American People* (1928). Though the section regarding Ellis Island immigration is titled "The Invasion from Southern and Eastern Europe," he added, "The labor services rendered by these aliens, men and women, were countless and invaluable." He also included a poem that discussed the immigrant contributions to the building of America. Still, Beard wrote, "They left their families behind them and remained loyal in heart to their native lands . . . Having no lasting interest in this country or love for it, they did not care whether it was well or poorly governed."[68]

In these textbooks, Asian Americans received virtually no treatment and only appeared briefly in descriptions of the Chinese Exclusion Act of 1882. Fish wrote, "in 1882 Congress forbade Chinese immigration." Tryon and Lingley said much the same: "another law forbade the immigration of Chinese laborers. This law, with some changes, has been in force ever since."[69] Perhaps assuming the reasons for Chinese exclusion would be obvious to readers, they provided no further discussion of Asian immigration.

Obviously, recent immigrants were not pleased with their depiction in these books. In response, the Knights of Columbus, a leading Catholic fraternal organization, decided to commission several books on the benefits of immigration. The series, reflecting the dominance of racial thinking during the early 1920s, was entitled, "Racial Contributions to the United States." Designed to counter the negative portrayal of newcomers, it clearly promoted the contributionist viewpoint, featuring volumes on the benefits brought by Jews, blacks, and Germans, as well as a number of other groups.

The Jewish volume, *The Jews in the Making of America*, by George Cohen, listed the contributions of Jews to the country dating to the colonial era. He discussed the benefits Jews brought to various parts of American life, ranging from military service to the arts. Cohen expressed a contributionist view that the Jews were changing American culture while also assimilating, adding, "The Melting Pot in the meantime is boiling and the Jew is thawing out. . . . They have absorbed both the good and bad elements of American life."[70]

Throughout the period from 1924 to 1965, ethnic organizations would be in the forefront of efforts to promote contributionism. In a broad array of forums, they would work to demonstrate how their constituents helped build the country. The Knights of Columbus foreshadowed similar educational efforts to detail immigrant contributions that would become prominent in the late 1930s.

∽

During the 1920s, policymakers and intellectuals clearly excluded southern and eastern Europeans from the "nation of immigrants." While the quotas established by the Johnson-Reed Act revealed that many appreciated the benefits of Irish and German immigration, contributionism did not yet extend to the Ellis Island immigrants. Public and private educational programs, as well as school textbooks, reinforced this dichotomy. Finally, Asians and Latinos were clearly even further beyond the boundaries of the "nation of immigrants."

Chapter 2

Contributionism in the Prewar Period

During the 1930s, the growing tensions between the United States and Nazi Germany inspired many government agencies and private organizations to sponsor programs to improve attitudes toward recent immigrants. Breaking from the World War I-era Americanization campaigns, some involved with these efforts stressed the accomplishments and contributions of different groups. Others believed this focus on the benefits of immigrants' native cultures to America only reinforced ethnic and religious differences and preferred a message emphasizing the more general need for Americans to exhibit greater tolerance toward different ethnic groups.

Despite these efforts, a combination of persistent domestic nativism, along with the economic problems wrought by the Great Depression, prevented any liberalization of the immigration laws. Not even the crisis faced by European Jewry provided an impetus for change. But it was during these debates over the relative advantages and disadvantages of immigration that the language of contributionism began to coalesce into a coherent pro-immigrant ideology in American politics and culture. By the beginning of World War II, a minority of legislators and intellectuals emerged to promote a contributionist vision of the United States as a "nation of immigrants" that included southern and eastern Europeans. This view suggested that these immigrants strengthened the American culture and economy while they themselves changed to adapt to their new environment.

The combination of the Johnson-Reed Act of 1924 and the Great Depression precipitated a dramatic decline in immigration to the United States, as only 528,000 immigrants entered the country during the 1930s, a significant drop from 4.1 million in the 1920s.[1] As a result, ethnic communities received fewer new arrivals to sustain their Old World ways and language, and the second generation began to acculturate faster. Many of the "foreign" customs that had drawn the ire of the proponents of restriction became less evident, contributing, perhaps, to a moderation in nativist sentiment.[2] A variety of politicians, academics, religious leaders, and intellectuals began to publicly promote greater tolerance for American ethnic and religious diversity and to embrace new immigrant communities.

President Franklin Delano Roosevelt led rhetorically in promoting a new sense of respect for recent arrivals. Roosevelt's support for immigrants was, in part, simple politics: unlike his Republican predecessors, he received strong electoral support from the new immigrants as they formed a central element of the New Deal electoral coalition. In his first reelection campaign in 1936, Roosevelt won 90 percent of the Jewish vote nationwide.[3] In New York City alone, he won 90 percent of the Jewish vote and 80 percent of the Italian vote.[4]

FDR emphasized the contributions of immigrants to America during his reelection campaigns. In a speech on Liberty Island celebrating the fiftieth anniversary of the Statue of Liberty in 1936, he declared, "For over three centuries a steady stream of men, women, and children followed the beacon of liberty which this light symbolizes. They brought to us strength and moral fibre developed in a civilization centuries old but fired anew by the dream of a better life in America." Roosevelt celebrated the diversity brought by immigrants, saying, "They brought to one new country the culture of one hundred old ones."

In speeches like this, FDR seemed to side with opponents of the 1924 legislation in his views of immigrant contributions: "We take satisfaction in the thought that those who have left their native land to join us may still retain here their affection for some things left behind—old customs, old language, old friends." In Roosevelt's mind, the retention of some affection for their homeland did not jeopardize their loyalty to the United States as long as their children learned English and adapted to American institutions. As he explained it, "Looking to the future, they wisely choose that their children shall live in the new language and in the new customs of this new people. And those children more and more realize their common destiny in America."[5]

Later that same day, FDR went from the Statue of Liberty to address an audience primarily composed of foreign-born citizens on New York City's Lower East Side. He applauded the diversity they brought to the city, as well as their willingness to adapt to their adopted country: "Many of the people who came past the Statue of Liberty settled in this section of New

York City. Here they wove into the pattern of American life some of the color, some of the richness of the cultures from which they came." The president continued, "They have never been—they are not now—half-hearted Americans. . . . They sought an assurance of permanency in the new land for themselves and their children based upon active participation in its civilization and culture."[6]

FDR made such comments on a regular basis, and his many public pronouncements in support of immigrants and their institutions marked an important shift from the political discourse around immigration for much of the 1920s. As FDR and others began to publicly discuss the merits of various immigrant groups, contributionist ideas became more and more part of the American fabric. Politicians' language both shaped and reflected changing popular attitudes toward immigrants, even if the remarks seem a bit condescending to a contemporary ear.

The shift in political rhetoric mirrored changing ideas about race in the academy as social scientists were working to undermine scientific racism. Disturbed by the rise of National Socialism in his native land in the early 1930s, Franz Boas fought hard to prevent the Third Reich's racial theories from gaining a foothold in the United States. After all, the Nazis were applying the same theories to justify their mistreatment of the German Jewish population that the United States had used to justify immigration barriers. By the end of the 1930s, more and more intellectuals were open to Boas's view that environment determined educational and economic success and that differences between races were not solely based on innate characteristics.

At the same time, liberal religious figures publicly began to encourage tolerance. Leaders from Protestantism, Catholicism, and Judaism came together to form the National Conference of Christians and Jews (NCCJ) in 1928, an organization created to combat religious bigotry and promote an appreciation for recent immigrants. The cultural battles of the 1920s, such as the rise of the Ku Klux Klan and the anti-Catholic bias that marked Al Smith's 1928 presidential campaign, provided the impetus for the NCCJ's creation. The organization attacked discrimination during the 1930s with its sponsorship of "tolerance trios" of groups of rabbis, ministers, and priests traveling throughout the country promoting understanding and fighting prejudice. These groups spoke at universities and on radio programs to discuss the nature of their faiths, as well as to correct misconceptions that some might have about a particular religion.[7]

The NCCJ began National Brotherhood Day in 1934 as an effort to promote tolerance and goodwill among Protestants, Catholics, and Jews with its theme "Have We Not All One Father?"[8] Brotherhood Day sought to promote school activities and various other educational efforts to promote harmony between people of different races and religions. In what became a presidential tradition, FDR issued a statement concerning Brotherhood Day: "This occasion presents an opportunity for concerted thinking on a vital problem of national welfare; it should help us all in our efforts to rise above ancient and harmful suspicions and prejudices and to work together as citizens of a democracy."[9]

The NCCJ, the National Association for the Advancement of Colored People (NAACP), and the New York Board of Education, disturbed by the lack of attention to minority accomplishments in the public schools, joined together to form the Service Bureau for Intercultural Education in 1934.[10] This organization promoted efforts to make foreign-born students aware of their groups' contributions to American culture. "This approach called for the separate treatment of ethnic groups in assembly programs, curriculum units and lesson plans—directing the attention of the students to one ethnic group at the time," according to Nicholas Montalto, author of the history of the intercultural education movement.[11]

Finally, some intellectuals began to stress the contributions of immigrants in order to aid their incorporation into American society. Louis Adamic, a Slovenian-born writer, became one of the leaders of this effort. Adamic had left his native Slovenia for New York City at age fifteen and became a nonfiction author, writing largely about the problems of the American working class. A trip back to his homeland in the early 1930s, however, inspired a new appreciation of his native roots, and he began to write and speak about the Ellis Island-era immigrants.[12]

Adamic believed second-generation immigrants were plagued by feelings of inferiority and low self-esteem. He thought that, while their parents at least had the benefit of belonging to their own indigenous culture, the second-generation felt caught between two worlds. "The chief and most important fact (the only one I shall stress here)," wrote Adamic, "about the New Americans is that the majority of them are oppressed by feelings of inferiority in relation to their fellow citizens of older stock."[13]

To ameliorate this problem, Adamic rejected the Americanization efforts of the post-World War I period: "By now it is obvious to many people interested in the problem that it is impossible, and what it is more undesirable to make the offspring of Lithuanians or Serbians into Anglo-Saxons; that the aim should be rather to help them become real men and women on the pattern of their own natural cultures." He suggested that the nation's goal should be to "try to harmonize and integrate, so far as possible, the various racial and cultural strains in our population without suppressing or destroying any good cultural qualities in any of them, but using and directing these qualities toward a possible enhancement of the color and quality of our national life in America."[14]

Adamic believed that educating Americans about immigrant contributions was essential to maintain the new immigrant culture as part of American society and to provide self-esteem to the second generation. In what could be considered an early version of multiculturalism, Adamic suggested revising history textbooks to include the accomplishments of immigrants from Eastern Europe and the Balkans.[15] He also recommended the formation of an organization to promote other activities, such as radio programs and essay contests, to spread awareness of the benefits of immigration.

He concluded this article with a paean to the contributions of recent arrivals, declaring that, "with the diverse racial and cultural backgrounds they inherited from their immigrant parents, they will enrich the civilization and deepen the culture in this New World."[16] Adamic would write numerous books and articles throughout the 1930s, such as *My America* and *Ellis Island and Plymouth Rock*, concerning the contributions of immigrants and ways to integrate them into American society.

❧

Though there were some attempts to promote more accepting attitudes toward immigrants, these efforts did not achieve prominence until the late 1930s. The rise of fascism in Europe provoked a strong reaction in the United States, as many on the Left joined together to support various progressive causes, such as the Republican effort in the Spanish Civil War. In addition, some feared the rise of pro-fascist "fifth columns" in the United States, similar to those that had aided the Nazi takeovers of various European nations. Other observers worried that the emergence of fascism abroad and the privations caused by the Great Depression at home were inspiring domestic bigotry. The appearance of anti-Semitic demagogues such as Father Charles Coughlin and the emergence of nativist organizations such as William Dudley Pelley's Silver Shirts and the German

American Bund amplified these concerns. Indeed, popular anti-Semitism was probably reaching all-time highs by the end of the 1930s.[17]

Fearing these trends, a number of public and private institutions began a series of programs to improve relations between different ethnic and religious groups.[18] These organizations included the American Jewish Committee (AJC), NCCJ, U.S. Office of Education, and Justice Department. Some of these groups had memberships that dovetailed with or received funding from each other, and they formed an informal coalition that worked to change attitudes toward immigrants. Given the threat from abroad, these efforts all stressed the superiority of America's diversity and democratic institutions over the uniformity and totalitarianism of Germany, Italy, and the Soviet Union.

Dispensing with the one-sided assimilation ideology that dominated World War I-era programs, these organizations all combined two separate but related themes when discussing the role of immigrants in America. The first followed an approach similar to that employed by Adamic and some of the earlier congressional opponents of restriction by stressing the contributions of immigrants to American society. Others involved in these programs felt that stressing the contributions of immigrants emphasized difference at a time when unity and intergroup cooperation were essential to the nation's health. As a result, their approach focused on the need to work together and, in particular, the need for tolerance of different ethnicities and religions. This universalist ideology diminished the differences between various groups and concentrated on their common bonds.

Both approaches avoided the racially charged rhetoric that often dominated the previous generation of debates over immigration. Increasingly, eastern and southern Europeans were not seen in the racial terms that they had been viewed in the 1920s. Furthermore, these programs did not focus on the need for the newcomers to learn English, reflecting the fact that restriction meant that there were fewer recent immigrants unfamiliar with the language. While there were fears in the late 1930s regarding the loyalty of the Ellis Island immigrants, they did not rise to the level of the concerns seen during World War I and the early 1920s.

In the fall of 1938 and the spring of 1939, the Federal Radio Project of the U.S. Office of Education, with assistance from the Service Bureau for Intercultural Education and the AJC, sponsored the radio series *Americans All . . . Immigrants All*. One of the early examples of educational radio, the program ran for eighteen weeks and encompassed both approaches. The program's designers aimed to prevent Nazi Germany from exploiting the ethnic differences that had plagued the country during World War I, while also building public support for allowing Jewish refugees from Europe to enter the country.[19]

The premier show, titled "Opening Frontier," aired on November 13, 1938. In the broadcast, Commissioner of Education John W. Studebaker invoked the idea that the United States was a nation of immigrants: "We are all Americans and as the President has said . . . We are all the descendants of immigrants." In contrast to the restrictionists of the 1920s, he said, "We believed men of diverse inheritances could become American and that belief has been justified." Studebaker sounded like Israel Zangwill: "It is the picture of millions of men forgetting ancient prejudices, learning to live with millions of others and making a new people into a new land. . . . Without their contributions, American democracy would have been impossible. With them it was inevitable."[20]

Later programs discussed the contributions of various ethnic groups to American society. While the transcripts of the broadcasts are unavailable, the press releases for each week indicate the programs often focused on unconventional contributions made by individual groups. For instance, military service was a major theme of week thirteen on Jewish Americans. In a press release on February 5, 1939, Commissioner Studebaker said, "There is not one episode or crisis in our national history in which the Jews have not played a part."[21] The release revealed the contents of the show, which included the Jewish role in the American Revolution, among other things: "Stirring episodes deal with the help given by Jews to George Washington; their heroic participation in the War Between the States and the World War and the battle against disease of misery."[22]

The Italian broadcast followed a similar approach. A press release of February 20, 1939, indicated that "While many Italians found their way into the industries, vineyards, truck farms and fruit groves of the United States, the survey reveals such men as Celofonte Campanini were adding to our artistic and cultural development." The release also dismissed the stereotype that most Italians were manual workers: "Italo-Americans play an important role in American professional fields. The facts reveal that there are more than 15,000 Italian doctors and dentists in the United States."[23]

Some *Americans . . . All* materials also stressed interethnic cooperation and tolerance as much as group contributions. For example, the Office of

Education created a handbook instructing teachers on how to use the series in their classrooms. The guide said, "Chapter after Chapter in this series shows how the heritage of those stalwart peoples of many countries were blended into the American nation. . . . At the same time these recordings will contribute towards the development of all-important attitudes: tolerance and goodwill to all peoples." The guide also states that the recording will help with a series of teaching enterprises, including, "How to develop new appreciation for cooperative action."[24]

The Office of Education's internal discussions reveal a debate over the different approaches. The first major meeting concerning the program focused on whether each week should examine the contributions of an individual group or more broadly focus on overall immigrant contributions to different categories such as art, music, and literature. Although the series used the former approach, some felt that the latter would be less likely to encourage division.[25]

These debates continued while the program aired, as some involved feared the show was reinforcing group identity. The incoming mail suggested that many listeners were learning only about their own heritage. Comments included, "We enjoyed all those programs especially today as my Mother's people were among the first Pennsylvania German settlers," and "Your program was very interesting. My parents are from Finland and I like to hear from their ol' land."[26] Some blamed the scripts for producing such reactions. "These programs seem to say: Germans did things, Irishmen did thing things, Jews did things, as Germans, as Irishmen, as Jews. The programs fail to say clearly that Irishmen who became Americans did things as Americans," wrote Chester Williams, whom Studebaker had asked to analyze the broadcasts. Williams recommended the program shift its focus to cooperation between different groups rather than their individual contributions.[27] Responding to these exchanges, William Boutwell, director of the Radio Division of the Office of Education, responded that "a close examination of the scripts will show that strenuous efforts have been made to report incidents revealing immigrants from specific groups working with Americans of other origins."[28]

In the final analysis, *Americans . . . All* was extremely successful as listeners sent 80,000 letters to Washington agencies regarding the series. It became the most popular radio program to air on CBS to that point, winning awards from the American Legion as well as the National Radio

Women's Committee. Furthermore, the program demonstrated that a bourgeoning market existed for educational programming on radio.[29]

Other signs of changing attitudes toward immigrants also emerged. For instance, the NCCJ Brotherhood Day became so popular that one day was no longer sufficient time for its activities. As a result, the NCCJ expanded the celebration to a week in 1939, and that year's edition demonstrated these same trends with its theme of "Make America Safe for Differences."[30] While Brotherhood Week was ostensibly concerned with improving relations among religious groups, the 1939 version also touched on racial and ethnic themes. According to the NCCJ materials for the week, America's immigrants represented a source of strength and provided an important contrast to the totalitarian regimes in Europe. Chief Justice of the Supreme Court Charles Evans Hughes is quoted on the first page: "When we lose the right to be different, we lose the right to be free." According to the "message" section of the introduction, "America, settled by peoples of many regions, races, colors, cultures and creeds, should lead the way in helping to make the world safe for differences."[31]

Again, Brotherhood Week materials reiterated that the contributions of immigrants, essential to America, should be maintained in some manner, rather than be eliminated by Anglo-conformism. The "meaning" section presents an ideology for assimilation similar to Horace Kallen's: "From such a brotherhood, there may develop an American culture composed, like a symphony, of choirs of many distinct instruments, each finding expression while contributing to the music of the ensemble."[32]

The NCCJ recommended several ways to pursue the goals of Brotherhood Week, including mass meetings, community dinners, and radio programs. Among other things, they encouraged schools to invite groups of rabbis, ministers, and priests to address school assemblies. The materials also suggested that schools showcase the different contributions brought by various ethnic groups, as well as to "Teach youth that the United States is fortunate to have many culture strains."[33]

In addition to the discussion of immigrant contributions, Brotherhood Week emphasized tolerance and intergroup cooperation. Newton D. Baker, President Woodrow Wilson's secretary of war, is cited next to Hughes's remarks on the opening page: "What this conference is interested in is not what a man believes, but what other people think about him, and do to him because of what he believes." The "meaning" section declared, "Religious tolerance is still to be won. The struggle for the greater good beyond tolerance, namely active appreciation of difference, has hardly begun." Furthermore, the "motive" section said that Brotherhood Week proclaims groups should cooperate and work together to achieve social justice.[34]

The American Left also worked to expand the definition of American identity beyond native-stock Protestants during the 1930s. The Congress of Industrial Organizations (CIO), a collection of progressive unions, aggressively reached out to organize immigrant workers that the more conservative American Federation of Labor (AFL) had previously ignored. Likewise, the American Communist Party joined with mainstream liberal organizations during the mid- to late 1930s in an anti-fascist alliance that became known as the Popular Front. The Popular Front's efforts influenced many artistic programs, such as New Deal cultural agencies and Hollywood films, which reiterated the idea that ethnic and cultural diversity was a source of national strength.[35]

The song "Ballad of the Americans," developed by the Federal Theatre Project, emerged from the Popular Front. The song, written by Earl Robinson, asked, "Am I an American?" and says "I'm just an Irish, Negro, Jewish, Italian, French and English, Spanish, Russian, Chinese, Polish, Scotch, Hungarian, Litvak, Swedish, Finnish, Canadian, Greek and Turk, and Czech and double Czech American." The song combines themes of ethnic and religious contributions: "And that ain't all, I was baptized Baptist, Methodist, Congregationalist, Lutheran, Atheist, Roman Catholic, Orthodox Jewish, Presbyterian, Seventh Day Adventist, Mormon, Quaker, Christian Scientist and lots more."[36] African American singer Paul Robeson performed this song over CBS radio in November 1939 and drew an enthusiastic response. According to *Time*, "In the studio an audience of 600 stamped, shouted, brayed for two minutes while the show was still on the air, for 15 minutes after." Listeners jammed CBS's Manhattan and Hollywood switchboards: "In the next few days bales of letters demanded words, music, recordings, another time at bat for *Ballad of Americans*."[37]

The New York World's Fair of 1939–40 featured an exhibit called the American Common, which was designed to contrast the United States with the totalitarian states of Europe.[38] Opened for the 1940 season, the Common was the brainchild of Robert Kohn, the second-in-command on the World's Fair Commission.[39] Resembling Chicago's "All-American Exposition" of 1919, it consisted of an open-air theater, with six booths displaying arts and crafts from different ethnic groups. According to the World's Fair materials, "Each week a different group will take over the giant band shell, the market-place, and the auditorium, and give its own distinctive 'county fair' with its old world bazaars and fiestas."[40]

Eleanor Roosevelt dedicated the Common on June 1, 1940, to "the people of every nationality, race, and religion who, as citizens of the U.S. by uniting their unique contributions to the land of their adoption, built here a living ever-growing Democracy devoted to Peace and Freedom."[41] A teaching guide for the World's Fair repeated the exhibit's themes: "Our culture is a composite of many peoples and has evolved by a democratic process which preserves the best of each. We hope it is to become in many ways the antithesis of the 'melting pot'."[42]

The displays at the American Common, like the *Americans . . . All* program, detailed the contributions of individual ethnic groups to the United States. The week featuring Italian Americans included two operas and a Neapolitan festival and concluded with LaGuardia and Mayor Angelo Bossi of San Francisco addressing the nation in a radio broadcast on Columbus Day.[43] The World's Fair, like *Americans . . . All*, also stressed themes of tolerance and intergroup cooperation. During the week celebrating Hungarian Americans, Frederick Sheffield, assistant United States commissioner to the exposition, explained that it was important that ethnic groups work together "so that as a unit and as a nation it [United States] can put forth its very best efforts."[44] Edward Corsi, director of the Italian celebration, hoped the program would "tend to dissipate the baseless prejudices that the unreasoning fears of small men tend to create."[45]

The Fair also featured a week describing the accomplishments of African Americans. The American Common's "Negro Week" included the same activities as the weeks concerning various immigrant groups, including speeches by W. E. B. Du Bois and A. Philip Randolph, as well as performances by a number of African American artists. The souvenir program for the week even contained a relatively progressive discussion of black history. The document, authored by Lawrence D. Reddick of the New York Public Library, praised the improvements made by Reconstruction-era southern state governments, adding that they were not as corrupt as the historical scholarship of the time suggested. Reddick also detailed how African American labor played a vital role in the development of the country during slavery and in the three-quarters of a century since emancipation, declaring "One of the most flagrant omissions from the usual history of the United States is the part the Negro has played in the making of the nation."[46]

Despite their inclusion in the American Common, other aspects of the 1939–40 World's Fair reaffirmed that blacks did not have the same status as recent immigrants. Several of the pavilions, including those sponsored by General Motors and Standard Brands, erected separate bathrooms for black and white employees.[47] According to the NAACP, blacks were also excluded from all jobs at the fair with the exception of maids and porters.[48] The NAACP vigorously protested these inequities, and one official wrote to Thomas Dewey, then New York City district attorney, urging him to combat discrimination in these areas: "The New York World's Fair, 1939 has been called 'the World of Tomorrow' and it is inconceivable that a pattern of life projected for the future should contain discrimination against any race or group because of race, color, and religion."[49]

Similar kinds of fairs took place in less publicized formats around the country.[50] The "Festival of Nations" in St. Paul, Minnesota, was among the best known of these efforts. Like the American Common, exhibits offered food from the different countries whose emigrants composed the population of St. Paul. The festival displayed architecture from various cultures, and groups performed dances or songs from their native lands.[51] The first festival, held in 1932, drew 3,000 people. By 1939, the celebration had grown to draw 31,000 people.[52]

Louis Adamic, who attended the 1939 celebration, said the festival's creators aimed to put on a "folk festival which would dramatize to the community the contributions and potentialities of its various elements and give people of different backgrounds an opportunity to mingle and work together." They faced the same dilemmas as other efforts of their kind: "Tolerance, which in practice means mostly that you and I refrain from insulting one another, was not enough. The thing to do was for the diverse elements to discover one another's racial, national, cultural, and spiritual values, instincts, and other attributes which they brought from the old country." Adamic added that the event's planners were not altogether pleased with the title, "Festival of Nations," because they felt it emphasized ethnic difference: "As I understood them, they felt that the word 'Nations' in the phrase might, in retrospect, still give the various groups too much of the idea of separateness."[53]

The Immigration and Naturalization Service (INS) and the Department of Justice began sponsoring "I Am an American Day" in 1939. The day was marked by induction ceremonies for new citizens and various other efforts to discuss the responsibilities of citizenship, featuring many of the same messages as programs such as the American Common. Two hundred communities across the country participated in the inaugural year, and Congress passed a resolution making the celebration an annual event in 1940.[54] Although the state of New Jersey referred to it as "Good Will Day," Governor Charles Edison issued a proclamation on I Am an American Day 1941, declaring, "Many national, racial, and religious groups have united to make worthy contributions to the American soul." The emphasis, however, remained on tolerance and intergroup cooperation: "We must ever be a united people. We must be determined that in this crisis of our history there will be no setting of group against group to destroy the singleness of our purpose. We must be determined to resist the propaganda of all totalitarian states."[55]

Similarly, an NBC radio program, *I'm an American*, aired in 1940–41 with the cooperation of the Justice Department. The program featured a series of interviews with prominent naturalized Americans from varying walks of life such as Thomas Mann, Albert Einstein, Kurt Weill, and Guy Lombardo. *I'm an American* emphasized the strengths of democracy vis-à-vis totalitarianism and discussed how recent immigrants valued America as much, or perhaps more, than native-born individuals.

In one program, Eleanor Roosevelt fielded questions from two young foreign-born American citizens from America's fascist enemies, Germany and Italy. The young Italian man asked the First Lady, "We read all the time that heads of countries are saying that democracy is too slow and clumsy to meet modern conditions. I guess we all know in our hearts that this isn't so. But we'd like to have you tell us how democracy can be made to work and how we can help to do it." Mrs. Roosevelt responded, "Of course, democracy can work but we must believe as passionately about preserving democracy as young Germans and young Italians do about their Nazi or fascist ideals, or young Russians about their Communist ideals."[56]

The program reflected the same themes as *Americans . . . All* and the American Common. At the outset of the majority of the interviews, the narrator said that the program would show "some of the duties as well as the privileges which are implied when we say, 'I'm an American'." Thomas

Mann discussed the loyalty of immigrants to America: "No one could live in America as long as my family and I have without realizing that America is the possessor of a definite national unity . . . a spirit of loyalty peculiar to itself. This national characteristic is to be found as surely in the men and women who are recent arrivals as in Americans whose forebears have lived here for generations."[57]

Echoing the rhetoric of Louis Adamic, the narrator said prior to some of the broadcasts that the show was "a program for all Americans from Plymouth Rock to Ellis Island."[58] Through these interviews with prominent naturalized Americans, listeners learned about the contributions of immigrant groups. A young German woman said to Mrs. Roosevelt, "We've been in this country long enough to feel like real Americans, but we can still remember our native countries. Isn't there some way we could help America by being sort of go-betweens and thus bring our nationality groups and native Americans closer together?" The First Lady responded with contributionist rhetoric: "I think one of the best ways is to never forget your own cultural background and use whatever skills and culture that background gives you to enrich what you acquire in the United States."[59]

Tolerance and cooperation, however, were equally, if not more important themes of the shows. One of the interviewers, Marshall Dimuck, second assistant secretary of labor, said to Thomas Mann, "The democratic virtue of tolerance today ceases to have merely an idealistic and academic meaning. It has become a matter of life and death concern for millions of people all over the globe."[60] Gregory Ziborosch, a Russian-born psychiatrist, said, "This very deeply rooted trend of tolerance and of judging men by what he does rather than by what his name is may and probably will be the guarantee against the unleashing of the savage instincts which rage in Europe today."[61] At the conclusion of some of the programs, the narrator noted that the Daughters of the American Revolution was giving out free copies of the Constitution, "in sympathy with the purpose of this program for a deeper consciousness of the privileges and responsibilities of citizens and more tolerance for Americans of all birthplaces."[62]

∾

Reflecting years later on his public school education during the 1930s, Nathan Glazer, a prominent public intellectual and scholar of immigration and ethnicity, recalled that "The public schools of New York City were then two-thirds or more Jewish and Italian in student composition, but no Jewish figure was to be found in our texts for reading or writing, for literature, for social studies, for history." He added, "While we learned about Columbus in elementary school, and Mazzini and Garibaldi made an appearance in high school European history, there was no implication that they had any connection with our Italian fellow-students."[63] As the 1930s progressed, however, and international conflict grew nearer, some teachers worked to incorporate immigrants into the classroom. By the eve of World War II, educators had joined in the effort to inform Americans about the benefits of immigration.

Glazer's recollections are confirmed by an examination of textbooks from the 1930s, such as the 1936 edition of *America and the New Frontier* by George Freeland and James Adams. The authors discussed how the source of immigration had shifted in the late nineteenth century from northern and western Europe to southern and eastern Europe, adding, "The Old World ways of the latter are less like those of America, and they have been slower to adopt American standards of living." Though they noted that "Many millions of immigrants have remained in the United States, however, and have become good American citizens," Freeland and Adams praised the Johnson-Reed bill: "In cutting down the number entering the country, we have been enabled to make a more careful attack on these problems." They concluded, "The immigrant has played an important part in the making of America in the past, but that phase of our history has probably ended."[64]

In his *History of the American People* (1938), John Holladay Latane described immigration blandly in terms of population flows without discussion of immigrant contributions to America. He approved of the 1924 legislation, saying, "At the outbreak of the World War it became evident that the 'melting pot' was not working as satisfactorily as had been sentimentally imagined and that our population of foreign birth had not been fully assimilated and Americanized."[65] *The United States in the Making*, written by several authors in 1937, also described the rise of immigration without discussing the newcomers' contributions. Primarily focusing on the social problems brought by immigration, they declared, "Living in colonies in the crowded slums of the cities, they continued to speak their own languages and preserve their own customs and institutions."[66]

The school texts continued to ignore Latinos and feature Asian Americans solely in the context of Chinese and Japanese exclusion. The authors of *The United States in the Making* appeared sympathetic to the concerns of American workers with regard to the Chinese: "American labor could not compete with the Chinese coolies, who worked for starvation wages and lived under conditions which Americans would not tolerate."[67] Ralph Volney Harlow went even farther, repeating the concerns about low Chinese wages, adding, "Their [the Chinese] vice dens and opium joints became so notorious that Congress sent a special committee to California to investigate them. Under the circumstances, it is not surprising that white mobs should have tried to drive the Chinese out by force."[68] Latane's *History of the American People* provided the only critique of exclusion: "The Chinese exclusion laws have been administered with undue severity, and overzealous officials have too frequently subjected Chinese gentlemen of culture and refinement to unnecessary hardships and indignities."[69]

The government's own program to educate immigrants about American history reflected the same concerns as the textbooks regarding immigrant life. The Bureau of Naturalization produced a three-part *Federal Textbook on Citizenship Training* during the 1920s and 1930s. The bureau designed the first two volumes to help citizens learn the English language and understand American laws. The third volume, titled *Our Nation*, concerned American history and contained the same description of immigration as the textbooks. "Because most immigrants settled in such colonies they had very little chance to get acquainted with Americans and it was very difficult for them to learn our language, customs, and ways," according to the 1932 edition.[70]

By the late 1930s, however, American educators made a greater effort to address the twin themes of ethnic contributions and tolerance as part of the growing quest for national unity in the late 1930s and early 1940s. The Service Bureau of Intercultural Education sent a guide titled "Out of the Many—One" to "citizens and educators who are enlisting in the American fight against intolerance." Distributed in the early 1940s, the pamphlet discussed the need to balance the concepts of contributions and tolerance: "Ours is the difficult mission of accenting those contributions without setting apart the nationalities which have made them; of giving to all children an opportunity to understand and respect them as elements which make the United States 'OUT OF MANY, ONE'."[71]

The Bureau instructed teachers to use the classroom to emphasize the need for unity as well as respect for all Americans. Similarly, they told administrators they could assist in this effort "by encouraging your faculty to imbue every part of the educational process with that true Americanism which seeks national unity in the recognition and use of cultural diversity." Parents were told to "help [your child] to widen his knowledge of the community's and the nation's heritage of culture contributions from many lands."[72]

During this time, some school districts were implementing curricula to improve students' knowledge of the recent immigrant groups and, to a lesser extent, African Americans. Rachel DuBois, one of the leaders of the Service Bureau, pioneered efforts to develop such programs, which became known as "intercultural education." Her formula, which she began while teaching history in Woodbury, New Jersey, in the 1920s, featured individuals from different ethnic groups talking to student assemblies about the culture of their groups. Then the students themselves put together programs portraying the accomplishments of an immigrant group.[73]

Such efforts spread during the Depression. The New York City Board of Education, which had rejected efforts to discuss immigrants' heritages in the early 1920s, adopted such a policy during the late 1930s. With the anti-Semitism of groups such as the Christian Front gaining influence in their community, the Board decided it was time to implement a program to combat this issue.[74]

Likewise, even as high school history textbooks generally ignored the contributions of immigrants, a few textbooks began to change course at the end of the decade. The evolution of Eugene Barker and Henry Steele Commager's textbooks demonstrates the subtle transition toward more positive portrayals of immigration. The 1934 edition of their book *Our Nation's Development* largely discussed immigration in terms of population flows and demographics. Still, the authors presented a more optimistic view of assimilation than did Charles Beard or the others: "Actually, the process of Americanization has proved much less difficult than was feared."[75]

Barker and Commager's 1941 book, *Our Nation*, reflecting the changing context brought by the quest for unity caused by the unstable international situation, emphasized the contributions of these new citizens to American society: "No description is more commonly applied to America than the term 'melting pot,' and none is more accurate. This term means that in America the different races of the world have been melted into a common product, which we know as American." They stressed that immigrants built America: "Indeed, the United States could not have progressed as rapidly as it did without the aid of the millions of immigrants who took up the task of helping to build the American society and economy we have today." Their rhetoric is similar to that of *Americans . . . All*: "It is clear that immigrants owed much to the country which offered them a home, freedom, and opportunity. But the debt was not entirely one-sided. The United States, too, owes much to the immigrant."[76]

In contrast to their 1934 textbook, the authors spent four pages in *Our Nation* detailing the contributions of immigrants to America. Most of the examples were from the "old" immigrant groups, such as the German John Jacob Astor and the Scot Andrew Carnegie. There were a few examples from eastern and southern Europe, such as the Serbian Michael Pupi and the Greek Nikola Tesla, who were experts in electricity. No Italians were mentioned, and the only Jew to surface was Samuel Gompers, "born in London of Dutch-Jewish parents." Commager and Barker concluded with a tribute to the contributions of immigrants: "In a sense, the United States is a nation made up of immigrants and the descendants of immigrants. . . . They came and planted farms, built railroads, and worked in the factories. They became American citizens and helped to build the nation. They made important contributions to the cultural life of our country."[77]

The leading academic scholarship of the time began to discuss recent immigrants as well. Marcus Hansen's groundbreaking work *The Atlantic Migration: 1607–1860*, published in 1940, focused largely on the process of how and why immigrants came to the United States and spent little time depicting the lives of immigrants once they had arrived in America.[78] When he did, however, Hansen seemed more sympathetic to immigrants and confident about their ability to assimilate into American society than the authors of the 1930s textbooks. According to Hansen, immigrants would sometimes "reproduce a part of their homeland and found a 'colony.' But in time the chemistry of the new scene dissolved even such Old World attachments."[79] *The Atlantic Migration*, which won the Pulitzer Prize for American History in 1941, also concluded at the Civil War and did not provide much analysis of the 1882–1924 wave of immigrants.

Hansen discussed eastern and southern Europeans a little more in *The Immigrant in American History*, also published in 1940. As in *Atlantic Migration*, he suggested that old ties faded quickly. "Time-honored ideals were blunted and the traditional culture was quickly forgotten," Hansen wrote regarding Italian Americans, "Only unusual vitality could preserve any part of it."[80] He included a brief section on the benefits brought by Italian immigrants, noting, "American diet is healthier and more varied because of Italian gardeners and Italian cooks."[81] In general, though, Hansen focused on the "old" immigration, as his death in 1938 precluded him from writing more about the "new" immigration.

Carl Wittke, however, analyzed the 1882–1924 immigration in great detail in *We Who Built America*, first published in 1939. Covering the history of immigration to the U.S., Wittke, a professor at Oberlin College, wrote about virtually every group that came to the United States. Embracing the benefits of immigration, he feared that some newcomers assimilated too quickly: "It is to be regretted that many immigrants conform so quickly and completely in all respects to 'American standards' and become genuinely ashamed of their heritage."[82]

Wittke included a section on each immigrant group that came to the United States. Like most books of the period, he largely viewed Chinese and Japanese migration in terms of their exclusion. In a brief description of their life in the U.S., Wittke noted that the Japanese were more likely than the Chinese to adapt to American norms.[83] He depicted Mexican migrants in a negative light, commenting, "Many look like Indians and live in a kind of fatalistic surrender to their lowly lot. . . . They live in unsanitary hovels; their children seldom attend school; and Americanization among them is a slow process."[84]

Conversely, Wittke wrote of the benefits provided by the Ellis Island-era immigrants, praising their role in the growth of the economy, suggesting, "cheap foreign labor was available in such quantities that immigration became a major factor in the rapid industrialization of the nation after the Civil War." He added, though, that this might have impeded technological advancements and helped bring about the Depression.[85] Wittke reviewed the immigrants' arrival in the country, discussed the industries they entered, and described their lives in the United States. For instance, he rejected critiques of the Italians, perhaps reflecting the growing critique of scientific racism: "Their problems in a new environment were complex social problems, but hardly biological." He concluded, "The Italians represented a stout-hearted, physically-fit peasantry, whose thrift and industry brought thousands unexpected success."[86]

∿

The growing appreciation on the part of some intellectuals for the immigrants' value to American life did not lead to any kind of support for liberalizing immigration laws. The economic and social problems spawned by the Depression, along with the increasingly dangerous international situation, reduced the importance of immigration as an issue. Throughout most of the 1930s, the only legislative action regarding immigration came from attempts to implement a Western Hemisphere quota, the occasional proposal to suspend immigration, or measures to strengthen the government's ability to deport aliens feared to be subversive.[87] For example, Representative Martin Dies (D) of Texas proposed lowering the quotas by 60 percent in 1935, alleging that immigration was responsible for the economic crisis. Without immigration, "It is reasonable to believe that the unemployment problem would never have assumed such serious and unprecedented proportions in this country," said Dies.[88] Though the Roosevelt administration frustrated Dies's attempt to reduce the quotas, few tried to weaken the national origins system during the Depression.

Congress's unwillingness to admit more Jewish refugees during the late 1930s demonstrated the intensity of the resistance to a more liberal immigration policy.[89] In response to the growing peril faced by European Jewry, representatives introduced a bill to provide asylum for Jews from Austria and Germany. The legislation, sponsored by Senator Robert Wagner (D) of New York and Representative Edith Nourse Rogers (R) of Massachusetts, became known as the Wagner-Rogers bill. It would have allowed 20,000 children to enter the United States as a humanitarian gesture outside the quota system.

Robert Wagner led the fight. Born in Germany in 1877, Wagner came to New York City as a young boy and rose from poverty to become one of the most influential senators of the twentieth century. He symbolized the emergence of the activist Democratic liberalism that would dominate American politics from the 1930s through the 1960s. He achieved his greatest influence after his election to the U.S. Senate in 1926. During the Great Depression, Wagner played an essential role in the passage of the New Deal. Most famously, he led the fight for the National Labor Relations Act, also known as the Wagner Act. This bill, passed in 1935, strengthened the collective bargaining rights of American workers, paving the way for the dramatic growth of organized labor in the 1930s. He also played a vital role in the passage of Social Security as well as laws regarding public housing, unemployment insurance, and the U.S. Employment Service. Commenting on Wagner's importance in 1938, President Roosevelt declared, "So often since

1933 has new legislation been described as 'The Wagner Act' that the phrase has become so confusing, because there have been so many Wagner Acts."[90]

But Wagner would not win this legislative battle. Scholars have seen the failure of the Wagner-Rogers bill as the inevitable result of the anti-Semitic climate of the period, and there is strong support for this perspective.[91] Most Americans were horrified by the barbarism of the Nazis during the anti-Jewish pogrom known as *Kristallnacht* in November 1938. This revulsion, however, did not translate into greater support for Jewish immigration to the United States. In a *Fortune* magazine poll in 1939, 83 percent of Americans expressed their unwillingness to admit more Jewish refugees into the country. These figures were even higher than they had been the previous summer.[92]

Despite the general public's lack of receptivity to Jewish immigrants in the face of crisis, there was a surprising amount of elite support for the Wagner-Rogers legislation. For example, numerous Southern newspapers supported the bill, and some backers of Wagner-Rogers entered their op-eds into the record during the congressional hearings. The *Montgomery Advertiser* editorialized, "Legally speaking, responsibility for these children does not rest with us. We could turn our backs upon them, if we like and seal our frontiers. But we should be guilty of a moral crime against the very things of which we most often boast." The *Galveston News* concurred, "It would dishonor our traditions of humanity and freedom, however, to refuse the small measure of help contemplated by the Wagner resolution."[93] A number of papers in the Midwest also supported Wagner-Rogers. "Not weepy sentimentality but common decency and common sense," declared the *Fort Wayne Journal Gazette*, "demand such action."[94]

The largest labor unions, often supporters of immigration restriction in the past, testified in favor of the Wagner bill. John Brophy, the national director of the CIO, strongly supported the legislation in his congressional testimony: "To my mind, it is incomprehensible that decent human beings in America should oppose this bill." He added, "Organized labor does not fear the alleged 'influx' of German children that the opponents of this bill say will descend upon us. On the contrary, organized labor welcomes the opportunity this Nation has to do a simple act of human charity in passing this bill."[95]

The more conservative AFL also supported Wagner-Rogers, leading to a testy exchange with opponents of the bill during the committee hearings.

Congressman Leonard Allen of Louisiana chided the AFL's representative for its support in light of its historical support for restriction. "In other words, you are a restrictionist until certain powers in the country clamor for a bill, and then you are ready to flop, is that right?" Allen alleged. He echoed the rhetoric of 1924: "The federation can do as it wishes to do, but I am going to stand for America." Joseph Paway, the counsel for the AFL, responded, "We are still as good Americans as you or anyone else, even though we support this bill. The difference between us is that we are for humanitarianism and you are not."[96]

Of course, there was very strong opposition to the bill, particularly from the patriotic societies. Some of these arguments were similar to the rhetoric of 1924. Mrs. Agnes Waters, who testified in front of both the House and Joint Committees, used particularly extreme language: "These refugees have a heritage of hate. They could never become loyal Americans." She added, "On Capitol Hill every now and then I see an army of people who speak foreign languages and insult the American flag, and are demanding more and more all the time. I submit that my children will be deprived of their liberty by this army." A few others employed a similar approach. Representative Charles Kramer of California said, "He [Hitler] has got rid of an awful lot of millionaires there because the Jews were the ones that originally financed him. I know that Hitler got his original support from the Jews and then he double-crossed them."[97]

Despite its heated rhetoric, the 1939 debate lacked the racial overtones of the 1924 fight. Placing economic issues in the forefront, Wagner-Roger's foes contended the country could not afford the burden of 20,000 additional children in the midst of the Depression. William Griffith of the Immigration Restriction League declared, "with 30,000,000 on relief and between twelve and thirteen million unemployed, and the President declaring 'over one-third of our population underprivileged, ill-fed, ill-clothed, ill-housed, we should first put our own house in order.'" "We are unable to build necessary schoolhouses, purchase equipment, or employ the necessary teachers," concurred Charles H. Hall, state secretary, Council of Pennsylvania Junior Order of United American Mechanics: "We have no right therefore, to add 20,000 more children to their rolls."[98]

Interestingly, the leading black newspaper of the time reiterated this line of argument. While expressing understanding for the plight of European refugees, the *Chicago Defender* called attention to the economic crisis faced by the country. "An increase in our population, especially when we have

nearly 12,000,000 people unemployed, would aggravate an already compli-
cated problem," argued the paper. The editorial even questioned the
motives of the bill's supporters, alleging they were more concerned about
the difficulties faced by Europeans than the injustices faced by African
Americans. "If the supporters of the bill to admit European refuges were
prompted by moral earnestness," argued the *Defender*, "they would be just
as concerned about the economic plight of the 15,000,000 blacks of this
country, half of whom may well be said to be starving."[99]

Opponents of Wagner believed that, once the children were admitted,
it would be impossible to resist the political pressure to admit their parents.
J. L. Wilmeth of the Junior Order of United American Mechanics said, "We
are apprehensive that if these children are brought into this country there
will be an effort made later on to reunite their families. That has been the
history heretofore." "The same cry will be used as an excuse for letting in
all the families of these children," agreed Francis H. Kinnicutt, president of
Allied Patriotic Societies. "It has been practically admitted by several wit-
nesses that that is exactly what they want to do."[100]

They also suggested that, if America admitted Jewish refugees on
humanitarian grounds, it would set a precedent for people from other
oppressive countries such as Spain and China. Herman A. Miller, national
secretary, Patriotic Order, Sons of America, declared, "Now if this bill is
enacted into law, the Congress will be morally obligated to pass a similar
bill for the relief of the children of Poland, the children of Rumania, the
children of Yugoslavia, the children of Spain." Hall said, "We oppose this
legislation because it establishes a precedent. Spain, Russia, China and Lord
only knows how many countries would have thousands of children for
Uncle Sam to take care of."[101]

The restrictionists worried above all that the legislation was the initial
step to overthrowing the quota system they had worked so hard to put in
place in 1924. The supporters of the national origins system espoused a
1930s version of the domino theory; once some part of the system was
knocked over, the rest would fall. James H. Patten of the Junior Order of
United American Mechanics said, "There is no question at all about this
resolution, but that it is a last stand attempt to destroy the quota act of
1924, in my opinion." "This provision of the bill, although it may not
appear so at first blush, is a serious blow at our present system of restriction," concurred Kinnicutt, "which has had the approval of the great
majority of our people and of both the great parties for over a decade."[102]

This objection proved key to the failure of the bill. Members of the immigration committee declared they were willing to pass the legislation— but only with an amendment mandating that the children would have to enter under the German quota. Wagner rejected this amendment because it would place the children in competition with adults for the already limited amount of available slots to leave Nazi Germany; as a result, the legislation never reached the floor.[103]

∼

In response to the rise of totalitarianism in Europe as well as domestic nativism, a synthesis of ideas merged during the Depression years to form a coherent philosophy that departed from the thought of the 1920s. This perspective stressed the importance of tolerance and cooperation between different groups, while also emphasizing the contributionist ideology that immigrants strengthened the country because they brought different cultures while retaining a commitment to common American ideals. This synthesis, developed by a small group of liberal elites, did not yet have a large or politically effective popular following, so the national origins system, which symbolized the exclusion of southern and eastern Europeans from American life, remained unchallenged. Once war broke out, though, the need to incorporate recent immigrants into the body politic would grow more urgent.

Chapter 3

The Quest for Tolerance and Unity

In November 1942, Louis Adamic wrote an article in the *New York Times Magazine* titled "No 'Hyphens' This Time." In this piece, Adamic commented on the lack of punitive action against recent immigrants during the war: "So far in this war—aside from the campaign against the Japanese group on the Pacific Coast, which was old-time exclusionism hitched to a potentially serious military problem—there has been no great hue and cry about the 'foreigners'."[1]

Adamic observed that this climate stood in sharp contrast with World War I, when prominent figures such as Theodore Roosevelt had led the attacks on the loyalties of recent arrivals. During that conflict, the government and private groups engaged in repressive actions against immigrants, especially German Americans. State and local school systems banned the German language, and, in one case, a jury found a lynch mob innocent in order to demonstrate their patriotism. A "100 percent Americanism" campaign, strong into the 1920s, demanded that immigrants abandon all ties with their homelands.[2]

Adamic believed the decrease in immigration between the wars, which produced a more assimilated population than there had been during World War I, was a major reason for this change. Due to the combination of the restriction law of 1924 and the Great Depression, the percentage of foreign-born had fallen from 14 percent of the country's population in 1920 to 9 percent by 1940.[3] He also credited FDR's administration and some of the educational efforts of the pre-World War II period, such as the *Americans All* program. "This was instrumental in creating through the country a general atmosphere in regard to the new immigrant groups which has been much sounder so far in this crisis than it was when we first set out to make the world safe for democracy," Adamic declared, adding, "It has tended to draw the 'foreigner' toward the main streams of American life."[4]

Adamic suggested that Americans were beginning to think anew about diversity:

> The result is the partial but continuing breaking down of the belief, held by many old-line Americans, that the great diversity of backgrounds in our population is a disadvantage to the United States as a nation. The gradual deterioration of this idea has apparently been enough to prevent anti-alien hysteria, in spite of considerable attempts not unrelated to Hitler's purposes to foment it.[5]

He went on to note, "It is possible that a few decades hence historians will regard this fact as one of our biggest present slices of good fortune."

Indeed, most historians agree that World War II accelerated the decline of nativism and the acceptance of immigrants from southern and eastern Europe and their children into American society.[6] Wartime migrations of Americans to different regions played an important role as 27 million citizens left their homes and neighborhoods for employment in wartime industries or to join the military.[7] Many left homogeneous rural communities and urban ethnic neighborhoods where they had encountered only individuals from the same nationality or religion.

The military experience brought disparate peoples into contact, as Americans of all racial and ethnic backgrounds fought and died together. In his 1944 book *A Nation of Nations*, which detailed the contributions of virtually every immigrant group, Louis Adamic wrote, "There is more getting together among Americans than ever before, more acceptance of people on the basis of their personal qualities regardless of background. This is especially true of the men in the services. There is nothing like being together in a foxhole, a bomber, or a submarine."[8] A *New York Evening Post* headline above the obituary of soldiers from March 25, 1943, demonstrated this effect: "Their Names Are Alien But—Their Blood Is All American."[9]

The war also weakened the foundations of the national origins system. Scientific racism, which had provided intellectual support to restriction in 1924, lost its legitimacy. The combination of the Nazis' use of master race theories to support their policies against Jews and other minorities, as well as earlier intellectual work by anthropologists such as Franz Boas and Ruth

Benedict, ended its respectability. Circulation of foreign-language newspapers and radio stations that had worried the restrictionists of 1924 also began to decline. The number of foreign-language radio stations fell from 205 in 1942 to 126 in 1948, and 15 percent of foreign-language newspapers folded between 1940 and 1945.[10]

As scientific racism lost its power, ethnicity rapidly replaced race in defining the position of the Ellis Island immigrants and their children. During the debate over Johnson-Reed in 1924, many supporters of restriction viewed Jews, Italians, and other eastern and southern Europeans as part of racially inferior groups. As these groups became "Caucasian," they were increasingly defined as being part of different cultures rather than as part of different races.[11] Indeed, the term "ethnic" first began to appear in circulation during World War II.[12]

The percentage of noncitizens in the country fell as the number of aliens becoming naturalized citizens doubled in 1940–44, as compared with 1934–39, from 148,000 to 296,000.[13] The Immigration and Naturalization Service *Monthly Review* observed in May 1944, "The unprecedented increase in naturalization in the past two years or so, deaths, departures, and deportations have greatly reduced the number of aliens in the United States."[14]

Large black migrations to the North, which had begun during World War I but slowed during the Great Depression, increasingly transformed black/white relations from a southern to a national issue. Seven hundred thousand African Americans left the South during the war, moving to take jobs in cities like Chicago, Philadelphia, and Detroit. This migration altered the demography of the major urban centers, as the population of the top ten war production centers grew by 19 percent, while the black population of these cities grew by 49 percent.[15] Many whites in the North fought with African Americans over housing and other resources in the often racially tense, wartime environment in northern cities. Eventually, these disputes boiled over into race riots in Detroit and Harlem in 1943. As black ghettos expanded and pushed toward ethnic neighborhoods, rivalries among different groups, such as Irish Americans and Italian Americans, diminished as they joined together to preserve the "whiteness" of their neighborhoods.[16]

As a result of these myriad changes, many children of the Ellis Island generation of immigrants remember World War II as a watershed in their acceptance as Americans. Paul Piscano, an Italian American architect, recalled that, after the war, "The Italo-Americans stopped being Italo and started becoming Americans. We joined the group."[17] Jewish American baseball player Hank Greenberg agreed: "When you joined the Army, you became an American. When I broke into baseball, every time they wrote about me it had something to do with my ethnic background. When the war was over, the ballplayers were no longer referred to by their religion."[18]

Of course, the inclusion of white ethnics came at the expense, to some extent, of other racial groups. While white ethnics fought together, African Americans and Japanese Americans served in segregated units. Wartime propaganda, such as the platoon films, largely excluded African Americans from this conception of American identity. Furthermore, government propaganda portrayed the Japanese enemy as a homogenous foe, sometimes using racialized rhetoric to compare them to apes and vermin.[19] This provided a sharp contrast with the propaganda images of Germans, who were not depicted in the same caricatured fashion.

As a result, the conflict produced mixed results for Asian Americans.[20] Most notably, the government forced 120,000 Japanese Americans, two-thirds of whom were American citizens, into internment camps, regardless of whether they were actually "disloyal." The vast majority were loyal and the internment episode remains one of the greatest violations of civil liberties in American history. Chinese Americans benefited somewhat from the contrast with their Japanese counterparts. They were viewed as the "good Asians" because of China's role as a wartime ally of the United States. *Time* even infamously instructed citizens on how to tell Chinese and Japanese apart under the headline "How to Tell Your Friends from the Japs."[21]

Congress repealed the Chinese Exclusion Act in 1943, its only major initiative regarding immigration during the war, and created a quota allowing 105 Chinese individuals to enter the country each year. Many in Congress resisted the bill, fearing, like the opponents of Wagner-Rogers in 1939, that it would lead to the breakdown of the entire quota system. The supporters of repeal represented the measure as a practical way to maintain China's support during the war, rather than as a humanitarian gesture.[22] FDR explained his rationale on December 17, 1943. "An unfortunate barrier between allies has been removed," he said. "The war effort in the Far East can now be carried on with greater vigor and a larger understanding of our common purpose."[23] Roosevelt, who had made many positive comments about immigrants from southern and eastern Europe, made no such remarks about the contributions of Chinese Americans to the United States. Nevertheless, this act marked the first change in the immigration system that policymakers had erected in 1924.

Before the war, educational and propaganda programs combined a new emphasis on the contributions of newcomers with calls for tolerance and interethnic cooperation. As a result of the need for national unity during wartime, propaganda and educational efforts shifted significantly away from the former and toward the latter. Contributionism did not disappear from wartime rhetoric, but moved into the background. This pattern continued during the immediate postwar period.

Many policymakers feared that the contributionist approach only increased ethnic tensions. The onset of the conflict made cooperation a paramount concern as the country needed to work together to defeat Japan and Germany. The Office of War Information (OWI), created by FDR in 1942 to explain the war to the American people, promoted an ideological view of the conflict as a battle for democracy and tolerance against totalitarianism and intolerance.[24] Private organizations such as the American Jewish Committee and the National Conference of Christians and Jews followed a similar philosophy. These groups sought to merge the practical wartime need for unity with the idealistic interest of eliminating nativism. As one OWI official put it, "By making this a people's war for freedom, we can help clear up the alien problem, the negro problem, the anti-Semitic problem."[25]

Wartime propaganda and its postwar counterpart emphasized that tolerance and cooperation represented an essential part of American identity. Various public and private organs labeled discrimination based on race, religion, and ethnicity as un-American and dangerous to the nation's stability and role as a world leader. To the proponents of this view, the war's goal was not merely to defeat the nation's military enemies but to create a more tolerant society without racial, ethnic, and religious discrimination. Tolerance and "teamwork" were not only essential to victory in World War II but also to the successful conversion to a peacetime economy and to fighting the Cold War.

Many Americans did not share this vision of the conflict. To them, the war's goal was simply to defeat the country's enemies, not to create a new world without discrimination. While many historians stress the liberalizing impact of the war, the social changes wrought by the conflict remained relatively limited. Although extreme bigotry lost respectability, American immigration policy remained largely unchanged as the national origins system went unchallenged.

FDR led the way in promoting the message of tolerance and national unity. As early as January 2, 1942, Roosevelt criticized employers who were firing loyal aliens, declaring that such actions were "engendering the very distrust and disunity on which our enemies are counting to defeat us."[26] In a fireside chat on February 23, he added, "We Americans will contribute unified production and unified acceptance of sacrifice and effort. That means a national unity that can know no limitations of race or creed or selfish politics."[27]

In his 1943 State of the Union Address, Roosevelt suggested the country had achieved wartime cooperation, saying, "We have given the lie to certain misconceptions—which is an extremely polite word—especially the one which holds that the various blocs or groups within a free country cannot forego their political and economic differences in time of crisis and work together toward a common goal."[28] Roosevelt often expressed an ideological view of the war's aims. "The United Nations are fighting to make a world in which tyranny and aggression cannot exist; a world based upon freedom, equality, and justice; a world in which all persons regardless of race, color or creed may live in peace, honor, and dignity," he declared on March 24, 1944.[29] Roosevelt repeated those sentiments in a campaign speech in Boston in the fall, saying, "They [our soldiers] also are fighting for a country and a world where men and women of all races, colors and creeds can live, work, speak and worship—in peace, freedom, and security."[30]

Propaganda posters by the OWI stressed the need for cooperation among all races, ethnic groups, religions, and classes. One poster declared, "TEAMWORK among all nationalities, groups and creeds made America great. That same teamwork now will spread our victory."[31] Others read, "In Unity There Is Strength" and "Together for Victory."[32] A poster represented an intact factory on one half with the caption "United We Stand." The other half showed a factory burning with the caption, "Divided We Fall."[33]

These posters promoted the idea that discrimination was un-American and deeply harmful to the war effort. One poster included a headline that said, "Our enemies' orders to their spies in the U.S.A," above a letter signed by Hitler, Mussolini, and Hirohito. The letter read, "Divide labor and management, turn class against class and spread religious hatred" as the caption instructed citizens to "FIGHT un-American propaganda." Another urged, "Don't fall for ENEMY PROPAGANDA—Against our Government—Against Our Allies—Against Catholics, Jews, or Protestants." The poster said below, "Remember—Hitler and the Japs are trying to get us to fight among ourselves."[34]

Echoing this sentiment, one poster displayed the text of President Roosevelt's Executive Order 8802 of 1941 banning racial discrimination in military production. Another showed a number of people working on a tank with names that represented a cross-section of ethnic groups, including Cohen, Lazarri, Kelly, and Du Bois, with the caption "Americans All." Below that, the poster paraphrased 8802: "it is the duty of employers and labor organizers to provide for the full participation of all workers without discrimination because of race, creed, color, or national origin."[35]

Although not the dominant message, traces of contributionism also appeared in these images. One poster showed what appear to be eastern and southern European immigrants and read, "This is America" in large letters, with "Keep it Free," scrolled at the bottom. In between, it described America as a "melting pot of liberty-loving people from all corners of the earth. People of different origins, faiths, cultures—all cemented together into one great nation by their passions for freedom. They have made America great—they have made America the hope of the world—This is your America." Another featured an immigrant saying, "I'm an Ellis Island American. I left the old country to be free—and nobody is going to take that freedom away. That's why I'm fighting on the production line—to help destroy the enemies of freedom. Let's keep 'em rolling."[36]

The posters also revealed the differing conceptions of the Japanese and the Chinese during the conflict. Posters routinely portrayed the Japanese in racist fashion, showing them with slanted eyes and large buckteeth.[37] One poster used this Japanese caricature with the caption, "SAVE A TAP . . . SLAP A JAP!"[38] On the other hand, the Chinese were depicted in a far more sympathetic light. One poster depicted a Chinese soldier with the caption "This man is your FRIEND . . . He fights for FREEDOM."[39] This representation accompanied several other identical posters with the same language, but featuring European allies of the United States.

The OWI delivered a similar message of unity to foreign-language newspapers concerning their coverage of the war. Future California Senator Alan Cranston, then chief of the Foreign Language Division of the OWI, told a group of editors and publishers on August 25, 1942, that, if their colleagues in underground newspapers overseas could send them a message, it would be "Unite! Stand together against the forces of aggression. Forget all differences until the forces of freedom are triumphant. Print nothing that will

Figure 1. A–C. World War II propaganda, such as the Office of War Information (OWI) posters shown, promoted tolerance for people of different faiths and nationalities as well as a more inclusive view of American identity. National Archives.

divert attention from the all-important task of defeating the Nazis and the Fascists."[40]

Believing the foreign-language press was more susceptible to enemy propaganda, the OWI provided them with a list of recommendations for their coverage, which are especially helpful in discerning the priorities and rationales behind government propaganda efforts. The first emphasized the ideological nature of the war: "This is not a racial or a national war, but a war against dictatorship and for the freedom of people of every race, color, and creed." The OWI also alerted the foreign-language press representatives to dangers they should avoid in their coverage, reiterating the need to diminish differences between ethnic groups: "We must close our ranks against the common enemy, the Axis. Strife within groups in this country weakens our war effort." It said they did not encourage any "news or discussion which tend to promote long-standing dissensions among Americans of different extractions. We must forget all differences until the forces of freedom are triumphant."[41]

Director Frank Capra's famous *Why We Fight* movie series contained similar messages. The films were a series of seven movies commissioned by the Pentagon to explain the reasons for the war and its goals. In episode 7, *War Comes to America*, Capra discusses religious life in America. The narrator says, "Churches. We have every denomination on earth. Sixty million of us regularly attend. And nobody tells us which one we have to go to." As the narrator reads this statement, the images of several churches appear on the screen, as well as one of a synagogue. In this film, a synagogue is simply another "church," rather than a place of worship for people of a different religion. This rhetoric and imagery promoted tolerance for non-Christian faiths by implying that all religions are essentially the same.[42]

The 1945 short film, *The House I Live In*, starring the young Frank Sinatra, expressed an almost identical point of view. Sinatra sees a mob of children attacking another young kid and asks them why they are picking on this one child. One of the children responds, "We don't like his religion," and another says, "Look mister, he's a dirty . . ." before Sinatra cuts him off. The singer tells them that they are behaving like Nazis:

Religion makes no difference. Except maybe to a Nazi or somebody as stupid. . . . God created everybody. He didn't create one people better than another. Your blood's the same as mine. Mine's the same as his. Do you know what this wonderful country is made of? It's

made up of a hundred different kinds of people and a hundred
different ways of talking and it's made up of a hundred different
ways of going to church. But they're all American ways.[43]

Sinatra, like the narrator of the *Why We Fight* episode, reflects the universalist approach of wartime propaganda. Both Sinatra and Capra largely
eschew discussing the disparate cultural contributions of various faiths;
instead, they cite the similarities between different religions as the primary
reason for religious tolerance.

Sinatra tells the children about the cooperation between Colin Kelly, a
Presbyterian pilot, and Meyer Levin, his Jewish comrade, when they
attacked a Japanese battleship after Pearl Harbor. "You think maybe they
should have called the bombing off because they had different religions?
Think about that, fellas. Use your good American heads. Don't let anyone
make suckers out of you," declares Sinatra. Ol' Blue Eyes concludes the
film by singing "The House I Live In," in which he pays tribute to the
contributions paradigm, crooning, "All races and religions. . . . That's
America to me."[44]

Sinatra's performance of the "The House I Live In" revealed that the
more inclusive wartime message encompassed Ellis Island-era immigrants
while largely excluding African Americans. One section of the song, which
contained references to black civil rights, was excluded from the film. This
version of *The House I Live In* spoke of "The words of old Abe Lincoln, of
Jefferson and Paine, of Washington and [Frederick] Douglass, and the task
that still remains!"[45]

Hollywood war films also featured themes of unity and cooperation.[46]
Movies such as *Bataan*, *Gung Ho*, *Guadalcanal Diary*, and *Pride of the
Marines* showed soldiers from different groups working together to defeat
the nation's enemies. Each of these "platoon" films had a variety of characters, usually including a southerner, a Jew, an Italian, and a native-stock
American. Like *The House I Live In*, the films demonstrated the limits of
the wartime message; blacks rarely appeared, and Asians were nonexistent
except as Japanese villains. African American groups protested their limited
presence in these movies; NAACP chief Walter White complained to OWI
director Elmer Davis that "the Negro has been very largely confined in the
films to comic or menial roles."[47]

These films downplayed the ethnic backgrounds of the characters and
simply presented a cross-section of ethnic types that were obvious to people

of the time. Sometimes, characters explicitly discuss the need for tolerance and cooperation. In *Gung Ho*, the commanding officer tells his troops to "cast out prejudices—racial, religious and every other kind."[48] In *Pride of the Marines*, a gun with both a Star of David and a shamrock painted on it depicts the importance of cooperation. More often, the message is simply implied. The audience sees soldiers from different ethnicities, religions, and regions working together without prejudice hindering their efforts.

Like other forms of wartime propaganda, the films underscored what Americans shared. One of the first images in *Guadalcanal Diary* is of a Catholic priest leading an interfaith service on a navy ship. One soldier says to another, "Say Sammy, your voice is OK." Sammy responds, "Why not? My father was a cantor in the synagogue."[49] The message is clear: people of all religions, or at least Jews, Catholics, and Protestants, are working together to fight the war.

National Brotherhood Week 1943 also reflected this perspective. Everett Clinchy, president of the NCCJ, invoked the same ideas as the OWI posters in a CBS Radio address. Clinchy discussed American soldiers in their training camps: "Do you realize what goes on in these camps? They make teams. Yes, teams like basketball teams and baseball teams, only these are fighting for our country's big ideas." Like the Hollywood films, Clinchy praised the ethnic platoon: "Listen to the roll-call of the families which have relatives in the service along with yours and mine,—Anderson, Bonet, Fernandez, Garcia, Goldstein, Jones, Kelly, Palegolos, Wysocki . . . the men who know that we don't have to fear anybody as long as the nation ticks together like the wheels of a clock."[50]

The motto for Brotherhood Week 1943 was "Brotherhood: Democracy's Shield Against Intolerance and Oppression," a significant shift from the "Make America Safe For Differences" slogan of 1939. The literature instructed religious groups to have a priest, a minister, and a rabbi deliver the message of tolerance to their congregations, so that all major faiths were represented. Declaring that all forms of prejudice must be rejected, one such trio reiterated that the mission was "to proclaim and illustrate by acting at home these principles of justice, amity, understanding and cooperation among men of all religious persuasions and racial origins upon which human brotherhood depends and to commend them to the world."[51]

Elements of Brotherhood Week, like government propaganda, stressed that prejudice and discrimination hurt the war effort. One radio program dramatized a discussion between the familiar triumvirate of a priest, rabbi, and minister. In one part, the priest says, "The Axis certainly recognizes this power of brotherhood. Their propaganda, you will have noticed, is designed to split up any united effort to create dissension, division, hatred of one group against another." The minister concurs that the Nazis use racial divisions to weaken their opponents, and the rabbi concludes this part of the discussion, urging that "It's up to us to resist this kind of attack with all our might. Not only that . . . it's up to us to attack with the greatest spiritual weapon we have . . . the fighting weapon of brotherhood."[52]

While emphasizing tolerance, Brotherhood Week did not entirely discard contributionism. Clinchy also asked rhetorically in his radio address, "What is the American Idea? It is the big idea that on a continent 3,000 miles wide people of 47 Old World nationalities have come to live together as one nation." He also noted that Americans can often be divided by religion and ethnicity and that these divisions did not necessarily present a problem. Expressing the contributionist idea that differences were acceptable, as long as everyone maintained a commitment to a common set of ideals, Clinchy argued, "The only danger is that each might build the walls of separation too high so that they do not know what their neighbors are thinking or doing and do not understand them or cooperate with them."[53]

I Am an American Day offered a similar wartime message. This observance grew dramatically during the war, from 200 participating communities in 1939 to 500 in 1943.[54] The INS published a guide to staging these ceremonies in 1943 entitled, "Gateway to Citizenship." The celebration centered on an induction ceremony for new citizens, speeches on the meaning of being an American, and patriotic songs.

The speeches, editorials and celebrations associated with the day offered familiar themes. One speech/editorial in 1943 read, "Hitler has moved heaven and earth to break our spirit by dividing us. His propagandists have tried to start American Catholics, Protestants and Jews quarrelling among themselves." It continued, "But they have lost their gamble. Our people have not lived in America as separated racial and religious groups. Instead they have fused into a single durable alloy . . . the American people."[55] Another speech, in 1944, stressed that tolerance was an essential part of being an American: "Real Americanism—the only Americanism any of us can accept without reserve—is based on respect for human beings, the conviction that the true worth of an individual has no relation to his birthplace, religion, or color."[56]

I Am an American Day featured the contributionist message more prominently than other celebrations. A stock speech in 1944 said, "America is a nation built by immigrants—and by the sons of immigrants . . . They enriched our science and culture, bringing with them their music, art, their hunger for learning and their appetite for the good life."[57] A radio spot agreed: "Since the founding of our nation, successive generations of new citizens, born in different countries and brought up with different cultures and religions have brought their gifts to our nation."[58]

As with the platoon films, I Am an American Day festivities revealed how African Americans could be excluded from the more expansive definition of American identity. While New York City Mayor Fiorello LaGuardia asked NAACP President Walter White to serve as a member of his holiday committee every year during the war, it seems likely that blacks played a less prominent role in many communities. Chester Gillespie, an attorney in Cleveland, wrote White before I Am an American Day 1942 to suggest an alternative version of the immigration celebration: "I believe Negroes all over the country should call May 17th 'I Am an American Too' day and in connection there—with huge mass meetings should be held. Such action seems necessary because the government has officially set Negroes apart from the American people."[59]

Still, some observers believed the tolerance message would eventually have implications for the status of American blacks. Most famously, Gunnar Myrdal's study *An American Dilemma* suggested that the World War II-era ideology exposed the contradiction between American ideals and practices. Myrdal, a Swedish sociologist analyzing race relations in America, noted that the war required the United States to profess ideas of tolerance and equality to combat the fascist doctrines of the Nazis and the Japanese. "The Negro problem has taken on a significance greater than it ever had since the Civil War," concluded Myrdal. "The world conflict and America's exposed position as the defender of the democratic faith is thus accelerating an ideological process which was well under way."[60]

I Am an American Day celebrations, like wartime propaganda, also illuminated the divergent fates of Japanese and Chinese Americans during the war. Organizers often excluded Japanese Americans from these observances, while Chinese Americans were sometimes included. For instance, in a 1943 holiday in San Francisco, Chinese Americans participated along with various Euro-American groups in offering examples of their native cultures.[61]

American education also entered the fight for tolerance during the war. In 1944, the National Education Association, the nation's largest teachers' union, made "education for tolerance" a priority for that year. Like other

groups, the intercultural education movement shifted from a contributionist approach to promoting unity and cooperation, as the Service Bureau
for Intercultural Education became simply the Bureau of Intercultural
Education.[62]

The AJC magazine declared, "The basic idea upon which intercultural
education rests is simple. It is that members of one culture group can be
taught to get along with members of other groups within the framework of a
democratic society." Unlike the Americanization campaigns of the World
War I era, intercultural education did not seek to eliminate group differences.[63] Instead, intercultural education exposed students to the cultures of
different immigrant groups. Students visited ethnic restaurants and neighborhoods, prominent figures from different groups appeared at classrooms, and
schools held joint celebrations of Christmas and Chanukah. These programs
focused on the similarities between peoples. "Folk dances, folk music, historical pageants, and native costumes emphasize the 'sameness' of all people in
their joys, sorrows, etc. rather than the 'strangeness' of different groups,"
according to the AJC.[64] A poster in one classroom summarized this perspective: "America—A Nation of One People from Many Countries."[65]

The military also promoted tolerance in its ranks. Every week, the Orien-
tation Section of the Information and Education Division, Army Service
Forces (ASF), distributed a discussion outline on important issues. Groups
were supposed to discuss the topic for a minimum of an hour a week during
a period called Army Talk.[66] The subject of Army Talk 70 for May 5, 1945,
was prejudice, and the message was a familiar one. "The man who spreads
rumors," ASF Manual M 5 declared, "particularly rumors about any group—
racial, religious, or national is doing Hitler's or Tojo's work." The manual
asked the soldiers why racial and religious discrimination was harmful. The
Army replied, "History has taught us that when we discriminate against one
segment of people, we set a pattern that may be used against other groups."[67]

Though Army Talk focused on fighting prejudice, elements of the contributionism paradigm appeared as well: "What many seem to forget is that
we are all immigrants or the children of immigrants. No one has a right to
complain about 'foreigners' unless it be the American Indian." The manual
went on to say, "Our country has been made great by people who came
from every land under the sun—people with names like Carnegie, Sikorsky,
Toscanini, Einstein, Osler—and thousands more."[68]

Army regulations also facilitated interfaith cooperation, as standard
operating procedure required chaplains to accommodate the religious

needs of soldiers from traditions different from their own. In fact, religious leaders would actively participate in the rituals and celebrations of other faiths; in one case, an Episcopal minister conducted a Passover seder when no rabbi was available. It was very common for a priest, a rabbi, and a minister jointly to lead funeral services for fallen soldiers. Cooperation did not always come easily, of course, and sometimes these policies forced religious conflicts to the surface. Declaring that his faith did not recognize the legitimacy of other religions, a Catholic chaplain once refused to provide volunteers for a seder. As a whole, though, military protocol, like Brotherhood Week, buttressed the idea that the United States was a "Judeo-Christian nation."[69]

"Car cards" appeared in buses, subways, and streetcars during the war with the same theme. These cards featured various protolerance and antiprejudice messages, such as, "If You Hear Anyone Condemn a Fellow American Because of Race or Religion . . . Tel 'em Off [sic]" and "We Fought Together . . . Let's Work Together." Another showed a child crying while saying, "I Am So an American!" The rest of the card responded, "You Bet, Sonny . . . No Matter What Your Race or Religion!"[70]

These messages were ubiquitous during the war. Dr. Samuel Flowerman, research director of the AJC, noted in a speech at the Waldorf Towers on November 30, 1945, "You have seen full page ads, you have seen billboards, you have seen match folders driving home the unity message; Catholics, Protestants, and Jews having fought together and lived together and died together and the need for unity in the post-war period." He noted the breadth of these efforts: "On the radio more than 216 individual stations broadcast every day some message of unity. . . . Way over a quarter million books have been distributed in libraries, hoping that people will understand and people will change their own ideas and get them across to others."[71]

Toward the end of the conflict and in its immediate aftermath, government and private organizations began to emphasize that the tolerance and unity essential to winning the war was also vital to the survival of postwar America. They feared that nativism, while submerged during the war, lurked beneath the surface and that domestic bigots were poised to take advantage of any instability that might occur while the country returned to a civilian footing. The AJC began to plan a program for the postwar world:

Twelve years of the Nazi propaganda of falsehood directed at this country have, unfortunately, aroused certain antagonisms between

groups of our population. . . . Today the time has come for informing the American people of the dangers to American life and to
American prosperity which the animosities resulting from this propaganda involve, and which will continue to use Hitler's methods
to promote their own selfish methods.[72]

The AJC discussed the need to use contributionism as a theme: "We are a
nation of all national origins, all religious faiths, all races. . . . During the
post-war era, it should be possible to publicize the contributions of men
and women of all these national, racial, and religious origins in the work of
making America a better place to live."[73]

Jewish groups were not the only ones concerned about intolerance in
the postwar world. Archbishop Francis Spellman of New York, the leading
American Catholic figure of the time, expressed similar fears in the fall of
1945. "Every true American and true Catholic must be the unequivocal
opponent of every species of bigotry," declared Spellman, adding "We must
be on guard lest hysteria following this war give rise to despotic bigotry,
political, racial, occupational or religious."[74]

Appeals during Brotherhood Week offered similar warnings about the
dangers of the postwar world. FDR's Brotherhood Week message for 1945
suggested, "It is a solemn duty for us to keep our country free of prejudice
and bigotry so that when our fighting men return they may find us living
by the freedom for which they are ready to give full measure of devotion."[75]
A speech for Brotherhood Week declared, "Though the battle moves in our
favor, we can lose it even in victory. Though we win by arms, we shall all
go down to destruction if the spirit of brotherhood dies."[76]

Concern about ethnic divisions following the war went beyond progressive and religious organizations. Eric Johnston, president of the U.S. Chamber of Commerce, a conservative business group, gave a speech stressing
that prejudice hindered economic growth. The AJC paraphrased a version
of his talk for distribution: "True economic progress demands that the
whole nation move forward at the same time. Prejudice does not pay," he
declared, "Discrimination is destructive. These are things that should be
manifest to the American people if we are to counteract the pestiferous
labors of race and hate-mongers."[77] Johnston's belief that discrimination
harmed prosperity would become a central theme after the war. He continued, "Let's not apologize for the amazing variety of our human material
here in America. Let us rather glory in it as the source of our robust spirit

and opulent achievements," adding that Americans need to be reminded that the country "receives more than it gives" from immigrants.[78]

Hollywood movies also began to highlight the need for tolerance in the postwar world. In *Pride of the Marines* (1945), another multiethnic platoon is fighting on Guadalcanal. The movie revolves around Al Schmid, a soldier who is blinded while fighting for his life during the battle. After he is wounded, he is sent to a military hospital to recover. He convalesces with a number of other wounded soldiers, who are concerned about their prospects in the postwar world.

Lee Diamond, a Jewish soldier wounded with Schmid, stresses the need to continue wartime cooperation: "One happy afternoon when God was feeling good, he sat down and he thought up a rich beautiful country, and he named it the USA. . . . Don't tell me we can't make it work in peace like we do in war. Don't tell me we can't pull together." The film reiterates the need for tolerance in postwar America. On a train back to the East Coast to receive a medal, Schmid fears his blindness will make him unable to obtain employment. Diamond tells him a lot of people will have problems after the war. Schmid replies, "What problems have you got? You're in one piece ain't you. . . . When you go for a job there ain't nobody gonna say we don't have a use for ex-heroes like you." Diamond explains: "There's guys that won't hire me because my name is Diamond instead of Jones. Cause I celebrate Passover instead of Easter. Don't you see what I mean. . . . You and me . . . we need the same kind of world. We need a country to live in where no one gets booted around for any reason."[79]

The war's conclusion did not relieve the anxieties of the protolerance coalition, as these groups continued to fear that ethnoreligious disunity and prejudice posed an imminent threat to the nation's social and political health. The Ad Council, an organization founded in 1942 to make public service announcements during the war, declared, "Our nation no longer has the supremely unifying cause of victory. The trend will be to stop pulling together, to stop working for the common good. Group clashes promise to be renewed, old hatreds revived; new war-born discords seem almost inevitable."[80] Some feared that unless wartime unity continued, the United States might undergo some kind of political cataclysm. The AJC added, "If the present system is allowed to proceed unchecked, it can undermine the American system. It may lead to revolution or dictatorship in which no cultural or economic group would be secure, in which freedom from fear and want would become a lost memory."[81] Flowerman said in his speech at the Waldorf Towers in November 1945, "the war of machines and bullets has ended temporarily, not in all parts of the world, but the war of ideas has not even begun. We are just in the early stages of the war of ideas." Referring to domestic bigots, Flowerman alleged, "The enemy is not over there; the enemy isn't in the Pacific, the enemy is here."[82]

National Brotherhood Week's growing popularity exemplified the continuity with wartime themes, and the NCCJ summary of Brotherhood Week 1946 suggested it was the biggest and most successful ever: "It topped all previous years. Never was it more evident that Brotherhood Week has been taken over by the nation at large, and made it its own."[83] Equally revealing was the message for 1946. The slogan, echoing wartime propaganda, was "In Peace as in War TEAMWORK!" President Truman wrote a letter in support of the goals of Brotherhood Week, declaring, "The teamwork of the armed forces won the war. The spirit of teamwork should extend to our national life. As we united for victory, we must unite for peace."[84]

The week focused on the common bonds between Protestants, Catholics, and Jews. Three Supreme Court justices of different faiths, Felix Frankfurter, Harlan Stone, and Frank Murphy, stood on the steps of the court for a newsreel in support of Brotherhood Week.[85] A radio roundtable between members of the three faiths emphasized the same idea. The Protestant says, "It's a strange thing, but what has become the burning necessity of modern times brings us back to the age-old teachings of the three religions we represent. The core of three religions is the brotherhood of men, under God."[86]

The promotional materials for Brotherhood Week repeated the theme. "Our national unity brought about by common peril is endangered now that the thunder of the guns is silenced. . . . Intergroup hatred slows up teamwork, kills the democratic spirit." Other materials suggested that prejudice was "America's Number One Problem." The literature cited polls showing that 13 percent of people surveyed said they would join a hate campaign against Jews and 7 percent wanted a campaign against the Catholic Church. Finally, the materials discussed the economic costs of discrimination: "Education for brotherhood costs money. But it does not cost nearly as much as bigotry, hate, riots, and war."[87]

Members of Brotherhood Week's distinguished Board of Governors weighed in with their views on the importance of tolerance. William Green, head of the AFL, said, "Prejudice and intolerance are crimes against democracy." Paul Hoffman of Studebaker Corporation added, "Tolerance must become something more than a passive word—it must become a fighting faith."[88]

There were traces of the contributionist message that was central to the 1939 celebration. Frankfurter declared in a newsreel, "The unfolding of our republic is the story of the greatest racial admixture in history. Foreign-born citizens from almost every land fought in the war for independence, helped to save the union, and in conspicuous numbers are found on the honor rolls of the two world wars."[89] The NCCJ also suggested that schools produce plays illustrating the contributions of various groups to American life.[90]

The overriding message, however, focused less on contributions than on intergroup cooperation. Truman's letter in support of Brotherhood Week 1947 reinforced this theme: "Democracy rests upon brotherhood. Justice, amity, understanding and cooperation among Protestants, Catholics, and Jews throughout the nation are cornerstones of our democracy. . . . With them we can maintain our national unity and keep up the teamwork needed in peace as in war."[91]

I Am an American Day followed a similar course after the conflict. The celebration continued its enormous growth, expanding to 1,100 communities by 1945.[92] In 1946, the Justice Department suggested a number of approaches for material to be published or broadcast on the day. It first emphasized the need to continue wartime unity during peacetime. Other suggestions included "draw attention to the rich contributions to American thought and life, to her arts and science, by her foreign-born citizens" and "combat the doctrines that would divide and weaken this Nation by pitting one group of Americans against another."[93]

Unsurprisingly, the celebrations tended to be concentrated in states with significant immigrant populations. According to the INS, 35 states had at least one city with multiple I Am an American Day celebrations, and such observances were usually in large and medium-sized cities in the Northeast and Midwest. Boston, New York, and Pittsburgh, as well as other major metropolitan areas, held festivities every year between 1939 and 1945. Smaller communities with diverse populations like Fort Wayne, Indiana, and Fall River, Massachusetts, observed the day at least five times in the same time frame. The 15 states that did not feature cities with multiple celebrations were predominantly in the South and the West.[94]

The Minneapolis observance of I Am an American Day 1947 provides an illustration of a typical community's celebration. The morning featured a music program followed by a talk by Mayor Hubert Humphrey and presentation of certificates of citizenship to new arrivals to the country. With the certificates, the new Americans pledged to protect the Constitution and "to oppose all efforts to divide the American people and to sow the seeds of bigotry and prejudice among them."[95] Humphrey added, "The United States of America owes its greatness as a nation to the diversity of the peoples of all races and nationalities who have, over the generations, migrated to our shores."[96] Detroit's observance offered a similar array of events. In addition to a talk by the mayor, academics lectured the new Americans on the responsibilities of citizenship, including the necessity of voting.[97] Both celebrations included speeches and radio performances by people of various racial and ethnic groups.

Materials surrounding the celebration of I Am an American Day repeatedly emphasized that Americans should not judge people on the basis of their race, color, or creed. One suggested editorial for 1947 exhorted, "Whenever a man is refused a job because of his parentage or religion; wherever a hooded gang can keep a man from voting; wherever folks are kept from speaking their minds without fear, American security is in danger."[98]

In 1948, the AJC used a play, *Do You Know the Score*, to illustrate the themes of I Am an American Day.[99] In the play, three young girls imagine they are informing "Uncle Sam" about racial problems by reenacting the development of the 1947 *To Secure These Rights* report. The Committee on Civil Rights, appointed by President Truman to propose solutions to America's racial problem, actually wrote the report. It proposed a series of measures, including a Fair Employment Practices Commission (FEPC), as well as anti-poll tax and anti-lynching legislation.

During the play, the fictional attorney general, secretary of state, and secretary of labor testify and reiterate anti-prejudice messages. After describing the nation's racial and religious problems, from lynchings to quotas in colleges and universities, one of the girls asks Uncle Sam if all Americans have the right to equal opportunity. Sam, having heard the testimony, responds, "I've got to admit that there is discrimination against Americans because of their race and religion; not only in finding jobs, but in getting into colleges and professional schools, too, and often in buying or renting a place to live."[100] At the conclusion of the production, the girls stress the importance of action not only on the part of government but on the part of individuals in their daily lives. One says, "Sure. You've got to practice what you preach. Once we learn the truth ourselves—that it doesn't make a bit of difference one way or the other, what a man's color or religion is—then we have to act up to our beliefs, every day, and in every way."[101]

By the late 1940s, celebrations such as I Am an American Day, Brother-hood Week, and ethnic festivals had become regular features of American life. In spring 1949, *Common Ground* ran a series of pictures depicting these festivals: "Whatever the occasion, the nationality costumes on parade are by now a colorful and thoroughly American phenomenon . . . a moving away from the old repressive type of Americanization toward acceptance and deep appreciation of the United States as the meeting-ground and working-together-ground of people from all over the earth."[102]

These festivals and holidays were only one of the ways organizations promoted the tolerance message. The AJC Department of Public Informa-tion sponsored the First American Exhibition on Superstition, Prejudice and Fear. The exhibition, held at the American Museum of Natural His-tory in New York in August 1948, contained an area known as the "Hall of Prejudice." This section featured, among other things, a quiz called "How Much Do You Know About the Human Races?" The answers to the quiz demonstrated that every nation is an amalgamation of different races and that the "strongest nation," the United States, contained the greatest mixture.[103] The exhibit also included illustrations from books such as *Races of Mankind* by Ruth Benedict, which criticized theories of scientific racism. One sign in the exhibit said, "Judge a person for himself, not for His Color, Race or Creed."[104]

The other elements of the prejudice section reflected this message. One section quoted Ford Frick, president of major league baseball's National League. "This is the United States of America and one citizen has as much a right to play as another," Frick affirmed.[105] The exhibit also urged Ameri-cans to "INSIST UPON NON-DISCRIMINATION in your own club, team, school, church, and other organizations."[106] The museum drew a record crowd for a summer exhibit, and the AJC planned to have the display shown throughout the nation.[107]

The emphasis on tolerance also continued in movies following the war, as Hollywood made a number of films decrying bigotry and anti-Semitism, most notably *Crossfire* and *Gentlemen's Agreement*. A wide array of people in Hollywood, both Jewish and non-Jewish, pushed for these films to be made. Interestingly, the AJC opposed making the movies because they feared they might precipitate an anti-Semitic backlash.[108]

The two films told very different stories about anti-Semitism but pro-moted the same message about the necessity of tolerance. In *Crossfire*, Rob-ert Young and Robert Mitchum play a policeman and a military officer who investigate the murder of a Jewish man. In *Gentlemen's Agreement*, Gregory Peck portrays a reporter who pretends to be a Jew to write a story about anti-Semitism in America. Both films were nominated for the Academy Award for best picture in 1947, with *Gentlemen's Agreement* receiving the award. While the films discuss anti-Semitism, they also pursue the broader theme of the universality of prejudice and its overall dangers to society.

In both films, traditional anti-Semitic stereotypes are visible. During the war, there were persistent rumors that a disproportionate number of draft-dodgers were Jews. In *Crossfire*, Montgomery (Robert Ryan), the soldier who turns out to be the killer, claims not to have met the victim, Joseph Samuels, until that evening. He tells Captain Finlay (Young), "Of course . . . seen a lot of guys like him." Finlay says, "Like what?" Montgomery responds, "Oh, you know, guys that played it safe during the war. Scrounged around keeping themselves in civvies. Got swell apartments. Swell dames. You know the kind." Finlay replies, "I'm not sure that I do. Just what kind?" Montgomery elaborates, "Oh you know. Some of them are named Samuels. Some of them got funnier names."[109] In *Gentlemen's Agreement*, a co-worker assumes Phil Green (Peck) must have been in public relations rather than in the trenches because he seems like a "clever guy."[110]

The impact of military service in World War II on attitudes toward ethnicity and religion can be seen in the reactions to these stereotypes. In response to Montgomery's comments, Sergeant Keeley (Mitchum) says, "He ought to look at the casualty lists some time. There a lot of funny names there too."[111] Indeed, Samuels turns out to have been a veteran who was wounded at Okinawa. In *Gentlemen's Agreement*, the primary Jewish character, a childhood friend of Green's, is a veteran who has difficulty buying a home because he is Jewish.[112]

The films both stress the need to look beyond the more odious forms of anti-Semitism and examine the genteel prejudice that exists in America among people who do not consider themselves bigots. In both films, even the most "harmless" form of prejudice is seen as equally threatening. In *Gentlemen's Agreement*, Green's editor tells him he wants to get beyond the overt anti-Semites and root out "the people who would never attend an anti-Semitic meeting or send a dime to Gerald K. Smith."[113] In *Crossfire*, Finlay says, "This business of hating Jews comes in a lot of different sizes. There's the you can't join our country club kind. And you can't live around here kind. And yes, you can't work here kind. And because we stand for all of these we get Monty's kind. . . . We don't get him very often . . . but he grows out of all the rest."

The movies emphasize the similarities between ethnic and religious groups. In *Gentlemen's Agreement*, Green's son asks him, "What are Jews anyway? I mean exactly." Green responds, "There are lots of different churches. The people who go to that particular church are called Catholics. Then there are people who go to other churches and they're called Protestants. And there others who go to still different churches and they're called Jews. Only they call their kind of churches synagogues or temples." This language echoes the approach of wartime films like *Why We Fight* and *The House I Live In*. Green adds, "You can be an American and a Protestant or a Catholic or a Jew. Religion is different from nationality." Green also reproaches his Jewish secretary for her shock when he reveals that he is a Gentile. In a variation on Shylock's "Hath not a Jew eyes" speech from Shakespeare's *The Merchant of Venice*, he declares, "Same face. Same eyes. Same nose. Same suit. Same everything. Here take my hand. Feel it. Same flesh as yours, isn't it? No different today than it was yesterday, Miss Wales. The only thing that's different is the word Christian."[114]

Along the same lines, *Crossfire* demonstrates that any kind of prejudice is the problem, not merely anti-Semitism. Finlay has to convince Leroy, a GI from Tennessee, to help him obtain evidence against Montgomery. Leroy says, "I don't see that this is any of my business anyway." Finlay asks, "Has Monty ever made fun of your accent?" Leroy replies, "Sure. Lots of times." Finlay says, "He laughs at you because you are from Tennessee. He's never even been to Tennessee. Ignorant men always laugh at things that are different. Things they don't understand. They're afraid of things they don't understand. They end up hating them."

Finlay also tells LeRoy that his grandfather was killed for being an Irish Catholic a century ago in Philadelphia. Perhaps reflecting the paucity of information in history books on immigrants, Finlay says, "That's history, Leroy. They don't teach it in school. But it's real American history just the same." He continues, "Thomas Finlay was killed in 1848 just because he was an Irishman and a Catholic. It happened many times. . . . And last night Joseph Samuels was killed just because he was a Jew." Further universalizing the experience of prejudice, Finlay concludes, "Hating is always the same. Always senseless. One day it kills Irish Catholics, the next day Jews, the next day Protestants, the next day Quakers, it's hard to stop, it can end up killing men who wear stripe neckties, or people from Tennessee."[115]

The films reveal the limitations of the expansion of American identity as the movies clearly focus on anti-Semitism. The inclusion of the white ethnic groups came, to some extent, at the expense of other racial groups. They were not yet seen as requiring the full attention of the country with regard to anti-prejudice efforts.

Nevertheless, national civil rights organizations reiterated Finlay's message that every kind of prejudice affected all minorities.[116] At its 1947 national conference, the NAACP passed a resolution on racial and religious tensions, declaring that "In defending the rights of Negroes, we recognize the fact that what happens to one minority group effects all the others," adding, "we must combat the continuing wave of anti-Jewish, anti-Semitic, anti-Oriental, anti-foreign born feeling in this country."[117] Rabbi Irving Miller, president of the AJC, discussed similar themes when he addressed the 1950 NAACP convention: "Through the thousands of years of our tragic histories we should have learned one lesson and learned it well: that the persecution at any time of any minority portends the shape, quality and intensity of the persecution of all minorities."[118]

This message remained visible in educational programs into the late 1940s. The Ad Council launched a campaign called United America in June 1946 to attack prejudice. According to the Ad Council's 1946–47 annual report, the campaign's "objective is to promote American unity by the lessening of inter-faith and inter-racial prejudices."[119] Like Brotherhood Week, the campaign echoed the wartime themes of unity, cooperation, and the dangers of prejudice and discrimination. The Council, however, was not simply motivated by altruism in this regard. Business leaders played a leading role in the organization, and many wanted to stress a message of "unity" because of the labor-management strife that emerged following the war, particularly the strike wave of 1946–47. As a result, some ads, which reiterated the necessity of cooperation between workers and business, also served to promote the message that assertive behavior by organized labor might threaten the nation's fragile postwar prosperity.[120]

All the 1949 ads concluded by emphasizing that tolerance was an essential element of American identity: "Make sure that you are not spreading rumors against a race or religion. Speak up, wherever you are, against prejudice, and work for better understanding. Remember that's what it means—to be a good American citizen."[121] One ad reiterated that rumors about different ethnic groups posed just as great danger to American unity today as they did during World War II, adding, "But perhaps we don't know that rumors are just as dangerous today as they were during the war. *Because*—rumors about other groups, other religions and other races always threaten our national unity—without which we cannot hope to survive."[122]

Another ad said in large letters "HOW TO COMMIT SUICIDE." The ad went on to say, "No not you!—but possibly your country. Nations have collapsed before because they allowed disunity to destroy them." The ad concluded by referring to the international consequences of discrimination: "If we discriminate against other people for any reason, we'll soon find others discriminating against us. Then what will we have? A family squabble—national disunity—and the enemies of our system laughing up their sleeves."[123]

By this time, international themes were becoming more prominent in these programs, partly to counter Soviet propagandists who were attempting to use the discrepancy between American rhetoric and practice as a tool in the Cold War.[124] During the *Do You Know the Score* play, the fictional secretary of state testifies, "Here we are trying to promote human rights all over the world and I have to explain away discrimination right here in my own country. . . . You cannot be a world leader when all these people distrust you! And they *will* distrust us if we continue to give raw deals to our own American citizens, just because of their race and their religion."[125] A radio spot for I Am an American Day in 1949 added, "Today they [immigrants] join with their fellow-Americans in telling the world that it's great to live in a land where bigotry and discrimination are on the run, where human rights and brotherhood are on the rise, where there's equality, opportunity and justice for all."[126] A speech from the conservative Veterans of Foreign Wars for Brotherhood Week 1949 echoed this sentiment: "The V.F.W. believes that [brotherhood] can be our effective answer to the communist and fascist enemies who foster DIS-unity among our own people in an effort to conquer the very foundation of American democracy."[127]

The VFW involvement in the antidiscrimination campaign reveals how much this language became part of postwar American thought and rhetoric, if not practice. Most programs promoting tolerance came from liberal organizations such as the NCCJ and AJC. The VFW rhetoric for Brotherhood Week 1949, however, was virtually identical to that of the progressive groups: "Some of our people forget that American Protestants and Catholics, Gentiles and Jews, Japanese-Americans, Negroes and men of many other racial origins have fought shoulder to shoulder under one flag—the Stars and Stripes."[128]

ᴄᴠ

World War II laid the groundwork for the greater inclusion of the descendents of southern and eastern European immigrants during the post-war period. The universalist message of tolerance and unity, however, facilitated this greater inclusion of white ethnics by emphasizing that these groups were little different from native-stock Americans or each other. Furthermore, the expansion of American identity conspicuously excluded Latinos, Asians, and African Americans. The contributionist ideology, which focused more on the unique cultural benefits brought by these different groups, faded into the background. This message would slowly gain strength during the 1950s and 1960s, as Americans grew increasingly appreciative of the cultural and economic assets brought by the "nation of immigrants."

Chapter 4

How Much Did the War Change America?

What impact did the combination of a war against racist enemies and cultural and educational campaigns promoting tolerance actually have on attitudes toward immigrants? Toward the end of the war, *Yank*, the Army weekly, used its open-forum section "The Soldier Speaks" to ask servicemen the question, "What changes would you like to see in post-war America?" M/Sergeant Joe McCarthy, managing editor of *Yank*, wrote a piece about soldiers' responses in the *New York Times Magazine* on August 5, 1945: "They mentioned, above everything else, the need for wiping out racial and religious discrimination." The soldiers' suggestions were quite similar to the language of wartime propaganda. "Make racial discrimination a Federal offense" and "We must learn to live together regardless of race, color, creed, customs, or domain" were among the comments.[1]

Nine states, including New York, Oregon, and Rhode Island, passed laws banning employment discrimination in the years following World War II.[2] By February 1946, the percentage of people saying they would support an organized campaign against Jews fell so low that the Opinion Research Corporation ceased asking the question in polls.[3] As Gunnar Myrdal predicted in *An American Dilemma*, the war did produce improvements for black Americans. President Harry Truman created the aforementioned Committee on Civil Rights in 1946, which recommended an aggressive civil rights program. In the spring of 1947, Jackie Robinson broke the color barrier in the national pastime when he started on opening day for the Brooklyn Dodgers. In 1948, Truman issued an executive order desegregating the military, and the Supreme Court ruled in *Shelley v. Kraemer* that restrictive covenants used to discriminate against minorities in housing were not enforceable in the courts.

Despite these advances, progress for blacks remained incremental. Race riots broke out in Detroit and Harlem in 1943. Black veterans returning home in 1945–46 were met with the largest wave of lynchings in a generation, and African Americans who attempted to vote in the South after the war faced violence and intimidation.

Asian Americans made small gains. In 1946, Congress created quotas of 100 slots for Indians and Filipinos, further weakening the elements of the Johnson-Reed Act of 1924 that had largely barred Asian immigration. The government also took minor steps toward correcting the injustice of the Japanese internment. Congress passed the Japanese American Evacuation Claims Act of 1948, which, while not admitting the wartime measure was unnecessary, provided limited compensation for lost property. Finally, voters in California defeated a referendum to strengthen laws against Asians owning land by a margin of almost 3–2.[4]

While there were notable improvements in attitudes by some measurements, the postwar period saw more continuity in attitudes than change. On the one hand, public displays of racism became less acceptable. Indeed, the cumulative effect of wartime propaganda and a conflict with genocidal governments seemed to reduce the respectability of overt bigotry and of figures who divided society along racial, religious, and ethnic lines. Nevertheless, certain traditional attitudes remained entrenched. School textbooks still neglected the accomplishments of southern and eastern Europeans, and most Americans resisted allowing greater immigration into the United States. As the 1950s dawned, support for the national origins system, as the debate over displaced persons following World War II revealed, remained strong.

∽

The fate of Senator Theodore G. Bilbo of Mississippi, nicknamed "The Man," illustrates the stigmatization of extreme bigotry in the postwar period. Bilbo, like many public officials before the war, had uttered racist comments and faced little reproach. In the aftermath of the war, however, "The Man" became a national symbol of bigotry because of his especially crude racist, anti-Semitic, and anti-Italian comments.

Bilbo enjoyed a long career in American politics before he became known as the nation's leading racist public official. Twice governor of Mississippi, he was elected to the Senate in 1934. He drew support from poor whites of Mississippi by persistently employing flamboyant, populist rhetoric to attack Wall Street. But it was his style as much as his legislative program that earned him devout followers and staunch enemies. Alan Brinkley described Bilbo's manner: "Stripped to his shirtsleeves, wearing a flaming red necktie with a diamond stickpin, he campaigned with a contagious passion, whipping crowds into frenzied excitement with his denunciations of 'Wall Streeters,' entrenched political interest groups, corporate monopolies and the establishment press."[5]

When Bilbo entered the Senate in 1934, many in the political establishment feared he would gain prominence as a populist demagogue along the lines of Huey Long of Louisiana. He remained, however, largely unknown during his early years in the Senate. He amassed a strong New Deal voting record, even supporting some legislation, such as public housing, that gave his more conservative Southern colleagues pause.[6]

"The Man" finally gained some attention in 1938 when he proposed a plan to repatriate blacks to Africa. Despite the audacity of this scheme, it drew only a few articles in the national press. When he ran for reelection in 1940, the *New York Times* described him as an obscure figure, saying "he was out of office for three years, then won election to the Senate. There he has seldom spoken on national affairs."[7] Moreover, Bilbo campaigned for Democratic candidates in states like Missouri where black votes held the key to victory. Before the war, his public bigotry drew little notice or condemnation.

Bilbo generated some controversy in 1944 when he made racist statements about African Americans. Bilbo, however, added anti-Semitism to his arsenal when Congress debated the Fair Employment Practices Commission (FEPC) again in June 1945. He delivered a long speech denouncing the legislation and submitted for the record a series of letters he had received from his constituents. The following letter came from a man Bilbo described as "an old friend of mine": "I continuously travel the United States and give my word from close examination that the birds behind all this social race equality stuff are Jews—from that rat [Walter] Winchell to the most illiterate second-hand man." Bilbo then proceeded to discuss the ethnic composition of the FEPC's employees, noting that many of them were black, Jewish, and Japanese. He asked, "Do Senators propose that we spend $446,000 of the people's money for 66 Negroes, 12 Jews, a few gentiles, and two Japs, just to be 'lollypops' for this country, 'sugar boys' going around pacifying?"[8]

Attacks on Bilbo reached the national level following this speech. *The Nation* wrote, "Senator Bilbo's exhibition last Thursday made it appear that at the cost of hundreds of thousands of lives we had destroyed Hitler's racial obscenity in Europe only to have it parade in all its shameless arrogance at the very center of our democracy." It added, "Perhaps we should warn the other nations that Bilbo is an atavistic survival and not an effective symbol of American democracy. . . . the challenge is nothing less than to extirpate from American public life all the evil intolerance that Bilbo and [Mississippi Representative John] Rankin personify."⁹

Anger at Bilbo only intensified in the summer of 1945 when it was revealed he wrote a letter to a New York woman, Josephine Piccolo, on July 1, with the introduction, "Dear Dago." Vito Marcantonio, Piccolo's representative in Congress, demanded that Bilbo apologize. Bilbo responded that he would apologize if she apologized to him for writing a "nasty, insulting, pusillanimous letter."¹⁰ Needless to say, this did not settle matters.

Samuel Dickstein, a Democratic congressman from New York City, continued the assault by attacking Bilbo for dividing the nation when he made public a letter he wrote to the "the Man" saying "a U.S. Senator, even from the State of Mississippi, should be the last person in the world to make himself the spokesman of dissension within America." Dickstein, repeating the theme of wartime propaganda, continued, "Indeed, by doing so you are playing the game of the enemies of this country who would like to see this nation split up into racial, religious, or nationalistic groups, thereby denying American unity and making this country a hodgepodge of groups and nationalities."¹¹

Undaunted, Bilbo continued to deepen his difficulties by engaging in unvarnished anti-Semitism. He replied to criticism from radio commentator Walter Winchell: "I have just heard this Sunday night's broadcast by you, the most limicolous liar and notorious scandalizing kike radio commentator of today."¹² Bilbo also attacked Leonard Golditch, executive secretary of the National Committee to Combat Anti-Semitism, in even more stark terms:

There are five million Jews in the United States and the majority of them are fine public citizens, but if Jews of your type don't quit sponsoring and fraternizing with the Negro race you are going to arouse so much opposition that they will get a very strong invitation to pack up and resettle in Palestine, the homeland of the Jews, just as we propose to provide for the voluntary resettlement of the American Negro in West Africa, their fatherland. Now do not pop-off and say I am in favor of sending the Jews to Palestine. What I am trying to say to you that there are just a few of you New York "kikes" that are fraternizing and socializing with the Negroes for selfish and political reasons and if you keep it up you will arouse the opposition of the better class of your race.[13]

Rhetoric this wild might have drawn some notice before the war, but Bilbo's statements had a more ominous tone only months after the liberation of the concentration camps. *Newsweek* recognized this fact: "But elsewhere in the nation, still with fresh memory of the savagery against European minorities, there was a murmuring of real concern . . . he [Bilbo] had chosen the aftermath of a war against the Nazis to invoke mob invective against 'dagos' and 'kikes' who had urged equal opportunity for the Negro." Other publications joined in the criticism. *Commonweal* called Bilbo "an incurably vulgar personage."[14] "Bilbo is a one-man chamber of horrors," *The Nation* wrote, "an unanswerable argument in favor of elimination of an obscene evil from a free society of men."[15]

A number of groups sharply criticized Bilbo in now-familiar language. The Committee of Catholics for Human Rights said, "Your conduct is a chilling deterrent to the world-wide belief that America is the symbol of democracy and human rights."[16] Senators Robert F. Wagner and James Mead of New York declared, "Statements insulting to one or more of the many diverse groups which make up our great nation are a disservice to the principles on which this nation was founded and to those of our boys of all races and creeds who during the past few years have fought and in all too many instances died for the preservation of these principles."[17]

New York State Senator Lazarus Joseph echoed this criticism: "I am one of those unfortunates whose kids did not come back [from the war]," he said. "And there were thousands of them, Catholic, Protestant and Jew, Negro and white, who died to keep this sweet land free. I hate and despise those bigots, like the nefarious Senator Bilbo of Mississippi."[18]

Cartoonist Bill Mauldin, who became noteworthy for his portrayals of enlisted men during the war, attacked Bilbo for the same reasons in a speech to the *New York Herald Tribune* on October 31, 1945. Stressing that many American soldiers had died during the war, he added, "But we were told it was worthwhile for some of us to get killed, so that our kids could grow up in a world free from hate, prejudice, force and intolerance." He compared Bilbo to the country's wartime enemies, saying, "I feel that as long as there are still the Bilbos who depend upon appealing to the beast in men to get power, the Rankins who preach distrust of the rest of the world to protect their own selfish interests, and the Gerald L. K. Smiths whose profession is preaching hate against fellow American citizens because of their color or creed, then the war is not won."[19]

Wagner's, Joseph's, and Mauldin's language was very similar to the messages by propaganda advocating racial, religious, and ethnic tolerance during and just after the war. By 1946, it was clear that Bilbo's rhetoric was out of place in postwar America. During the summer of 1946, he encountered an entirely different situation from the one he had faced in 1940. Northern and border state Democrats no longer wished to campaign with him. An extraordinarily broad coalition of elites, including both *The Nation* and the *Saturday Evening Post*, the Communist Party and the Jewish War Veterans, Robert Wagner *and* Robert Taft, desired or seriously considered his expulsion from the Senate. While "the Man" won reelection, Congress used statements he made encouraging violence against blacks attempting to vote in the Mississippi Democratic primary to prevent his return to the Senate.

Bilbo's fate was not an isolated incident in the postwar period. The Anti-Defamation League (ADL) reported that the 1948 elections revealed "(1) the marked diminution in the use of anti-Semitism as a campaign weapon and (2) the defeat of most candidates who tried to make political capital out of minority prejudice and intolerance." According to the ADL, 28 anti-Semitic candidates were on the ballot in 1944. By 1948, the number had fallen to 21, a modest but statistically significant decline.[20]

Furthermore, ethnic groups continued to make political gains as eight Italian Americans were elected to Congress in 1948, double that in any previous year. In 1950, Rhode Island made John Pastore the first Italian American senator. Catholics and Jews continued to make up a growing share of the federal judiciary in the early postwar period, rising from a mere 9 percent of appointments during the GOP administrations of the 1920s to almost 40 percent under Truman.[21]

While Bilbo was rejected for his extreme racial rhetoric, he was also a symbol of the limits of the changes caused by the war. Though "The Man" was a figure respectable people would reject, old prejudices and attitudes still existed below the surface. In *Gentlemen's Agreement*, Phil Green's female co-worker attacks his fiancée and her country-club friends who believe they are progressive: "They scold Bilbo twice a year and think they've fought the good fight for democracy in this country. They haven't got the guts to take the step from talk to action."

As this comment suggests, efforts to promote tolerance and intergroup cooperation left much unchanged in the immediate postwar years. Many Americans focused on personal concerns as they feared a return to the mass joblessness of the 1930s. With the stimulus of war production gone, some economists forecast that unemployment would reach 13 percent by early 1946.[22] Though these kinds of predictions proved to be alarmist, the nation did endure the pain of postwar inflation and economic reconversion in 1946–47. Other distractions emerged in the following years as the postwar economic boom began and most Americans started to participate in the burgeoning consumer culture. Some Americans began to make the journey to the suburbs as the number of single-family homes built each year rose from 114,000 in 1944 to almost 1.7 million in 1950.[23] Calls for tolerance were not the highest priority for many citizens.

Policymakers also had more pressing issues. The Cold War gradually became an important element of American political life in the late 1940s. The wartime alliance with the Soviet Union slowly dissolved as Joseph Stalin consolidated his hold on Eastern Europe and attempted to push the Western allies out of Berlin. Several stories about communist espionage in the United States made internal subversion a concern to many in Washington.

At this time, the major immigration issue concerned the fate of seven million people displaced by the conflict. This group included Jewish survivors of the Holocaust, as well as millions of Christians and others who became refugees. In addition, Eastern European governments began expelling 12 million ethnic Germans from their territory after the war's conclusion. Many entered Displaced Person (DP) camps constructed by the United States and other Allied forces.

Public opinion polls revealed little appetite among the American people for greater immigration. In December 1945, Gallup asked, "Should we permit more persons from Europe to come to this country each year than we did before the war, should we keep the number about the same, or should we reduce the number?" Only 5 percent of respondents wanted more immigration, while 32 percent wanted to maintain the same level, 37 percent wanted fewer, and 14 percent none at all. Analyzed by education level, the numbers reveal an even stronger animus toward immigration. College-educated individuals were the only demographic group in which a majority wanted to maintain or increase the current level. A majority of respondents with a high school education or less wanted reduced immigration or none at all.[24] Perhaps most revealing, 56 percent of World War II veterans wanted less immigration or none at all. One might have expected that veterans fighting in multiethnic platoons abroad would have developed liberal attitudes toward immigration. Most ex-servicemen, however, were concerned about resuming civilian life and obtaining employment and housing on their return home. Reflecting this sentiment as well its own traditional anti-immigration policy, the Veterans of Foreign Wars (VFW) called for a ten-year moratorium on immigration.[25]

Given this background, it is not surprising that, when President Truman made it known in the summer of 1946 that he was considering legislation to allow more displaced persons from Europe into the United States, the congressional reception was not exactly welcoming, even within his own party. Senator Charles Andrews (D) of Florida declared, "in my judgment the Immigration Committee will not be in favor of increasing the quotas." Other opponents were even more direct. John Rankin (D) of Mississippi, a virulent anti-Semite who could compete with Bilbo in racist bile, said there had already been "too many so-called refugees pouring into this country bringing with them communism, atheism, anarchy, and infidelity." Ed Gossett of Texas, ranking Democrat on the House Immigration Committee, opposed Truman's efforts and said he would work to cut the existing quotas in half for the next ten years.[26]

This is not to suggest there was no support for allowing more DPs into the country. Progressive Senator Glenn Taylor (D) of Idaho, who became Henry Wallace's running mate in his 1948 presidential campaign, called Truman's proposals "commendable," adding, "The population problems in Europe are insoluble. Unless the gates of all countries, including our own, are opened to allow a fair and proportionate number of these victims of Hitlerism."[27] A number of elite newspapers and magazines, as well as liberal religious groups, supported these initiatives.[28] *Newsweek* wrote, "Mr. Truman's desire to open wider the 'golden door' had support from numerous organizations, Catholic, Jewish and Protestant."[29]

The opponents of the DP legislation, like the opponents of the Wagner-Rogers bill in 1939, feared that any change would precipitate the end of the national origins system. In December 1946, Senator William Revercomb (R) of West Virginia, who was designated to become chairman of the Senate Judiciary Committee's Subcommittee on Immigration when Republicans assumed control in January, said any new law would "break down the whole quota system."[30] Senator Richard Russell (D) of Georgia also expressed concern that the 1924 legislation was in jeopardy.[31] As the Cold War intensified, anticommunism, which had been a factor in 1924 and 1939, became more prominent in the arguments of the restrictionists. Revercomb argued, "Certainly it would be a tragic blunder to bring into our midst those imbued with the Communist line of thought when one of the most important tasks of this government today is to combat and eradicate communism from this country."[32]

Some people erroneously believed that most DPs were Jews, and they opposed the legislation out of anti-Semitism. As a result, Jewish organizations formed a group called the Citizens Committee on Displaced Persons (CCDP) that worked to educate Congress about the nature of the DP problem. In order to build public support, the CCDP stressed that the majority of DPs were Christians.[33] For example, on the second anniversary of V-E Day, the CCDP published an editorial that described the demographics of the DPs: "They are, these 80 percent, of the Christian faith, a good many of them Polish and Baltic Catholics. Another portion of them, by far the smallest number, only one out of five, is of the Jewish faith."[34]

In addition to the CCDP educational efforts, a number of congressional delegations visited the DP camps in 1947. These trips caused many lawmakers to switch to support of DP legislation, and by the spring of 1948, the political dynamics of this issue had shifted: "Where the problem had once been whether or not Congress should pass DP legislation, it now became how far the legislation should go," declared Newsweek on May 10, 1948.[35]

The debates and the final bill that emerged revealed more continuity with the debate over Jewish immigration in 1939 than differences. Any legislation would have to leave the basic foundations of the quota system untouched. As in 1924, many representatives feared that further immigration would increase the urban character of the country. Senator Revercomb said of the refugees, "when they reach this country and disembark from ships 89.9 percent go into the cities, approximately 50 percent into New York City alone. I want to say that the bill reported by the committee endeavors to take care of that very situation." Senator James Eastland (D) of Mississippi concurred: "it should be pointed out that 95 percent of those aliens have located in the city of New York, where they fill up the slums, whereas only one percent have gone to the farms of the United States, where they are needed."[36]

In the aftermath of the Holocaust, the bill gave preference to German refugees who had been expelled from Poland and Czechoslovakia at the end of the war. The legislation allotted them 50 percent of the regular German and Austria quota. William Langer (R) of North Dakota made the case for the ethnic Germans: "They were Wendell Willkie's forefathers, Harold Stassen's forefathers, Carl Schurz's forefathers, and thousands more that I could name." Revercomb concurred: "I want to say that it is absolutely inescapable as a matter of right and fairness, that the people to whom the Senator from North Dakota referred are genuinely displaced people. . . . They had been in those countries for generations."[37]

Of course, many of these ethnic Germans had collaborated with the Nazis during the war. The Nazis justified the invasion of Czechoslovakia in 1938 on the pretext of protecting Germans in the Sudetenland, most of whom welcomed their arrival. A number of congressmen objected to giving preference to those who may have aided America's wartime enemies. "Whether all of them were willing parties to circumstance [sic] which accelerated the war, I do not say but some of them were parties and they were one of the causes of the beginning of the war," declared Senator John Sherman Cooper (R) of Kentucky, adding, "I do not believe that they belong in the same category for consideration as displaced persons as do those who were victims of the Nazis."[38] Benjamin Epstein, national director of the ADL, agreed: "It's the original Hitler fifth column the Congress now wants in our midst."[39]

Not only did many politicians want to give preferential treatment to groups of people who may have collaborated with the Nazis, but the legislation made it more difficult for Jewish DPs to enter the country. The bill allowed 200,000 individuals who had entered the DP camps by December 22, 1945, to enter the United States. Most of the Jewish DPs who still needed a new home, however, had entered the camps in 1946 following pogroms and renewed anti-Semitism in Poland. The Senate defeated an amendment to extend the deadline to April 1947. Epstein wrote, "This is a polite way of saying, in effect, to hell with the 15,000 Jews who fled the Polish pogroms of January 1946."

In addition, the legislation mandated that farmers compose 30 percent of the DPs. This part of the bill was designed to appeal to congressmen from rural states who wanted to offset population losses they had suffered during the war. The bill also required that 40 percent of the DPs come from countries that had been annexed by a foreign power. This element was designed to enable a large number of individuals from the Baltic States, which, unlike Poland and other European states, had been annexed by the Soviet Union, to enter the country. Senator Leverett Saltonstall (R) of Massachusetts suggested these provisions did not treat Jews fairly: "There are few farmers among the Jews—only about four percent and only a small percentage of them originated from areas now considered by the bill as annexed areas."[40] Moreover, opponents of the clauses exclaimed that many in the Baltics had also been collaborators. Epstein wrote, "Also, they are as fine a collection of Naziphiles as you could point to during the heyday of the Hitler bloodbath."[41]

Ignoring opponents such as Saltonstall and Epstein, the final bill passed by Congress allowed 205,000 DPs to enter the country and included the provisions favoring potential collaborators over Jews.[42] The anti-Jewish aspects of the legislation drew some criticism. The *New Republic* wrote, "The Senate's bill to admit displaced Europeans to the US is a classic model for discrimination against Jews."[43] President Truman reluctantly signed the bill, but said in his message about the law, "The bill discriminates in callous fashion against displaced persons of the Jewish faith." He criticized the cutoff deadline: "By this device more than 90 percent of the remaining Jewish displaced persons are definitely excluded. . . . For all practical purposes, it must be frankly recognized, that this bill excludes Jewish displaced persons, rather than accepting a fair proportion of them along with other faiths."[44]

The public supported the limitations on Jewish immigration. In September 1948, a Roper Poll showed that, while a majority of respondents supported allowing some DPs to enter the country, 60 percent responded "yes" to the question, "If most of these refugees turn out to be Jews, do you think we should put a special limit on the number of them we let in?"[45]

Support for the national origins system seemed as strong as ever. Just as in 1939, some representatives were frightened that a small liberalization of the immigration laws was merely a prelude to its destruction. Some still believed that the quota system kept out groups that would be difficult to assimilate. "The displaced persons in Europe, except persons of German nationality, are all from countries of southern and eastern Europe," declared Senator Revercomb, "which have relatively small quotas because immigrants in those areas have been found during the course of our history to be less assimilable [sic]."[46]

༄

History textbooks also illustrated that attitudes toward immigrants, though more liberal, had changed only slightly. Most, such as John Holladay Latane's *History of the American People* (1948) and *The United States in the Making* (1946), written by several authors, did not alter their accounts of immigration between 1880 and 1924. They continued to discuss immigration in terms of population flows while endorsing the restriction legislation.[47]

These textbooks also continued to discuss Asians only through the prism of Chinese and Japanese exclusion, while Latinos began to draw some unflattering references in a few books. *America's Progress in Civilization*, by George Freeland and James Adams, now noted that "Mexican immigration became a grave problem during the 1920's," adding, "they would work for low wages and were satisfied with very simple ways of life."[48]

Ralph Volney Harlow's *Story of America*, however, took a significantly different approach after the war. The book's 1937 edition contained little discussion of the contributions of immigrants. In contrast, the 1947 version included a section titled "Immigrants made important contributions in American life." Harlow discussed the role immigrants played in the growth of American industry: "the new heavy industries needed strong men who could work hard, long and steadily." He also discussed their contributions to American culture. "Well-known conductors of symphony orchestras have come here from Russia, Germany, Italy, and Holland," said Harlow, followed by several examples.[49] Harlow's section on immigrants, like that of Henry Steele Commager before the war, emphasized newcomers from northwestern Europe.

Before the war, Harlow seemed favorably inclined toward the Johnson-Reed Act. "This restrictive policy," his text from 1937 read, "was adopted partly as an economic measure, to keep out cheap labor, and partly as a social measure, to prevent America from being flooded with too many different elements. It seemed desirable to give the country a chance to Americanize those already here, a process which would be difficult if untold thousands kept pouring in."[50] By 1947, Harlow appeared less certain: "We can take up this new policy later. There is still some question as to the wisdom of the restriction." He concluded by suggesting that the new immigrants weakened unions, but "At the same time these new arrivals made some valuable contributions to American life."[51]

Other textbooks were also taking a more sanguine view. Glenn Moon's *Story of Our Land and People* (1949) discussed assimilation: "Could these newer immigrants [from southern and eastern Europe] learn a new language and new ways? In general they did. And their children who have grown up in the United States are thoroughly American." Moon also stressed the contributions that immigrants had made to the country, including those from southern and eastern Europe: "In return for greater freedom and a chance to better themselves, immigrants have made a greater contribution to the American way of living."[52]

The 1950 edition of *History of the American Way* by several authors took an even more detailed look at the contributions of eastern and southern Europeans, devoting two pages to the benefits of Jewish and Italian immigration. The authors were not sympathetic to the fears of the 1924 restrictionists, noting, "Concern over the 'new immigration' was probably greater than it needed to be. As a matter of fact, the new immigrant found his way in America almost as readily as the older immigrant. Given half a chance, he was only too glad to adopt the American way of life."[53]

Despite these examples to the contrary, most history textbooks continued to neglect immigrants from southern and eastern Europe. Edward Saveth, a member of the American Jewish Committee, discussed the issue before the National Council of Social Studies in January 1950. Saveth said, "Let us make this generalization about textbook treatments of immigration: It may be said that the peoples of the 'old immigration' who came from the countries of Northern and Western Europe in the early 19th century are treated rather favorably in textbooks." He added, "However, when the 'new immigration' from the South and the East of Europe which came to the United States after 1880 is considered, the attitude of the writer changes markedly." Saveth noted that the old immigrants are portrayed as having come to America for idealistic reasons, while new immigrants are depicted as having made the journey for economic reasons and are often blamed for social problems such as crime and urban slums.[54]

Louis Adamic perceived similar problems in the teaching of American history at this time: "The record written into the standard textbooks portrays the U.S.A. as a white Protestant Anglo-Saxon country with a white Protestant Anglo-Saxon civilization patched here and there with pieces of alien civilizations." He added, "This is the prevailing view, and it reaches beyond the textbooks and the teachers. It is taken for granted by almost everybody; it is breathed in from the atmosphere and exhaled back again into the air around us."[55]

☙

Calls for racial, religious, and ethnic tolerance were ubiquitous during World War II and the immediate postwar period. Nevertheless, the national origins system remained intact and largely unchallenged. The reasons for these continuities are not entirely clear. Such attitudes were deeply ingrained in American culture, and even the most prolonged propaganda campaign would not necessarily erase them. Research after the war suggested that the efforts of advocates of tolerance had not been much heeded and that many Americans, including veterans, were not much aware of the ideological rationale of the war. Furthermore, some of the factors promoting liberal ideals, such as the Holocaust, had not yet made an impact on the nation.

After the war, the AJC, looking at one aspect of the problem—anti-Semitism—conducted a study in Chicago that revealed that most veterans did not share the ideological view of the conflict. "It is estimated that only about 30 percent of the veterans who knew what this war was about anyway," declared Samuel Flowerman, research director of the AJC.[56] The AJC's research on veterans dovetailed with its fear of increased domestic bigotry and demagoguery following the end of the war. Flowerman commented:

> If we are to understand these reports, our men in our army of occupation do not know what it is all about. They see the French as poor, starving dirty people; they are annoyed with the English. Now the Germans—they are a people like us, they say, and they are being well-indoctrinated, and the word "fraternization" has taken on an entirely new meaning. We are worried about the veterans because there are over 12,000,000 of them and they can be a force for good or for evil, depending upon how they are used and what the economic circumstances are.

Flowerman described the veterans' attitudes: "In the first 10 or 15 minutes, the first half hour he is all for democracy. He is all for unity. He is all for the United States; he has learned something in this war. He fought alongside negroes, he fought alongside Jews and Catholics, and everybody is wonderful." Flowerman added, "Then the stuff begins to come out. From where, nobody knows. But the most vicious, the most violent hatred of all sorts."[57]

Indeed, the AJC's Chicago study of veterans demonstrated the persistence of prejudice. Its survey showed that 4 percent of veterans could be labeled "Intense anti-Semites." "These were spontaneously out-spoken in wanting or demanding restrictive action against Jews *even before the subject was raised by the interviewer.*" The study identified 27 percent as "Outspoken anti-Semites" who "did not spontaneously ask for restrictive action against Jews but held a wide range of unfavorable and stereotyped opinions about Jews." Finally, the survey considered 28 percent of the veterans "Stereotype anti-Semites" who did not express a desire for hostile action against Jews but "did express a wide variety of stereotyped notions about Jews, both favorable and unfavorable." Only 41 percent could be labeled "tolerant."[58]

The early depiction of the Holocaust in the American press is another reason attitudes toward Jews and other minorities may not have changed dramatically. Scholars believe the Holocaust played a major role in the greater tolerance of the postwar era, suggesting that the exposure to this atrocity reduced the respectability of racism and anti-Semitism.[59] The initial newspaper and magazine reports on the Holocaust, however, did not represent the Nazi atrocity as an attempt to annihilate European Jewry. The media simply wrote that the Nazis used brutal and murderous tactics against their political opponents. As a result, the Holocaust probably did not have a significant impact on racial attitudes in the immediate postwar period.

As Allied troops marched east toward Berlin in 1945, they encountered Nazi concentration camps such as Buchenwald and Dachau. The Germans had erected these camps during the early 1930s to hold political prisoners, Communists, labor unionists, and others who opposed the Nazi regime. Jews eventually began to compose a significant part of their population in the late 1930s. Though these camps were brutal, they were not primarily dedicated to the extermination of Jews like Auschwitz and Treblinka in Poland. Thus, the nation's first encounter with the Holocaust did not reveal the full depredations of Nazism.[60]

Nevertheless, the first reporters to see these camps were shocked. On April 15, 1945, CBS radio newsman Edward R. Murrow broadcast his famous account of Buchenwald, telling his audience in advance that the discussion would be graphic: "It will not be pleasant listening. If you are at lunch, or if you have no appetite to hear what the Germans have done, now is a good time for you to switch off the radio, for I propose to tell you of Buchenwald." Among his observations, "As we walked out into the court-yard, a man fell dead. Two others—they must have been over sixty—were crawling toward the latrine. I saw it but will not describe it." Murrow said that he saw piles of bodies and asked his listeners, "I pray you to believe what I have said about Buchenwald."[61]

Murrow's reporting suggested that the camp's residents came from every nationality that opposed the Nazis, rather than from specific racial and ethnic groups. He met Czechs, Frenchmen, and Austrians: "Men kept coming up to speak to me and to touch me, professors from Poland, doctors from Vienna, men from all over Europe. Men from the countries that made America."[62] He never used the word Jew. This perspective would characterize the early coverage of the Holocaust.

The *New York Times* front page story on April 18, 1945, described Allied soldiers forcing the local German population to view Buchenwald. The article referred to the camp's population: "It included doctors, professors, scientists, statesmen, army diplomats, and an assortment of peasants and merchants from all over Europe and Asia." There were limited references to Jews: "it was also at Auschwitz that Jewish women among the 30,000 once here at Buchenwald were sent to be exterminated after they had become pregnant."[63]

A newsreel highlighting the Nazi atrocities described Buchenwald as the "most dreadful of all the camps," saying, "Poles, Greeks, Russians—any non-Germans, were systematically slaughtered."[64] An article in *Newsweek* about the visit of an American congressional delegation to the camps did not mention Jews.[65] *Time* published an article about all the camps in Germany, describing them as "a series of concentration camps for political prisoners from most of the nations the Nazis had conquered, including the German nation."[66]

The *New Republic* concurred, explaining that the Nazis perpetuated crimes "against Allied prisoners of wars, foreign political enemies, as well as against Germans themselves," elaborating, "The Nazis did not distinguish between the German people and foreign peoples, they distinguished only between those who resisted their barbaric regime and those who did not."[67] A *New York Times Magazine* article on May 6, 1945, described one camp as "for political prisoners," adding, "this was what happened to people who had opposed Hitler or said indiscreet things or were Jews or had been caught in the resistance movements of their native lands."[68]

Even the exposure of the death camps in Poland did not alter the general tenor of the coverage, as the Soviets espoused the identical view when they revealed the discovery of Auschwitz in May 1945. C. L. Sulzberger wrote in the *New York Times*, "This slaughter exceeds in barbaric intention and method not only the greatest brutalities of such infamous conquerors as Genghis Khan, but also surpasses even Germany's own record in her previous prize exhibitions at Maidanek, Dachau, and Buchenwald." Sulzberger continued, "According to the Soviet commission, 'more than 4,000,000 citizens' of the Soviet Union, Poland, France, Belgium, the Netherlands, Czechoslovakia, Yugoslavia and other countries, including the non-Allied lands of Hungary and Rumania, were exterminated in Oswiecim [Auschwitz]."[69]

There were some exceptions to this trend. Gideon Seymour, executive editor of the *Minneapolis Star Journal*, visited Dachau and Buchenwald as part of a group of U.S. editors who traveled to Europe to view the camps. He saw that the Nazis operated under a theory of a racial hierarchy "with Russians and Poles at the bottom of the scale." Seymour added, "They just didn't waste any time on the Jews. They put them to death."[70]

The Nazi atrocities may also have been overshadowed by other events toward the end of the European phase of the conflict. The liberation of Buchenwald occurred at roughly the same time as the death of FDR. The discovery of other camps coincided with the deaths of Benito Mussolini and Hitler, as well as V-E Day, most likely blunting the immediate impact of the Nazi campaign against European Jewry.[71]

For these reasons, early reports of the Holocaust did not change attitudes toward Jews. In March and June 1945, Opinion Research Corporation (ORC) polls asked, "Have the mass killings of the Jews in Europe caused any change in your attitudes toward the Jews of this country?" In March, 77 percent of those polled said that the revelations caused no change, while 79 percent said "no" in June. Similarly, an ORC poll asked, "Has your own feeling toward the Jews become more friendly or less friendly during the last few years?" In 1945, 10 percent said the war made them friendlier, while 26 percent indicated it made them less friendly.[72]

∾

American propaganda and educational efforts, aimed in large part to promote unity, combined with a war fought against intolerant regimes, sought to buttress an ideological view of the conflict as a battle for a more tolerant world where individuals of all religions and ethnicities would work together toward common goals. The impact of these campaigns was limited as this view of the war, however, did not prevail during the late 1940s. Then, as during the war, attitudes toward eastern and southern European immigrants seemed—as textbooks and small legal changes suggest—somewhat more liberal. Still, many Americans resisted allowing large numbers of displaced persons to enter the country, particularly if they were Jews. Due to the nature of media coverage, the Holocaust did not have an immediate impact on public attitudes. Finally, the national origins system remained intact, and pressure for significant changes in the status of ethnic and religious groups appeared weak.

Chapter 5

The Reemergence of Contributionism

By 1950, the Cold War dominated American foreign relations and shaped the domestic political debate. A series of international events, such as the Czech coup of 1948 and the Soviet atomic bomb test in 1949, alarmed many Americans and prompted vigorous American policies to contain the USSR. When President Truman sent American troops to defend South Korea from the North Korean invasion in June 1950, there was no longer any doubt that the United States was involved in another major war, a mere five years after the end of World War II. In addition, traditional American fears of radicalism merged with the new confrontation with the Soviet Union to lift internal subversion to a source of national discord. By 1946, politicians such as the young Richard Nixon were using "communism-in-government" as a wedge issue to win congressional elections. Eventually, the guilt or innocence of Alger Hiss and the Rosenbergs became the subject of intense debate. Attacks on domestic communist influence were not limited to the Republican side of the aisle, as President Truman issued an executive order calling for loyalty tests of government employees. When Senator Joseph McCarthy (R) of Wisconsin made his accusations about communism in the State Department in Wheeling, West Virginia, in June 1950, he was a latecomer to the issue.

For many Americans, however, the Cold War and the bomb were distant fears. By the late 1940s, the greatest economic boom in American history had begun. Millions of Americans continued to make the move from the central cities to the suburbs and were enjoying the fruits of postwar prosperity. New car sales grew from 69,500 in 1945 to 7.9 million in 1955; by the end of the 1950s, 60 percent of families owned their own homes, up from half of families at the end of the war. Americans were also making up for time lost during the war, marrying younger and having large families as

the "baby boom" continued. The number of live births per 1000 population, the so-called "birth rate," remained between 18.4 and 19.4 during the
Depression years. This rate rose to 26.6 in 1947 and held at 24 or higher
until 1959.[1]

Scholars are divided as to which elements are most important to understanding the 1950s. To many historians, the Cold War hovers over the
entire decade, influencing everything from politics to popular culture.[2]
They see the period as "The Age of McCarthy," in which the civil liberties
of a good many Americans were violated.[3] Another school of historians
suggests that suburbanization and postwar prosperity were more important
to most Americans than the Cold War and McCarthyism.[4] Peter Filene
summarizes this perspective best: "They [Americans of the 1950s] may have
been more worried about grocery prices than the fate of Czechoslovakia or
the treason of Alger Hiss."[5]

Ordinary citizens may not have dwelled on the U.S./Soviet confrontation, but the propaganda battle with the Soviet Union was foremost in the
minds of the congressmen, intellectuals, and policymakers who dealt with
issues of immigration and ethnicity. Communism was an issue in virtually
every political debate, public celebration, and film that broached the subject. Those who supported liberalizing the immigration laws emphasized
how the national origins system hurt our international standing in the
world. Those who supported maintaining the current system had many
arguments, among them the fear of communist espionage and the desire to
maintain the demographic composition of the country.

Congress fought over the McCarran-Walter bill in 1952, the most
important debate concerning the nation's immigration laws since 1924. The
legislation upheld the status quo, maintaining the national origins system.
Continuing a pattern established during World War II, both sides used the
language of tolerance during the debate and assured the American people
of their respect for different ethnic groups. McCarran-Walter became law
despite a presidential veto, but the firestorm over the bill emboldened those
who opposed the current system to attack it more directly. After 1952,
supporters of liberalizing the immigration laws called for abolishing the
national origins system. The Cold War created sympathy for refugees from
behind the Iron Curtain, and Congress passed special legislation to allow
many into the country.[6] Though immigration remained relatively low on
the national agenda in the late 1950s, some supporters of reform believed
it was increasingly likely that policymakers would eliminate the quotas.

The language of supporters of immigration reform changed as they revived contributionism during the McCarran-Walter debate, promoting the idea that immigrants changed the culture while also accepting a minimum of American norms. Departing from the universalist message of World War II, they used contributionist rhetoric with a frequency not seen since the late 1930s, as the phrase "a nation of immigrants" began to appear more often in political debates, school textbooks, and public celebrations. Along these lines, some intellectuals rediscovered liberal interpretations of the melting pot.

New ethnic groups were also altering how Americans thought about immigration as the 1950s progressed. While the idea of a "nation of immigrants" encompassing southern and eastern Europeans gained increased acceptance, other groups began to draw the ire of restrictionists. An upsurge of Latino immigration, particularly from Mexico, occurred in the mid-1950s and by the end of the decade, they were rapidly emerging as the group that most concerned nativists. Even as the "nation of immigrants" expanded to include the Ellis Island-era immigrants, it continued to leave Hispanics and Asians well outside its boundaries.

∾

National Brotherhood Week reiterated the themes of tolerance and teamwork that marked the celebration during and after World War II. By 1950, the Cold War dominated its events, and programs emphasized the necessity of tolerance and cooperation to fight communism and avoid nuclear holocaust. Radio commentator Robert Montgomery gave a speech in City Hall in New York City during Brotherhood Week in February 1950 repeating those themes. "For the greatest ammunition Communism has, always has had, always will have, is not a super-bomb," declared Montgomery, "but the hatreds of one man for another—because he worships in a different form—because he speaks with a different accent—because he comes from a different walk of life." Mongtomery also said that "no bomb yet made could destroy New York so completely than if this city forgot tolerance for 24 hours."[7]

Editorials for Brotherhood Week 1950 also discussed the bomb. Syndicated columnist Marquis Child wrote that brotherhood had always been an important concept, but, "on August 5, 1945, it became more than that. It became an imminent necessity for the survival of mankind. For man, with all his prejudices, his greed, his blindness, has today the capacity for self-destruction. Only in the concept of Brotherhood is there any hope for human life on this planet."[8]

The rhetoric of tolerance and cooperation continued to have broad support across ideological lines. George W. Craig, the commander of the American Legion, said, "We have urged and shall continue to urge upon our members a participation in the observation of Brotherhood Week with the idea of cementing the intent of all of our citizens, without regard to race, color, or politics, to maintain our American way of life."[9]

With the European colonial empires crumbling, the United States found itself competing with the Soviet Union for the loyalties of nonwhite peoples around the world. America's treatment of its own minorities became relevant to the nation's foreign policy, and Asian nations and Asian Americans began to be discussed during Brotherhood Week.[10] In particular, the beginning of the Korean War in June 1950 placed American attitudes toward its own racial minorities under the microscope. Eric Johnston, president of the Motion Pictures Studio of America and the honorary chairman of Brotherhood Week 1951, said in a speech on November 11, 1950, "The Asian people happen to be on the dark-complexioned order. Their religions are mostly strange to us. How much trust do you think they put in Americans when we play *up* the color line and look *down* our noses at one another's faith?" He added that, while many Asians had misgivings about communism, this fear did not necessarily translate into support for the United States. Johnston also reiterated how the bomb made tolerance a necessity: "Have you heard 'The Atom Song'? If you haven't, I recommend the record to you, for in it, Old Man Atom tells us that we'd better get together—or disintegrate. And I'm taking his advice."[11]

War films also began to have a more multiracial character than in previous years. There were few combat movies between 1945 and the release of *Sands of Iwo Jima* in 1949, and John Wayne's famous war film was one of the last pictures to feature a solely Euro-American platoon with a mix of ethnic characters almost identical to movies made during the war. Again, the audience sees soldiers from different ethnicities working toward common goals, and similar tributes to pluralism appear. One soldier says "Shalom Aleichem" to another as their ship approaches Iwo Jima. A soldier dies on the island saying the holiest prayer in Judaism, the Shm'a.[12] With the onset of the desegregated military and Korea, the platoon film began to take on a new and more racially diverse shape.

The 1951 film *Go for Broke!* dramatizes the experience of the 442nd combat division, the all-Japanese American unit during World War II. Taking up the mantle of *Gentlemen's Agreement* and *Crossfire* in exposing the evils of racism and the importance of tolerance, the film opens with patriotic music and displays a quote from FDR emphasizing the ideological nature of Americanism. "The principle on which this country was founded and by which it has always been governed is that Americanism is a matter of the mind and heart," Roosevelt noted. "Americanism is not, and never was, a matter of race and ancestry."[13]

In the film, Van Johnson plays a white Army officer who is given command of the platoon during the war. Johnson's character, Lt. Michael Grayson, is from Texas and requests a transfer to his old unit from his home state, saying he always expected to return to it after officer training. His superior asks, "And you're sure that's the only reason you have for wanting a transfer?" Grayson replies, "Yes, sir." The superior says, "No objection to working with the kind of troops we have here?" Grayson responds, "Because they're Japs. Oh no, sir, nothing like that at all." The superior reproaches him for the ethnic slur: "Now, let's get a couple things straight, lieutenant. First, there's not going to be any transfer. You're staying here. You got that?" Grayson accepts, and his superior continues, "And second, they're not Japs. They're Japanese Americans. Nisei. Or as they call themselves, Buddhaheads." After this exchange, Grayson goes outside and appears uncomfortable when he sees some of the soldiers engaging in traditional Japanese dances. He also seems fearful that his soldiers will be able to use live ammunition in their training exercises.

The army sends the 442nd to Italy, and Grayson remains aloof from his troops. He complains to another superior at one point, "A guy gets in to fight the Japs and winds up fighting with them." The officer lectures him that Japanese Americans are no different from other immigrants, "A lot of us had parents who were born in enemy countries, Italian Americans, German Americans." Grayson replies, "That's different, sir, and you know it." The officer responds, "Why?" Grayson struggles for an answer: "Well, it's just . . ." The officer mockingly says, "The shape of their eyes? Or is it the color of their skin?" Grayson says, "Tell the truth, sir, wouldn't you rather be with some other outfit?" The superior responds, "If I knew of a better outfit, but I don't."

In true Hollywood fashion, the heroism of the Japanese American troops begins to change Grayson. At one point, the platoon captures some

German soldiers. The Germans are perplexed when they see the Asian soldiers and ask if they are Chinese. "Japanese. Didn't Hitler tell you?" Grayson jokes. "Japan surrendered and they're fighting on our side now."

The 442nd proceeds to the south of France. Grayson now appears at
ease as his troops engage in the same dance that bothered him in the beginning. He finally runs into his unit from Texas and discovers they are suspi-
cious of the Japanese American troops. His old platoon sergeant calls them
"Japs." Angered, Grayson takes him outside and repeats his superior's
speech from the beginning: "They're not Japs. They're Japanese Americans.
Nisei. Or if you prefer Buddhaheads. But not Japs. They don't like it and
neither do I." The sergeant lashes back, "What are you a Jap lover or something?" The verbal battle eventually turns into a physical fight as Grayson
beats up his old friend. Grayson's transformation from racist white to a
crusader for racial and ethnic tolerance, like Gregory Peck's Phil Green in
Gentlemen's Agreement, is complete.

Though the film revolves around the white officer Grayson, the Japanese soldiers are portrayed as heroic soldiers who fight for their country
even while they face discrimination at home. The images in the film are a
world removed from the racist depictions of the Japanese during World
War II, which had occurred less than a decade earlier. In a device that seems
designed to reinforce the idea of Nisei loyalty, one of the Japanese soldiers
is always eager to fight Imperial Japan because he lost his parents at Pearl
Harbor. As in *Crossfire* and *Gentlemen's Agreement*, the fact of military service in World War II serves to incorporate a group into the national community. Only this time it is not Jews, but Japanese Americans.

Go for Broke! revealed that Japanese Americans were increasingly seen
through a different lens of race than before war. The scientific racism of
the prewar period was being superseded by a concept of race based on
physical differences and culture. By the 1950s, the racial labeling of "Japs"
during the war had been replaced by more inclusive terminology like "Japanese Americans." Writing in the *Anti-Defamation League (ADL) Bulletin* in
October 1956, Stanley Jacobs observed, "In fewer than a dozen years, our
Japanese-Americans have risen, Phoenix-like, from the ashes of homes,
stores, and farms, lost after Pearl Harbor, to gain a new eminence and
acceptance on the American scene probably unmatched by any other racial
minority."[14] Nevertheless, Japanese Americans and other Asian Americans
largely remained outside the "nation of immigrants," as inclusive discussions of race and ethnicity still largely focused on white ethnics.

Brotherhood Week 1951 and 1952 continued the focus on teamwork and tolerance in the context of the Cold War and the bomb. One radio spot declared, "Ladies, there are plenty of men in your future—over two billion of them! Yes, the atomic age has made the welfare of men everywhere our business."[15] Radio spots also noted that the rest of the world was looking at American behavior, particularly in Asia and Africa: "All over the world, in fact, there are people—brown people, yellow people, black people—who can choose either democracy or communism. To help them decide we've got to prove we consider them equals." The spot continued, "And how do we prove that? By seeing that the folks of our own country, the *Americans* of other races and religions from our own, get the same opportunities we expect for ourselves."[16]

Other groups placed unity and teamwork in a Cold War framework. One Ad Council ad shows Joseph Stalin with his hand over a man with the title "That's My Boy" over their heads. The ad elaborated, "Uncle Joe would jump with glee if he thought he could divide the United States—Management against labor—Christian against Jew—White against Negro."[17]

The national origins system and the Iron Curtain combined to keep immigration relatively low, and the percentage of foreign-born in the country continued its gradual decline, from 7 percent in 1950 to 5.4 percent in 1960.[18] The quotas for large quota countries such as Great Britain and Ireland went unfilled because of relatively low demand. Meanwhile, countries such as Italy and Greece had small quotas that were oversubscribed, creating long waiting lists for their citizens to enter the United States. Greece, for instance, had a limit of 310 and a waiting list of 24,000 in 1952.[19] Others living behind the Iron Curtain simply had no opportunity to leave their home country. The continued decline in immigration and fading of the old ethnic neighborhoods helped pave the way for the growing acceptance of the Ellis Island immigrants and their descendants.

The emergence of the displaced persons issue, the Cold War, and America's new role as leader of the "Free World" led many to recommend a reexamination of the country's approach to immigration. In 1947, the Senate, at the urging of Senator William Revercomb (R) of West Virginia, passed a resolution calling for an investigation of the nation's immigration laws. A subcommittee of the Senate Judiciary Committee conducted the investigation, which resulted in the first major congressional study of the subject since the Dillingham Commission in 1911. The subcommittee released its findings in 1950, laying the groundwork for the nation's most important discussion of immigration in thirty years.[20]

The subcommittee's report recommended maintaining the national origins system. In doing so, however, the subcommittee rejected the racialist underpinnings of the Johnson-Reed Act of 1924 and supported the status quo on cultural grounds:

> The subcommittee holds that the people who had made the greatest contribution to the development of this country were fully justified in determining that the country was no longer a field for further colonization and henceforth, further immigration would not only be restricted but directed to admit immigrants considered to be more readily assimilable because of the similarity of their cultural background to those of the principal components of our population.[21]

While upholding the system, the report revealed a greater appreciation for immigrant institutions than earlier restrictionists had shown. About the foreign –language press, the report said, "The millions of immigrants who could not otherwise be reached until they had learned the English language have been reached through the foreign-language press, which has been an important educational agency for the immigrant." The subcommittee was not entirely positive in its assessment, adding, "Its very existence tends to preserve the alien language of the immigrant and to sustain nationalist and particularist tendencies, and may even create antipathy toward the American way of life."[22] The subcommittee thought much the same way about the role of religion in the lives of immigrants: "While the church may be conservative and stand in the way of assimilation in some measure, it also serves as a stabilizer. Under its influence, the assimilation process has moved ahead, slowly, but on a firm basis."[23] The report shows the growing tolerance and appreciation of immigrant culture—like rhetoric during National Brotherhood Week and in war films—that characterized the postwar period.

By 1952, when new immigration legislation reached the floor of the Congress, McCarthyism was at its peak. Legislators constantly alleged that domestic subversion remained an imminent threat, and Senator McCarthy was not alone in attacking virtually any left-of-center legislation as Communist-inspired. Senators William Jenner (R) of Indiana, Karl Mundt (R) of South Dakota, and Pat McCarran (D) of Nevada could all easily match McCarthy's bile. McCarran joined with Representative Francis Walter (D) of Pennsylvania, chairman of the House Subcommittee on Immigration, to sponsor new immigration legislation to strengthen the government's ability to keep subversives out and maintain the national origins system.

McCarran's Senate career began when, after many unsuccessful attempts to reach Washington, he won a seat in the Senate in 1932, the same year fellow Democrat Franklin Roosevelt was elected president. Almost from the outset, though, McCarran's Jeffersonian state's rights philosophy put him at odds with FDR and his New Deal programs. At this time, McCarran's intense anticommunism came to the forefront as he, like many of FDR's harshest critics, attacked the New Deal as communist-inspired. During Felix Frankfurter's confirmation hearings for the Supreme Court in 1939, the senator from Nevada grilled him about his views on Marxism and asked him if he had ever been a member of the American Communist Party.[24] McCarran's philosophy naturally led him into an important role in McCarthyism during the 1950s, when he sponsored the Internal Security Act, which banned anyone with a previous membership in a Communist or Fascist party from entering the United States. Some have gone so far as to theorize that the senator's role in the "Second Red Scare" was greater than that of McCarthy himself.[25]

McCarran's resistance to immigration dovetailed with his virulent anticommunism, as he was convinced communists were using the immigration system to enter the country.[26] While McCarran himself came from an immigrant family of Irish Catholics, he became the leader of the congressional forces attempting to keep the door closed to the next generation of new arrivals. Oscar Handlin, a leading historian of American immigration at the time, suggested that McCarran's nativism also stemmed from a desire to affirm his own Americanness: "The venom McCarran now directs against the aliens was generated by the hatred of foreigners that was all about him in his youth and by the dim, recalled fear that he himself might be counted among them."[27]

Francis Walter, like McCarran, was a staunch anticommunist whose support for the national origins system was inextricably linked to his fears of communist subversion. He later became chairman of the House Un-American Activities Committee (HUAC), which led investigations into domestic communist influence during the 1950s. Walter represented the Lehigh Valley of Pennsylvania and held to his anti-immigration stance despite criticism from many leading figures in his district.[28]

By upholding the national origins quotas, McCarran-Walter maintained a 154,000 limit on immigration from the Eastern Hemisphere. Strengthening the security provisions prescribed by the Internal Security Act, the bill made it easier for the government to act against suspected subversives, giving the attorney general the right to deport an alien convicted of a crime if he deemed the alien dangerous. In another Cold War measure, the legislation removed race as a bar to naturalization, allowing all Asian nations into the origins system. Previously, most Asians had been barred from entering the United States because they were ineligible to become citizens. The bill now provided every country in Asia with a quota of 100 immigrants per year, except Japan, which received 185. These nations, which the law organized into an entity known as the Asia-Pacific Triangle, received roughly the same quota already given to China, the Philippines, and India. McCarran-Walter specified a limit of 2,000 total immigrants that could arrive each year from the Asia-Pacific Triangle.[29] Although the bill preserved the nonquota status of the Western Hemisphere, it created a new set of restrictions for British holdings in the West Indies. Previously, immigrants from Jamaica and other British colonies had entered the country under the United Kingdom quota. In a measure seemingly designed to reduce black immigration into the country, McCarran-Walter now limited each colony to 100 spaces.

During the congressional debate, a few supporters of McCarran-Walter used the old restrictionist rhetoric from 1924. Representative John Wood (R) of Idaho defended the ideology of racial superiority: "It seems to me that the question of racial origins—though I am not a follower of Hitler—there is something to it. We cannot tie a stone around its neck and drop it into the middle of the Atlantic just because it worked to the contrary in Germany." Wood also repeated old fears about the concentration of immigrants in urban, ethnic communities: "They read their own newspapers. It has been my impression from the short space of time spent in those eastern cities that it takes almost three generations to make a good American citizen."[30]

McCarran and his supporters cited anticommunism as a key rationale. As usual, John Rankin offered the most extreme expression of this view, declaring, "Nine out of every ten of the Communists that have been convicted of treason have been foreign-born." Walter made the same point in less incendiary language: "The loopholes in our own old statutes have gradually become larger and larger, so that while fighting communism abroad we have actually become powerless in fighting its infiltration into our own country." He added, "I believe that the Congress is under the obligation—under a mandate—to provide for better protection of our country from subversives, gamblers, narcotic peddlers, stowaways, ship jumpers, and foreign agents who know only too well how to slip in and remain in our country."[31]

Anticommunism also gave supporters a way to weaken the opposition, as the climate of the McCarthy era sometimes placed advocates for progressive legislation, such as a more liberal immigration policy, under suspicion. Mundt noted that the National Lawyers Guild, which he called a communist front group, opposed the bill "presumably because it believes that this bill, in turn, would curb the activities of Communists in this country."[32] McCarran said in McCarthy-esque fashion, "I hold in my hand also, Mr. President, a stack of several hundred cards issued by the American Committee for Protection of Foreign Born, which likewise vigorously opposes the instant bill."[33] He alleged that the group was also a communist-connected organization. Mundt added that "the *Daily Worker*, the official Communist newspaper, has been launching a tirade of attack and invective against this proposed legislation." Opponents of the bill grew impatient with this line of argument. John Pastore (D) of Rhode Island, referring to *Daily Worker* opposition, fired back: "I do not care who is for or against the bill. But, certainly because I am against it, it does not prove that I am a fellow traveler. I dare anyone to stand up and say that I am."[34]

McCarran also reiterated that allowing immigrants from southern and eastern Europe would change the nation's culture because they would have a more difficult time assimilating. "If we scrap the national origins formula, we will, in the course of a generation or so, change the ethnic and cultural composition of this nation," McCarran declared. He added that "the cold, hard truth is that in the United States today there are hard-core, indigestible blocs who have not been integrated into the American way of life, but who, on the contrary, are its deadly enemy."[35]

Supporters of the legislation stressed that the bill did not discriminate, even though it upheld the origins system. In fact, they emphasized their antiracist credentials, declaring that McCarran-Walter did away with discrimination against Asians in the immigration laws. "Under the terms of the bill, national-origin quotas will be available to all countries of the world and no immigrant will be barred solely because of race, nor will aliens be barred from naturalization because of race," said McCarran.[36] Representative Walter H. Judd (R) of Minnesota declared, "it takes out of the hands of the Kremlin its most powerful and effective propaganda weapon against us all 'round the world."[37]

Opponents of the McCarran-Walter bill did not propose the abolition of the quota system. Their bill, cosponsored by Democratic Senators Hubert Humphrey of Minnesota and Herbert Lehman of New York, sought only to change the base year used to estimate the quotas from the 1920 census to the 1950 census. Under the formula created by the Johnson-Reed Act in 1924, Congress specified the overall limit for Eastern Hemisphere immigration to be equal to one-sixth of 1 percent of the total census. By shifting the base year, total immigration under the quotas would rise from 155,000 to 250,000. The bill also proposed to increase migration from southern and eastern Europe by pooling the unused quotas for nations such as Great Britain and Germany and redistributing them to countries where the quotas were oversubscribed, such as Italy and Poland. Lehman regretted the failure to attack the national origins system directly, saying that, if he could have written the bill himself, "It would have been more generous, and more humane; it would have abolished entirely the present blood-stock quota system, the so-called national origins system."[38]

Just as in 1924, most of the opponents represented northeastern states that contained significant immigrant communities. By this time, the children and grandchildren of the Ellis Island-era immigrants had become the base of support for the New Deal coalition that sustained the Democratic Party.[39] Lehman, Humphrey, and others were also trying to maintain the support of these ethnic groups by advocating for removing the stigma of the quotas.

The foes of McCarran-Walter, like its supporters, invoked the Cold War to buttress their argument. Pastore said opposition to the bill would encourage other peoples "to join with us in opposition to Soviet domination." Lehman concurred: "I beg of you Senators not to exclude those who are refugees from Communist tyranny, who seek haven in this land of freedom."[40]

While the Cold War rhetoric represented a new tactic, many of the arguments against McCarran-Walter were similar to those made twenty-eight years earlier by those opposing Johnson-Reed. This debate revived the contributionist message that had been deemphasized during World War II and the immediate postwar period. Representative Peter Rodino (D) of New Jersey, who was later to gain fame as chairman of the House Judiciary Committee during Watergate, argued that immigrants strengthened the nation economically: "We know that the five states with the largest populations of foreign born—New York, Massachusetts, Rhode Island, New Jersey, and Michigan—are also among the most prosperous of all the states." Lehman echoed this contributionist sentiment: "There can be no doubt that not only the period of our nation's greatest growth, but also its greatest prosperity, was during the time when immigration was on a very large scale."[41]

Opponents retorted that the restrictionists' arguments simply repeated the ill-founded views of earlier generations that wanted to limit immigration. "The story is not new," said Pastore. "It goes back 100 years prior to 1920 when racists and scaremongers in this country urged that the frontiers for American expansion had closed and that this nation should restrict the entry of all immigrants, or at least, certain types of immigrants." Rodino concurred: "The arguments in favor of a closed-door policy have been repeated over and over again since the days of John Adams."[42]

They cited the military service of immigrants as evidence of their strong sense of loyalty to America. Representative Emanuel Celler (D) of New York City, who had been outspoken in his opposition in 1924, said, "Many have gone through the valley of the shadow of death in Korea and through our wars after 1890 who bore Polish names, Italian names, Czechoslovak names, Rumanian names, and Jewish names." Some extended this argument to Japanese Americans. Senator Paul Douglas (D) of Illinois declared of the 442nd division, "That unit was composed of Japanese-Americans, who went into the service with two strikes against them and demonstrated, by their heroism, that they were as fine soldiers as we could have."[43]

Reflecting the growing prominence of black/white racial divisions in the immigration debate, a few attacked the measures limiting West Indian migration. In his speech concerning McCarran-Walter, a young John F.

Kennedy cited this provision among several different reasons he opposed the bill.[44] The *New York Times* concurred, editorializing that the bill "sets up brand-new barriers against West Indian Negroes."[45] Not surprisingly, Representative Adam Clayton Powell (D) from Harlem, one of the few African Americans in Congress, used far more forceful language: "To ensure that only a token number of colored persons may enter the United States, the proposed legislation further strikes directly at the major modern source of this population flow." Powell compared the new quotas to Nazi Germany's Nuremberg Laws, concluding "Under these bills, if they are passed by Congress and signed by the President, the United States will itself become an iron-curtain country. We will become the western counterpart of the Union of South Africa's apartheid."[46] While observing that "Negroes have shown little excitement over the racist provisions" of the McCarran bill, the NAACP sent letters to many in Congress, forcefully opposing the West Indian provisions of the legislation.[47] This part of the debate seems to suggest that the old ethnic divisions were fading and that the dichotomy between African Americans and whites was rapidly becoming the central racial/ethnic issue in American society.[48]

Finally, the supporters of the Humphrey-Lehman bill reiterated the contributions that immigrants made to American culture, suggesting that the country was "a nation of immigrants." Lehman rejected the philosophy of the restrictionists: "This rather quaint philosophy forgets the fact that America was settled and peopled entirely by immigrants, and built to greatness by immigrants, from many lands and many continents." He added, "I know it is not the philosophy we speak of on the Fourth of July or on I Am an American Day." Douglas concurred, "They [immigrants from southern and eastern Europe] have made a splendid contribution to America as their circumstances, the time they have been here, and the difficulties under which they have labored have all made possible."[49]

Both the House and Senate passed McCarran-Walter by overwhelming margins with widespread support from both political parties.[50] President Truman denounced the legislation in strong language and vetoed it. In the message explaining his veto, Truman praised the measures that removed racial bars to naturalization and allowed alien wives to bring their spouses into the country outside the quota framework. He justified his actions on the grounds that the bill retained the origins system, which Truman called a relic of the 1920s: "The idea behind this discriminatory policy was, to put it baldly, that Americans with English or Irish names were better people and better citizens than Americans with Italian or Greek or Polish names. . . . Such a concept is utterly unworthy of our traditions and our ideals." Truman went on to say, "The basis of this quota system was false and unworthy in 1924. It is even worse now. . . . It is incredible to me that, in this year of 1952, we should again be enacting into law such a slur on the patriotism, the capacity, and the decency of a large part of our citizenry."[51]

The president also referred to the Cold War to justify his veto. He noted that the bill afforded only small quotas to NATO allies such as Greece and Italy, damaging our relations with those nations. Saying that communism and the rise of the Iron Curtain made the idea of excluding southern and eastern Europeans antiquated, Truman declared, "We do not need to be protected against immigrants from these countries—on the contrary we want to stretch out a helping hand, to save those who have managed to flee into Western Europe, to succor those who are brave enough to escape from barbarism."[52]

McCarran fired back in anger, calling the veto "one of the most un-American acts I have witnessed in my public career," adding that the president "has adopted the doctrine that is promulgated by the *Daily Worker*."[53] He also attacked the veto on progressive grounds, declaring that, if it were sustained it "would dash for the second time the hopes of 86,000 Orientals within our borders who have been our friends and neighbors for a quarter of a century."[54]

Congress responded by overriding the veto. The voting patterns were remarkably similar to those of 1924, as the congressmen from the South and the Far West provided the backing for the legislation. The Northeast, home to the largest communities of first- and second-generation immigrants, led the resistance. Nevertheless, the region's representatives opposed the bill by a margin of only 10–8 in the Senate and 66–56 in the House.[55] Some observers were dismayed at the breadth of support for McCarran-Walter. The *New York Times* editorialized, "This legislation is unfair and unwise. It is hard to understand how so many legislators with fairly good voting records stood with it."[56]

Truman did not give up the fight and issued an executive order in September 1952, creating a national commission to investigate immigration policy. Solicitor General Philip Perlman chaired the President's Commission on Immigration and Naturalization, and Earl Harrison, a former U.S.

commissioner of immigration, served as vice-chairman. The commission conducted thirty hearings in eleven cities during the fall of 1952 to ascertain the American public's view of immigration issues.[57]

Despite the passage of McCarran-Walter, the atmosphere of 1952 was more favorable to immigrants than the atmosphere of 1924. Restrictionists no longer argued that immigrants were racially inferior. By supporting the removal of the bars against Asian immigration, many stressed that they were racially tolerant. They relied instead on cultural arguments and, in particular, the fear of communism as their rationales. While World War II had brought about a significant change in attitudes toward immigration, support for the national origins system remained remarkably durable. Opponents of the system did not dare attack it legislatively. Congress not only supported the current format, it was able to maintain it in the face of a presidential veto. The quota system appeared to be unassailable. Or at least, that was how it seemed.

∽

By 1952, the Truman presidency had fallen into serious difficulty. The Korean War had stalemated, and many Americans were growing tired of the conflict. Several small scandals were plaguing the administration. Despite the fact that Truman and his foreign policy team had created NATO and the Marshall Plan, and had sent troops to defend South Korea from the communist North, Republicans and even some Democrats alleged that he was "soft on Communism" and responsible for the fall of China to Mao Tse-Tung. Some historians have suggested that Truman had already decided not to seek another term.[58] Even if he had decided to run, he would have had difficult time winning reelection. Truman stepped aside in favor of Governor Adlai Stevenson of Illinois, who was a hero to many in the liberal intelligentsia.

The Republicans, despite Truman's difficulties, were not particularly confident of their chances. After all, a GOP candidate had not been elected president since Herbert Hoover in 1928. Many in the Eastern liberal wing of the party feared that, if the Midwestern conservative wing of the party had its way and nominated Senator Robert Taft of Ohio, they would go down to defeat yet again. They recruited General Dwight D. Eisenhower, commander of U.S. forces during World War II, to be their candidate. Both parties had sought out the general in the past, though no one was sure of his party affiliation. In any case, Ike accepted their call and defeated Taft's forces at the GOP convention. Republican leaders hoped that Eisenhower's tremendous personal popularity would help them overcome the stigma their party still carried from the Depression era.

No one expected immigration to be an issue in the fall campaign. The war in Korea, inflation, and concerns about internal subversion seemed likely to dominate the race between Eisenhower and Stevenson. But Truman, though not running himself, placed the issue on the front pages of every newspaper in the nation and made the McCarran-Walter Act an important part of the political debate. The president took an active role in the campaign because he was infuriated by Eisenhower's attacks on his foreign policy, believing it was hypocritical for Ike to attack policies he himself had shaped as supreme commander of NATO.

Truman's attack began with a speech in Buffalo in early October. He lashed out at the GOP for supporting McCarran-Walter and the national origins system, "based on a discredited and un-American theory of racial superiority," adding, "There is no logic in it—but there is plenty of prejudice—prejudice against people with foreign names and foreign backgrounds." He concluded by stressing the threat such policies posed to American unity: "Once these deep forces of prejudice and unreason are set loose, no one can tell where they will go. They could tear our nation apart, setting group against group, creed against creed, the older immigrant stocks against the newer."[59]

Truman criticized Eisenhower and his running mate, Senator Richard Nixon of California, for supporting restrictionist immigration laws: "The Republican candidate for president was asked about immigration, but he didn't have any views on the subject. The Republican candidate for Vice President was one of the Senators who voted in favor of this unjust law, and to override my veto."[60] Truman repeated these charges a few days later in New York City, invoking an ideological interpretation of World War II: "What do these add up to? They add up to the philosophy of racial superiority developed by the Nazis, which we thought we had destroyed when we defeated Nazi Germany and liberated Europe." Truman also linked Eisenhower with what he called the intolerance of the right wing of the GOP, including William Jenner, Joseph McCarthy, and William Revercomb: "the champion of the anti-Catholic, anti-Jewish provisions of the original D.P. bill, these men have been embraced by the Republican candidate for President."[61]

After these initial volleys by Truman, Ike tried to neutralize the issue by criticizing McCarran-Walter. The general stated, "we must strike from our statute books any legislation concerning immigration that implies the blasphemy against the democracy that only certain groups of Europeans are welcome on American shores." In the same speech, Eisenhower expressed his belief in the importance of tolerance and unity: "Unity of our own people implies a host of great tasks and duties. It demands—on all fronts and in all senses—the keenest guard against divisive propaganda, the sternest watch against divisive prejudice."[62]

A few days later, Eisenhower attempted to place the onus on Truman, accusing the president of calling him anti-Semitic and anti-Catholic. The next day in Boston, he repeated his opposition to discrimination and again called for a repeal of "the unfair provisions of the McCarran-Walter Act" without citing a particular aspect of the bill.[63] The following week he used an ideological narrative of World War II to reject the charges, declaring, "Surely, my reckless and desperate opponents cannot expect the American people to have forgotten how my professional life came to a climax. It was in the defeat of Hitler, the destruction of Nazi and Fascist hordes, and the governments which propagated doctrines of racism."[64]

As Ike's remarks suggested, the rhetoric of tolerance appeared frequently during the campaign. Stevenson's running mate, Senator John Sparkman of Alabama, a supporter of Jim Crow, said McCarran-Walter "perpetuates in our laws the most unwholesome kind of discrimination." Stevenson, who himself was no ardent opponent of Jim Crow, spoke about the history of racial and ethnic minorities in the United States: "There have been many injustices and inequalities. For some, because of race, religion, or color, a special and unfortunate fate has been decreed. But happily, we are now removing even those stubborn old stains from the fabric of our national life."[65]

During this time, the language of tolerance emerged as a central aspect of American public discourse, if not national practice. Of course, one has to be wary of such rhetoric, particularly when it is not always accompanied by actions. It is, however, noteworthy that politicians felt the need to separate themselves from intolerant behavior and pay attention to the contributions of immigrants.

Despite Eisenhower's attempt to distance himself from McCarran-Walter, Truman continued to attack the GOP for its support of the legislation and its opposition to immigration in general since the 1920s. He criticized McCarran and other Democrats who supported the bill. Stevenson did the same, pointedly refusing to call for Francis Walter's reelection when he campaigned in his Pennsylvania district toward the conclusion of the campaign.[66]

In the end, Eisenhower's tremendous personal popularity, fatigue over the Korean War, and twenty years of Democratic rule produced a Republican landslide in November 1952. Truman's attacks on McCarran-Walter and Ike's unwillingness to defend the bill wholeheartedly, however, portended changes in the future of immigration policy. The bill, which Congress had passed by an overwhelming margin with bipartisan support a few months earlier, had now been disowned by the leaders of both political parties. "As the year came to a close," Oscar Handlin wrote in May 1953, "hardly a voice was heard in defense of the new law."[67]

∾

During the McCarran-Walter debate, the candidates talked of visions of the United States as a "nation of immigrants." Truman used contributionist rhetoric: "Ours is a nation of many different groups. Of different races, different national origins and different religions." Stevenson sounded like Israel Zangwill, declaring, "They were of every racial stock and every religious faith and each brought something of the old country to the new country. And different though they were they became one."[68] Increasingly, advocates of a more liberal immigration policy became more forceful as they called for the abolition of the national origins system. They did so by using the kind of contributionist rhetoric employed by opponents of McCarran-Walter.

Whom Shall We Welcome, the report by President Truman's Commission on Immigration and Naturalization, revealed the evolution in language and attitudes. Issued in 1953, *Whom Shall We Welcome* served the same function as *To Secure These Rights*, the report issued by Truman's Committee on Civil Rights. Both documents laid out blueprints for reform that policymakers would implement years after their release.[69]

Whom Shall We Welcome used contributionist language similar to the *Americans All . . . Immigrants All* radio program. Sounding much like the opening show, the report said, "Our growth as a nation has been achieved, in large measure, through the genius and industry of immigrants of every race and from every quarter of the world. The story of their pursuit of happiness is the saga of America." The report continued, "Scarcely one aspect of our American economy, culture, or development can be discussed

without reference to the fundamental contribution of immigrants."[70]
Whom Shall We Welcome then listed, like the progressive textbooks of the
time, a number of prominent immigrants from various parts of the world,
including southern and eastern Europe.

The report also echoed traditional arguments concerning the benefits
of immigration, declaring that the newcomers benefited society while they
also adapted to American ideals. Like the opponents of restriction in 1924
and 1952, *Whom Shall We Welcome* rejected the idea that immigration
weakened the nation's economy: "Whether immigration was cause or
effect, it is true today, as it was in Revolutionary times, that the richest
regions are those with the highest proportion of recent immigrants."[71] The
report also rejected the idea that immigrants were unable to assimilate into
American society: "Each new group or category of immigrants evoked fear
that they could not assimilate, but nonetheless, with the passage of time
each of the various succeeding groups became full participating members
of the American community."[72]

Whom Shall We Welcome called for abolishing the national origins system. The report said the system had been implemented based on now-
discredited theories of racial superiority and that the quotas hurt the country's international standing in the Cold War.[73] The Commission on Immigration and Naturalization proposed replacing the national origins system
with a unified quota system that would allocate the same number of visas
using a different criterion. Rather than distributing visas by country, entry
into the United States would be determined by whether an individual
immigrant fit into a set of five categories, including political asylum, family
unification, skill needs of employers, assisting with the problem of overpop-
ulation in the "free world" and general immigration ("aliens who may be
desirable immigrants merely because they are good people whom we should
be happy to welcome"). The commission also recommended continuing
the nonquota status of the Western Hemisphere.[74]

Though he did not endorse the commission's findings, Eisenhower
addressed immigration in his first State of the Union address. Repeating his
campaign statements concerning the importance of tolerance and the need
to reform McCarran-Walter, he added some contributionist language: "It
is well for us to remind ourselves occasionally of an equally manifest fact:
we are—one and all—immigrants or sons and daughters of immigrants."[75]

Eisenhower also proposed and Congress passed the Refugee Relief Act
in 1953, which allowed 209,000 immigrants to come into the country from

outside the quota system. Again reflecting the influence of the Cold War, the bill favored refugees who were escaping Eastern European Communist countries that had low quotas. Ike invoked the Cold War in his letter to Congress proposing the law, noting that, "these refugees and escapees [from behind the Iron Curtain] searching desperately for freedom look to the free world for haven."[76] The Senate passed the bill by a vote of 63–30, with many senators who had supported McCarran-Walter also endorsing the relief legislation. McCarran and William Jenner led the opposition to the bill because they believed it would aid Communist attempts to infiltrate the United States.[77] The Relief Act continued a process, begun with the Displaced Persons Act of 1948, by which emergency legislation weakened the importance of the system. By allowing more and more immigrants to enter the country outside the quota framework, the special bills reduced the national origins system's centrality in American immigration policy.

Public events celebrating immigration were yet another manifestation of the growing popularity of contributionism. In 1952, I am an American Day and Constitution Day merged together to become Citizenship Day, which thereafter was normally held on September 17 each year.[78] An American Legion pamphlet explained the logic behind the change: "the ideals and objectives underlying the citizenship observance [I Am an American Day] and celebration of Constitution Day are so identical that each will give strength to the other. On both occasions Constitutional rights and the necessity for their preservation are emphasized."[79] The programs involved remained largely the same as in earlier years, featuring induction ceremonies and pageants displaying immigrant contributions.

In 1954, naturalization ceremonies could not be held September 17 because federal law prohibits naturalization in the sixty days before an election. As a result, Citizenship Day and the concomitant ceremonies were held on Veterans Day, November 11. The celebration moved to a national level on this occasion as 48,000 Americans from New York City to Hawaii took the oath of citizenship.[80] According to *Life*, "It was the first time in U.S. history that citizenship was conferred upon so many people in so many mass ceremonies."[81]

The largest of these gatherings were held in Ebbets Field and the Polo Grounds in New York City and Herbert Brownell, Eisenhower's attorney general, addressed both groups. Immigration, Brownell proclaimed, was a sign of America's strength: "living proof that America still stands before all the world as the greatest symbol of freedom." Striking a more inclusive tone than Woodrow Wilson had at a similar gathering forty years earlier, he added: "Your oath of allegiance to the United States required your renunciation of all former allegiance. This solemn pledge does not obligate you to forgo your natural affection for the land of your birth. Rather, it exacts from you a sincere promise of unswerving loyalty to this nation above all others."[82]

⁂

Intellectuals and history textbooks also reflected the growing appeal of contributionism. Leading thinkers were returning to the debates held by Horace Kallen, Randolph Bourne, and Israel Zangwill in the first two decades of the twentieth century. Increasingly, they were developing a modified version of Zangwill's melting pot that embraced how immigrants remade American culture while also assuring that new arrivals themselves changed and embraced basic American ideals. The impact of these intellectual changes could be seen in the rhetoric of organizations such as the American Jewish Committee and in the political dialogue of the period.

Oscar Handlin, himself the son of Jewish immigrants, clearly disagreed with Kallen and Bourne about the endurance of immigrant culture in his 1951 telling of the immigration experience, *The Uprooted*. Starting with a cover that portrays downcast immigrants about to make the journey to America, *The Uprooted*, which won the Pulitzer Prize for History, concentrates on the difficulties faced by immigrants in America. Though Handlin was clearly sympathetic to immigrants, his book pays little attention to the benefits brought by the Ellis Island-era newcomers and depicts a painful adjustment experience, fraught with economic and social difficulties. "Strangers in the immediate world around them," Handlin wrote, "the immigrants often recognized, in dismay, the loneliness of their condition. Their hesitant steps groped around the uncertain hazards of new places and exposed them ever to perilous risks."[83]

Handlin observed that the immigrants attempted to recreate aspects of their Old World life in their new environment. "In the fluid and free life of America," he wrote, "they found the latitude to join with one another, to contrive institutions through which they could speak, means of expression that would speak through them."[84] Handlin believed that these institutions, such as the church, the mutual aid societies, and the foreign-language press, could not sustain themselves in America and that assimilation would largely erase native traditions. Though he suggested that the immigrants' contributions changed the country's culture, Handlin disagreed with pluralists like Kallen, concluding that the newcomers would "struggle to preserve the old associations. But their sons were not likely to make the attempt."[85]

Nathan Glazer, a prominent New York intellectual of the 1950s who later coauthored *Beyond the Melting Pot* (1963), an important book about American ethnicity, also weighed in on this debate. He believed immigration was responsible for a more profound transformation in the national culture than Handlin allowed. While he thought Kallen and Bourne had exaggerated the endurance of ethnic subcultures, Glazer suggested that they were correct in "seeing that the American culture that had been created by the descendants of English immigrants was undergoing large changes."[86]

In Glazer's mind, the immigrant cultures altered America by removing the sense of homogeneity that had prevailed in the years before the turn of the century. Previously, a writer like Mark Twain could "assume a general measure of understanding in his audience." By the mid-1950s, there were now numerous American subcultures—"the life of the big cities, of the urban Negro and the rural Negro, of the Jews and the Italians, of the midwestern farmer, of the city middle classes and the self-conscious intellectuals"— that were too different to understand each other.[87] Glazer, a child of Jewish immigrants, did not bemoan this change and expressed contributionist views: "They have changed American culture: within this changed culture, they, as well as the long-settled groups of English, Irish, and Germans, are now quite at home."[88]

Harvard law professor Louis Jaffe summed up the changing ideologies of immigration in an article in the journal *Law and Contemporary Problems* in 1956. Observing that the melting pot had evolved with the times, he wrote, "The present day version is apt to emphasize unification a little less and diversity a little more."[89] He suggested that many now considered the melting pot ideology too conformist. Of course, many immigrants had expressed a similar view when Zangwill's play was released forty years earlier. Jaffe added a clear expression of contributionism:

It is more correct—and in the mind of some, morally superior—to speak of pluralism. The premise is that everyone will satisfy the basic minima of American citizenship. But beyond that, each will be free to practice his diversities, among which may be those of a racial character. This, like the Melting Pot, is thought of as not merely tolerated, but positively beneficial. It "enriches" the society.[90]

School textbooks began to reflect this perspective. *Our Nation's Story* by Everett Augspurger and Richard McLemore (1954) discussed the positive impact the "new" immigrants had made on American culture: "Anglo-Saxon elements no longer entirely dominated in the emerging American culture. Items that appeal to the tongue, the ear, or the eye are generally accepted for their true worth, whatever their origin." Augspurger and McLemore continued, "Americans were soon to discover that foods like spaghetti, strudel, and paprikash were welcome additions to any menu. On festival occasions, the colorful native costumes pleased the eye as polkas and other folk music delighted the ear. Variety enriched, rather than weakened, the capacity for enjoyment."[91]

Ralph Volney Harlow's textbooks continued their evolution toward contributionism. The 1953 version of *Story of America*, like the 1947 version, mentioned the achievements of various immigrants. Harlow now went farther, declaring, "It is strange that almost from the beginning of our nation, there have been people who feared and hated the newcomers. We are a *nation of immigrants*. All of us are immigrants or the descendants of immigrants."[92]

Some textbooks, such as *History of the Free People* by Henry W. Bragdon and Samuel McCutchen, did not go this far in describing the benefits of recent immigrants. Nevertheless, their language was markedly less hostile than the textbooks of the 1920s and 1930s: "The 'new immigration' tended to concentrate in cities. . . . They usually formed compact communities of the same national origin, so that every great metropolis had a 'little Italy,' a 'little Poland,' a 'little Greece,' and so forth. This gave rise to the charge that the new immigration was difficult to Americanize."[93] These books largely ignored Latinos and only referred to Asian Americans with regard to exclusion legislation.

Ethnic organizations that were advocating for immigration reform, such as the American Committee for Italian Migration, also played a role in promoting the contributionist viewpoint. Judge Juvenal Marchisio, the committee's national chairman, promoted this ideology on a television panel in Cleveland in 1952, noting that the states with the highest per capita incomes were also the states with the highest percentages of immigrants as well as vice-versa. Rejecting stereotypes of Italian Americans, he added, "in proportion to their number, less Italians have been convicted of crime than any other race, even as more Italians in proportion to their number fought and died in the Armed Forces of the United States in the last war."[94]

The American Jewish Committee's speeches and editorials regarding public holidays expressed a similar message as they called for the abolition of the origins system. An editorial for Independence Day, 1955, detailed the difficulties faced by refugees fleeing the Iron Curtain: "Let's junk the unfair quota system. It's based on bigotry. It discriminates against members of certain races. It runs contrary to all our ideals of liberty and equality." Referring to proponents of national origins quotas, "Seems they've forgotten that, since the time when immigrants and the sons of immigrants affixed their signatures to the Declaration of Independence, millions of other newcomers have contributed mightily to keeping America strong and free."[95]

The AJC, in cooperation with several other liberal organizations, distributed a booklet called *The Fence* (1956), which contained a series of cartoons that used both the Cold War and contributionism to illustrate the inequities of American immigration policy. One showed a police officer standing with a young boy next to a gate. The police officer tells the child, "That fence means keep out, sonny. Leave the gate alone, and be on your way. Go on back home." The boy responds, "Please Officer, it looks so nice in your country—like our home in Europe. We lived in a free country too—until the Communists came. Now we have no home. Wherever we go, there's always a fence." Another cartoon depicted a Native American, with a caption that read "Fact is, except for the Indians, we're all immigrants— or descendants of immigrants. President Eisenhower says: 'The immigrant has brought greatness to our land.' . . . We need immigrants as much as they need us."[96]

In 1956, the United States Information Service produced a document titled *In Quest of Freedom*, which listed the accomplishments of immigrants. The booklet featured several newcomers from eastern and southern Europe, including Arturo Toscanini, Igor Stravinsky, and Joseph Pulitzer, among others. Reflecting the greater discussion of nonwhite newcomers, *In Quest of Freedom* also detailed the lives of a few Latino and Asian immigrants, such as José Martí, a Cuban resistance leader, and Hideyo Noguchi, a Japanese American bacteriologist.[97] The introduction and conclusion of *In Quest of Freedom* included the typical paeans to the gifts of immigrants. The introduction said, "In these pages you will meet a few of the millions who found a home in the United States. . . . each used his talent to the fullest, and in return gave something of himself to his new homeland and to the world. America is the richer for their coming."[98]

Though there were important differences between these thinkers, they all broke with wartime universalism and espoused the contributionist vision. In their minds, the "new" immigrants brought different cultural and economic benefits that strengthened the country. On the other hand, they all believed that the immigrants adapted and were changed by the transition to life in the United States.

Though immigration reform remained a relatively minor part of the political agenda, contributionist language also increasingly became part of political rhetoric when immigration was discussed in the mid- to late 1950s. Eisenhower proposed new legislation to allow more immigrants from southern and eastern Europe into the country in 1956, declaring, "Throughout our history immigration to this land has contributed greatly to the strength and character of our Republic."[99] Even politicians unsympathetic to reform were praising immigrant contributions. In an article defending the national origins system, Francis Walter declared that what united Americans as a nation was not race, but a common ideology and cultural heritage. Walter elaborated, "That we are a 'nation of immigrants' is indeed a part of that heritage, but the emphasis is on the word 'nation'." He added, "We are 'immigrants' who have fused into one people, with one national loyalty—to the United States of America."[100]

❧

Even as many Americans grew increasingly tolerant and appreciative of immigrants from southern and eastern Europe during the 1950s, racial tensions increased as the black civil rights movement began to garner national attention. The Supreme Court's decision in *Brown v. Board of Education* and the success of the Montgomery Bus Boycott provided evidence that racial change was coming. With the growing prominence of civil rights as a national issue, black/white divisions were gradually superseding conflicts between the Ellis Island-era immigrants and native-stock Americans.

For example, the 1955 film *Blackboard Jungle*, which provided a dramatic look at the problem of juvenile delinquency, depicted a school with Irish, Italian, Puerto Rican, and black students. When it came to issues of race and ethnicity, however, the focus was on the problems faced by an African American student played by the young Sidney Poitier and, to a lesser extent, Hispanics. Glenn Ford, who plays Richard Daidier, an idealistic young teacher, gives a lecture to his students after one calls a classmate a "spic." "I want to get one thing very clear in this classroom," declares Daidier. "There's not going to be any name-calling here. Not today. Not tomorrow. Not ever." Later in the film, Poitier's character, Gregory Miller, tells Daidier that he does not really try to excel in school because there are few opportunities for blacks: "We talking from different sides of the fence, Mr Daidier. You're not black, remember." Daidier responds, "That's not a good enough excuse, not nowadays, and you know it, Miller. Dr. Ralph Bunche proved that, George Washington Carver," as he went on to list other successful blacks of that era.[101]

Civil rights for African Americans, however, still received relatively little attention during National Brotherhood Week and other celebrations of American heritage. As late as February 1955, Senator William Fulbright (D) of Arkansas, a segregationist, chaired the Brotherhood Week activities. It would not be until the 1960s that the causes of immigration reform and civil rights became inextricably intertwined. Although civil rights received little attention in discussions over immigration in the 1950s, issues of race were becoming more prominent in these debates, as restrictionists were growing more and more apprehensive about the growing number of Latinos, particularly Mexican Americans, who were entering the country.

There had always been a significant Latino presence in the Southwest, dating to the U.S. seizure of California, Texas, and New Mexico during the Mexican-American War in 1848. Migration from Mexico renewed during World War I, when war production and the cutoff of immigration from Europe precipitated labor shortages. Most of these new arrivals went to the Southwest, although some made the journey to urban centers in the Midwest and Northeast.

Though there was no quota on the Western Hemisphere, Mexican immigrants needed to apply for visas for entry into the United States, and the State Department often made this process difficult and time consuming in an attempt to limit immigration. Officials also used the "public charge" provision, which allowed immigration authorities to deny individuals entrance to the United States if they were deemed unable to support themselves, to prevent Mexicans from making the journey north. As a result, many Latinos entered the country illegally during the 1920s.[102] During the Depression, the federal government engaged in a massive effort to repatriate Mexican immigrants, both legal and illegal, because they were blamed for undercutting wage levels and exacerbating the unemployment crisis. This process contributed to a sense that Mexicans were a different race, despite the fact they did not face a specific quota.[103]

World War II precipitated another wave of Mexican migration into the United States. Farmers in the Southwest claimed they faced a labor shortage because their employees were moving into war production or the military. The U.S. and Mexican governments worked out an agreement to begin what would be called the bracero program in 1942. Under this program, a fixed number of Mexican workers would come into the United States under contracts that provided them protection from the exploitation many migrant workers faced. The 1942 agreement specified that braceros were guaranteed, among other things, to be paid the prevailing wage in their region, as well as decent free housing and free transport back to Mexico when their contract expired.[104]

The program had problems from the outset. Migrant workers had to make long journeys to the border to receive their contracts. Because the number of braceros allowed to enter the United States was capped, many were denied the opportunity to work. Rather than return to the poverty of their villages, some chose to enter the country illegally. Employers in the Southwest were only too willing to hire them, avoiding the red tape and labor protections of the bracero program.[105] As a result of the bracero program and economic changes in Mexico, illegal immigration from the south grew dramatically. In 1944, the Border Patrol arrested approximately 34,000 illegal entrants; by 1952, the number had grown to almost 532,000.[106]

National newspapers and magazines described the changes along the border, portraying the Mexican migration as a dangerous "invasion."[107] A New York Times article by Gladwin Hill in January 1954 reveals these attitudes: "down here on the Mexican border the dawn of each day, seven days a week, brings the renewal of an unremitting if bloodless battle to stem a never-ending invasion of the United States." Hill went on to discuss how these migrants lowered the wages of native-born American workers, raised the costs of public services, and found protection in the agricultural Southwest, or "in the Latin-American colonies of big cities and proceed to stay here indefinitely, contributing to such problems as poverty and illegitimacy." Hill concludes by declaring that "each dawn the battle against them is renewed."[108]

Hill's words, in a leading organ of liberalism, were noteworthy because they were similar to the language restrictionist politicians and thinkers had used to describe southern and eastern Europeans during the 1920s. Immigrant communities are again isolated "colonies" where they remain outside the mainstream of American life. Newcomers again threaten the living standards of native-born American workers.

Some politicians, sensing the growing concern about the so-called "wetback" in the early-to-mid 1950s, proposed penalties on employers who hired illegal immigrants. These bills garnered support not only from restrictionists in Congress, but from others who had opposed McCarran-Walter. Unions and many pro-labor liberal politicians, such as Paul Douglas and Hubert Humphrey, feared that illegal workers were lowering the wages of American citizens. Urging the passage of new legislation to control the border, Walter Mason, national legislative director of the AFL, declared that illegal immigration had "produced chaos in American agriculture, deprived American workers of opportunities for obtaining employment, and seriously undermined the wage standards which Americans have worked to establish."[109]

Mexican American organizations also supported the legislation because they believed illegal immigrants exacerbated discrimination against Latinos.[110] Despite the efforts of this disparate coalition, Congress did not pass legislation addressing the problem in the 1950s. Large agricultural organizations, such as the American Farm Bureau Federation, had a vested interest in maintaining the status quo and lobbied to prevent the passage of any bill that penalized employers for hiring illegal immigrants.[111]

As the congressional debate dragged on in 1954, Attorney General Brownell planned and executed a massive roundup of illegal immigrants along the border. This program, known as "Operation Wetback," represented a dramatic effort to control the border. The INS started in California, using roadblocks and other methods to capture illegal aliens and return them to Mexico. The operation moved to Texas and other border regions and eventually sent approximately one million illegal immigrants to their home country in 1954.[112] Operation Wetback seemed to have succeeded as illegal immigration fell and remained relatively low for several years. Most of those desiring to enter the country switched to using legal means, and immigration through the bracero program climbed between 1954 and 1960.[113]

Despite the more stringent barriers to illegal immigration, restrictionist politicians increasingly turned their attention to Latinos. Francis Walter expressed his concerns in a Memorial Day speech to the Sons of the American Revolution in 1956. He suggested that immigration from the Western Hemisphere was becoming a major problem, observing that legal migration from Mexico had increased 347 percent in 1954 and 525 percent in 1955. Walter added that, if Congress changed the base year for the quotas for Eastern Hemisphere migration from 1920 to 1950 while immigration from Mexico continued to rise, the United States would lose its cohesiveness as a nation. "I believe that it would be entirely safe to assume that by, say 1980, we will have much difficulty making ourselves understood in the English language in some parts of this country," he declared, adding, "we must resist with courage and determination the attempt to convert this country into a disorganized, multilingual, overcrowded dumping ground."[114]

Though the restrictionists clearly depicted Hispanics in a negative light, their rhetoric was not nearly as racialized as it was during the 1920s and 1930s. Increasingly, they based their objection to Latino immigration to the United States on physical differences and cultural grounds, like the lack of a common language, rather than on older theories of racial inferiority. In the 1920s, restrictionists worried about the decline of English as the American language, but they had been concerned about Jews and Italians speaking their native tongues. By the 1950s, restrictionists were turning their attention to Spanish-speaking newcomers.

∾

It appeared that the system might be on its last legs as the winds of public opinion seemed to be blowing in the direction of change. A Gallup Poll in 1955 indicated that Americans with some awareness of immigration issues wanted reform. The survey asked, "Have you heard of or read about the McCarran-Walter Immigration Act?" Only 15 percent replied yes. Half of those who said yes believed the law should be changed. Of that subset, 68 percent wanted the current law to be liberalized.[115] While this is not evidence of a dramatic dissatisfaction with the law, it showed that most people who were conscious of the current policy disapproved of it.

The AFL-CIO, which had traditionally supported immigration restriction, moved toward opposing the national origins system. Many of the union's members were now the descendants of Ellis Island immigrants, and the umbrella of labor organizations increasingly adopted the contributionist language rejected by their forefathers. In testimony before the Senate in 1959, Hyman Bookbinder, the AFL-CIO legislative representative, explained that the labor organization did not view immigrants as an economic threat to its members: "It must not be forgotten that only a portion of all immigrants—sometimes no more than a fourth or a third—are job seekers. But every immigrant is a potential customer for the products of American workers." "And, of course," he added, "every employed immigrant is a producer who contributes to our total wealth." Bookbinder repeated familiar arguments that immigrants strengthened the national economy and that every wave of immigrants had been met with suspicion only to be seen eventually as an essential part of the national polity. "Despite the initial distrust of new peoples, the record of adjustment, of integration, of accommodation is a glorious story," declared Bookbinder in contributionist language. "What we once used to refer to as the 'melting pot' of America is now more appropriately and accurately described as the 'mosaic' of American culture"[116]

Many observers believed it was simply a matter of time before Congress enacted new legislation. Harry N. Rosenfield, executive director of Truman's Commission on Immigration and Naturalization, remarked that the politics of the issue had undergone a dramatic transformation in the four years since the passage of McCarran-Walter: "From the partisan jockeying of 1952 there seems to have developed substantial agreement by both major parties in 1956 that the basic features of the McCarran-Walter Act need thoroughgoing changes." A coalition of groups had emerged to support reform of the immigration laws. Religious groups, including the National Council of Churches, the Catholic Church, and Jewish organizations, supported change. Special measures such as the Refugee Relief Act weakened the system as more and more immigrants entered the country outside the quota framework. The Cold War, America's role as a world leader, and the declining respectability of scientific racism fostered a climate favorable to the advocates of reform. Rosenfield concluded, "By 1960, it seems safe to predict, the American people will have set their sights on a complete and thorough revision of our immigration law. . . . They will demand a positive, liberalized immigration policy consonant with our great traditions and our role as a world power."[117]

At the same time, Ike's views on immigration reform had evolved to the point that his position was almost identical to that of liberal advocates during the McCarran-Walter debate. He called for the quota base year to be raised from 1920 to 1950 and for the remaining openings to be distributed on a first-come, first-served basis to other parts of the globe. Meanwhile, Senator Lehman proposed a bill that would carry out the recommendations of *Whom Shall We Welcome.*

Despite these signs of change, the national origins system continued to have many important defenders who believed the quotas served a vital purpose by protecting the country from communism and preserving the demographic continuity of the nation. Francis Walter, the leading congressional proponent of national origins following Pat McCarran's death in 1953, continued to have little patience with advocates of reform: "Spearheaded by the Communists, their fellow travelers, Congressional 'liberals' and spokesmen for the so-called ethnic minority blocs, the assault on America's immigration system is increasing in intensity every month." He added that, "all of these proposals are thinly veiled attempts to wreck the 'national origins' quota system, which is vital to the preservation of the basic cultural composition of our society."[118] The *Saturday Evening Post* agreed in a more restrained fashion, editorializing, "We should open the door for as many worthy aliens as we can. But we must hold fast to our policy so that the cultural characteristics of our population will not be materially altered."[119]

Patriotic societies such as the American Legion and the Veterans of Foreign Wars, though they often offered rhetorical support for contributionism during public celebrations like National Brotherhood Week and I Am an American Day, remained firmly in favor of the current system. Robert Alexander, who had worked on immigration issues for the State Department, made the argument for preserving cultural continuity as the centerpiece of the nation's immigration policy in the *American Legion Magazine*. In doing so, he exposed an important dilemma faced by those who wanted to abolish the national origins framework. Alexander declared, "Those who object to our national origins quota system obviously disapprove the national origins of our people." He concluded by rhetorically asking that supporters of reform "should tell us 'What is wrong with our national origins'."[120]

John F. Kennedy's book *A Nation of Immigrants*, published in 1958, exemplified many of the changes and trends of the 1950s. Kennedy wrote the book with the assistance of his staff and Arthur Mann, a historian supplied by the Anti-Defamation League.[121] *A Nation of Immigrants*, like his earlier *Profiles in Courage*, burnished JFK's image as a thoughtful politician concerned about major national and international issues.

Stressing contributionism, Kennedy wrote, "Another way of indicating the importance of immigration to America is to point out that every American who ever lived, with the exception of one group [Native Americans], was either an immigrant himself or a descendant of immigrants." He added:

> The effects of immigration—to put it another way—the contributions of immigrants—can be seen in every aspect of our national life. We see it in religion, in politics, in business, in the arts, in education, in athletics and in entertainment. There is no part of America that has not been touched by our immigrant background.[122]

Like the progressive school textbooks of this era, Kennedy listed the contributions of southern and eastern Europeans on the same level as earlier arrivals from northern and western Europe. JFK then went on to delineate the accomplishments of several famous immigrants, citing the same individuals described in *Whom Shall We Welcome*.[123]

Kennedy criticized the national origins system, noting that the large quotas for Great Britain and Ireland were undersubscribed while the demand came from small quota nations such as Greece and Italy. He observed that special pieces of legislation, such as the Displaced Persons Act and the Refugee Relief Act, were required to deal with humanitarian emergencies because of the inequities of the current framework. JFK declared that these bills repaired some of the damage to America's international image caused by the quotas, but "the effect of these actions is diluted by the very fact that they are viewed as exceptions to our national policy rather than as part of that policy."[124]

Endorsing Senator Lehman's reform proposals, Kennedy called for abolishing the current system. He emphasized that there would continue to be overall limits on immigration, but "Instead of using the test of where the immigrant was born, the Lehman bill would have made the applicant's individual training and qualifications the test for admission." "The most serious defect in the present law is not that it is restrictive," he argued, "but that many of the restrictions are based on false or unjust premises." JFK concluded by saying about the reform proposals, "With such a policy we could turn to the world with clean hands and a clear conscience. Such a policy would be but a reaffirmation of old principles."[125]

A Nation of Immigrants summarized the evolution of liberal thought concerning immigration in the 1950s. Moving past the universalist ideology of the World War II-era, many Americans embraced a contributionist perspective that emphasized that newcomers from southern and eastern Europe had helped to build the U.S. economy and enhance its culture while they also adapted to American norms. Though they were no longer described in the racialist language of the 1930s and 1940s, Asians and Hispanics remained outside the broader view of American identity. At the same time, liberals believed the national origins system was antiquated. Immigration from Mexico, which was not covered by the quotas, also undermined the system and created consternation among restrictionists. As the nation headed toward the 1960s, it seemed that reform of the 1924 law was increasingly possible.

Chapter 6

The Cold War and Religious Unity

In his book *Protestant, Catholic, Jew* (1955), sociologist Will Herberg declared, "The same basic values and ideals, the same underlying commitment to the American Way of Life, are promoted by parochial school and public school, by Catholic, Protestant, and Jew, despite the diversity of formal religious creed."[1] He asked rhetorically, "After all, are not Protestantism, Catholicism, and Judaism, in their sociological actuality, alike 'religions of democracy'?" Herberg's suggestion that the three major religions in the United States shared the same fundamental values summarized the major theme of religious pluralism in the 1950s. During this time, many intellectuals and politicians invoked the common bonds of the three faiths and developed an American identity that emphasized a belief in God while diminishing doctrinal differences.

The roots of this philosophy lay in the propaganda of World War II. During the conflict, wartime organs such as the Office of War Information (OWI) repeatedly suggested that the three major religions shared a basic ideology far greater than what divided them. The interfaith movement, led by organizations such as the National Conference of Christians and Jews (NCCJ), continued to promote this message during the early postwar period. By the 1950s, the exigencies of the Cold War created the need to construct an American identity distinct from that of the Soviet Union. The religiosity of many Americans contrasted sharply with the state-sponsored atheism of the Soviet Union and policymakers and intellectuals wanted to emphasize the faith of Americans in a way that would not divide the nation. Though contributionism composed part of this ideology, the 1950s era message focused more on what different groups had in common and stressed faith in a unifying manner.

At the same time, church attendance and religious identification increased while spiritual pronouncements became a central part of the political culture. Americans grew increasingly tolerant of different faiths, although they largely kept close to their coreligionists in the growing suburbs. While policymakers and intellectuals emphasized the similarities between Judaism, Protestantism, and Catholicism, John F. Kennedy's 1960 campaign for the presidency revealed that many voters still feared the possibility of a non-Protestant president. Religion remained an issue in the campaign throughout the year, and traditional fears regarding the persistence of ethnic and religious identity played a significant role in the outcome of the election.

∾

No story better illustrated the presumed unity of the three faiths than the tale of the four chaplains who died serving aboard the troopship USS *Dorchester* during World War II. In February 1943, a German submarine torpedoed the *Dorchester* near Greenland as it carried supplies across the North Atlantic. As sailors scrambled for their lifeboats, the four chaplains gave up their seats so that others might live and were last seen on the deck of the sinking ship holding hands while bowing their heads in prayer. Six hundred men died on the *Dorchester*; only three hundred survived. The four chaplains represented the diversity of American religion at that time: Clark V. Poling and George L. Fox, ministers; John P. Washington, a priest; and Alexander Goode, a rabbi.

The story of the four chaplains became ubiquitous during the 1950s. Every year, private organizations such as the American Legion and the American Jewish Committee sponsored "Dorchester Day" commemorating the loss of the chaplains. The speeches offered that day explicitly connected the wartime message with contemporary events. A suggested speech for the American Legion on Dorchester Day 1950 stated, "We were battling an enemy who fought under the vile banner of racial and religious hatred; and these four chaplains symbolized the unity of free men under God—the unity that the enemy had set out to destroy—the unity that was bound to win." The speech alluded to the Cold War: "Part of the answer to the communist menace, is to bind up the wounds of democracy, for the communists cling like leeches to these sore spots. They exploit every grievance, every sign of corruption within."[2]

In 1951, President Truman dedicated a memorial to the four chaplains in Philadelphia. A Baptist church contained the memorial, which included a revolving altar with three parts representing Protestantism, Catholicism, and Judaism. At the opening, Truman remarked on the common ideology of the three religions: "These four men represented the Protestant, the Catholic and the Jewish beliefs. Each of these beliefs teaches that obedience to God and love for one's fellow man are the greatest and strongest things in the world." He used some contributionist language: "We must never forget that this country was founded by men who came to these shores to worship God as they pleased. Catholics, Jews, and Protestants all came here for this great purpose."[3] Radio carried the ceremony across the nation, and a newsreel concerning the memorial declared effusively, "Perhaps nowhere in America will there ever be a monument to the brotherhood of man so symbolic of American ideals."[4]

Even at this ceremony celebrating the chaplains, signs of serious differences between faiths appeared despite rhetoric to the contrary. No official representative of the Roman Catholic Church attended the ceremony because the Church prohibited sharing a house of worship with another faith. Catholic services could not be held in the building because it was a Baptist church.[5]

Numerous other tributes to the chaplains appeared throughout the 1950s. The United States Military Academy created a window at its chapel to commemorate the chaplains in 1952.[6] At the same time, the American Legion initiated its annual Back-to-God campaign at the Chapel of the Four Chaplains.[7] The veterans' organization hoped the campaign would strengthen America's religious faith during the Cold War. Major political and religious figures such as President Eisenhower, Bishop Fulton Sheen, and Norman Vincent Peale spoke at these ceremonies over the years.[8] In 1953, Representative Peter Rodino (D) of New Jersey proposed a resolution to make every February 3rd "Dorchester Day."[9] Rodino spoke on the House floor: "In the last wild moment on the deck of the flaming Dorchester, these four men of different religious belief, with their arms linked in prayer as they sank into the deadly waters, gave a demonstration of faith, courage, and brotherhood such as the world has seldom seen." He concluded, "For what an understanding of their heroic action might mean toward the improvement of human relations, we should endeavor to establish and perpetuate in the minds of men everywhere a knowledge of their sacrifice and its meaning."[10]

The decision to add the phrase "under God" to the Pledge of Allegiance also emerged from this combination of ecumenicism and the Cold War. Catholic groups such as the Knights of Columbus passed resolutions calling for Congress to add references to God in the pledge in the early 1950s. These statements resonated more because they occurred at the peak of Senator Joseph McCarthy's influence.[11] The immediate impetus for the move, however, came from a Presbyterian minister, George Docherty of the New York Avenue Presbyterian Church. On February 7, 1954, he delivered a sermon suggesting that something was missing from the Pledge of Allegiance. Docherty said that the pledge, as currently conceived, could be recited by the citizens of any republic, even by those in the Soviet Union: "In fact, I could hear little Muscovites repeat a similar pledge to their hammer-and-sickle flag in Moscow with little solemnity. Russia is also a republic that claims to have overthrown the tyranny of kingship. Russia also claims to be indivisible." Docherty emphasized that the phrase "under God" needed to be added to demonstrate the true difference between the two nations. This sermon seemed to make an impression on one member of the audience—President Eisenhower.[12]

Congress moved rapidly to address the issue. In May 1954, the Senate passed a resolution to add "under God" to the pledge, and the House began to debate the measure in June. The representatives discussed the rationale for the proposal, and the decision to make the change was unanimous. The members emphasized the Cold War and the need to win the ideological battle with the Soviet Union. Representative Overton Brooks (D) of Louisiana declared, "In adding this one phrase to our pledge of allegiance to our flag, we in effect declare openly that we denounce the pagan doctrine of communism and declare 'under God' in favor of free government and a free world." Rodino agreed, "Though a completely peaceful act, it would be the most forceful possible defiance of the militant atheism and 'dialectical materialism' that are identified with Russian and international communism."[13]

Congressmen took pains to celebrate the religious diversity of America and emphasize that the addition of "under God" did not exclude any group. Representative Hugh Addonizio (D) of New Jersey employed some contributionist rhetoric, explaining that "Never before in our national history have so many diverse groups enjoyed such a complete measure of religious freedom as exists in the United States today," adding that the major religions in America shared much in common: "No matter what our religious belief or affiliation, we have embraced the common faith of

America." Rodino concurred, ending his remarks, "Let us join together, Protestant, Jew, and Catholic, in taking this action."[14]

Other official expressions of a generalized belief in God appeared often during the mid-1950s. In April 1954, the Post Office issued the first stamp with a religious message. The stamp pictured the Statue of Liberty with the caption, "In God We Trust." President Eisenhower and Secretary of State John Foster Dulles attended the ceremony commemorating the release of the stamp, the largest such gathering in the history of the Post Office. The narrator of the newsreel of the event suggested, "The new stamp will carry to the world America's message of liberty and faith."[15]

In 1955, Congress passed legislation to place "In God We Trust" on all national currency and coins. Again, the Cold War loomed large in the thinking of legislators. "In these days when imperialistic and materialistic communism seeks to attack and destroy freedom," said Representative Charles Bennett (D) of Florida, the sponsor of the bill, "we should continuously look for ways to strengthen the foundations of freedom. At the base of our freedom is our faith in God and the desire of Americans to live by His will and His guidance." Bennett added, "As long as this country trusts in God, it will prevail. To serve as a constant reminder of this truth, it is highly desirable that our currency and coins should contain these inspiring words, 'In God We Trust'."[16]

National Brotherhood Week, 1955, echoed this trend with its theme of "One Nation Under God." The materials for the celebration urged churches and synagogues to play a role in the fight against the Soviet Union. The National Conference of Christians and Jews, which sponsored Brotherhood Week, wrote, "The moral struggle against the onslaughts of Communism and war begins with your congregation. And this year, during Brotherhood Week, you have the opportunity to do significant and important work."[17] The literature for Brotherhood Week frequently referred to the Cold War and the dangers of the atomic age: "Every day the newspapers bring us ominous warnings of the dangers that lie ahead. Scientists predict an atomic war would wipe out civilization. The red tidal wave is spreading over vast areas of the world."[18]

The materials for Brotherhood Week 1955, as had often been the case in previous years, emphasized the need to diminish the differences between faiths. The NCCJ issued guidelines for speakers during the celebration. Among them were "*Never discuss differences of theology and church policy. Refer to those differences only in explaining that we respect them as matters* of conscience. The Conference was not founded to debate the 'pros' and 'cons' of ANY religion."[19] Other materials promoted the similarities among the three major religions: "Protestant, Catholic, and Jew are united in the religious idea that forms the conceptual basis for the unity in diversity that characterizes our American heritage—the Brotherhood of Man under the Fatherhood of God."[20] Along the same lines, the NCCJ suggested that local communities dramatize one of the greatest symbols of interfaith coopera-tion, the story of the four chaplains.[21]

The radio spots for Brotherhood Week 1955 made frequent mention of the need for tolerance. One said, "There should be no room for prejudice in this nation of ours. Give every man the dignity of his color and creed. Judge every man solely as an individual. Remember, we're one nation under God." Another mentioned the international ramifications of prejudice: "With the eyes of the world upon us, there's no place in America for group prejudice."[22]

The announcements commonly featured contributionist rhetoric: "There are hundreds [of radio stars], all with different names, different religions, different races—they're all Americans! And that's the American way of life in work and play. . . . all races, all religions, all colors get together." Another spot used noted: "Each person apart is of different color, different race, different religion . . . but all together—Americans."[23]

The suggestion that the three major faiths shared a basic philosophy dovetailed with the emerging idea that the United States was a Judeo-Christian nation.[24] Previously, many observers had spoken of a "Christian" America, but this language was discredited when various extremist groups appropriated it during the 1930s.[25] Increasingly, intellectuals and policy-makers referred to the similarities between faiths and emphasized that the Judeo-Christian ethic was an essential part of American identity during the Cold War.[26] Roger Strauss, honorary president of the National Federation of Temple Brotherhoods, declared that the greatest threat facing the world was the "world-wide clash of two divergent beliefs: the Judeo-Christian philosophy and the crass materialism of communism."[27] Most famously, President Eisenhower remarked that "Our form of government makes no sense unless it is founded in a deeply religious faith, and I don't care what it is." What is less well known is that he added, "With us of course it is the Judeo-Christian concept but it must be a religion that all men are created equal."[28]

❧

Herberg's *Protestant, Catholic, Jew* provided the most thorough formulation of 1950s religious pluralism. Like a number of intellectuals, Herberg flirted with communism during the Great Depression. Eventually, he rejected Marxism and embraced his Judaism, becoming a professor of Judaic Studies at Drew University. In this capacity, he authored several books and papers emphasizing the similarities between Judaism and Christianity.[29]

Herberg rejected the notion, put forth in the early years of the century by Woodrow Wilson and Theodore Roosevelt, that Americans could not retain Old World ties while identifying as Americans. TR had declared, "The immigrant cannot possibly remain what he was, or continue to be a member of the Old World society." Wilson concurred, saying, "I certainly would not be one even to suggest that a man cease to love the country of his origin . . . but it is one thing to love the place where you were born and it is another thing to dedicate yourselves to the place to which you go. You cannot dedicate yourself to America unless you become in every respect and with every purpose of your will thorough Americans."[30] The restrictionists of 1924 had expressed a similar dismay about immigrants retaining aspects of their native culture.[31]

Citing the research of sociologist Ruby Kennedy, Herberg demonstrated that intermarriage in religious groups reduced the salience of ethnic identity. In the America of the 1950s, he said, Irish and Italian Catholics were marrying in significant numbers, as were British and Scandinavian Protestants. As a result, he believed third-generation immigrants were shedding ethnic identification in favor of religious affiliation: "The principle by which men identify themselves and are identified, locate themselves and are located, in the social whole is neither 'race' (except for Negroes and those of Oriental origin) nor ethnic-immigrant background (except for recent arrivals) but religious community."[32]

Herberg suggested that this group identification posed no threat because all three major faiths shared a set of common values he called the American Way of Life: "If the American Way of Life had to be defined in one word, 'democracy' would undoubtedly be the word. . . . On its political side it means the Constitution; on its economic side, 'free enterprise.'" Herberg added that progress, belief in education, and optimism were also essential parts of the American Way of Life. He remarked that a tendency to view issues as battles between good and evil formed part of this philosophy: "Americans tend to be moralistic: they are inclined to see all issues as plain and simple, black and white, issues of morality. Every struggle in which they are seriously engaged becomes a 'crusade'."[33]

Herberg wrote that Protestantism, Catholicism, and Judaism shared a basic commitment to these values. Over time, he explained, the pressures of Americanization were forcing the three faiths to adopt similar philosophies: "That is, at bottom, why no one is expected to change his religion as he becomes American; since each of the religions is equally and authentically American."[34] These ideas reflected the concept of "consensus" espoused by many intellectuals during the 1950s in books such as Louis Hartz's *Liberal Tradition in America* and Daniel Bell's *The End of Ideology*. These thinkers suggested that Americans shared a set of common values across a relatively narrow political spectrum that spared the United States from the extreme political divisions that plagued many European nations.[35]

Herberg elaborated that the nation increasingly believed religion played a vital role in strengthening American values:

> The Christian and Jewish faiths tend to be prized because they help promote ideals and standards that all Americans are expected to share on a deeper level than merely "official" religion. Insofar as any reference is made to the God in whom all Americans "believe" and of whom the "official" religions speak, it is primarily as sanction and underpinning for the supreme values of the faith embodied in the American Way of Life.[36]

Along these lines, he believed the fear of communism in the 1950s fed the desire for religious identification. "Confronted with the demonic threat of Communist totalitarianism," Herberg wrote, "we are driven to look beyond the routine ideas and attitudes that may have served in easier times."[37] Increasingly, religious leaders viewed faith as a bulwark against the Soviet Union and internal subversion. The Cold War shaped a message that emphasized tolerance while at the same time lauding the contributions different groups made to American society. Religious ideology, though, stressed tolerance and the "sameness" of different faiths more than contributionism.

Herberg observed that religious attachments appeared to be growing in importance during the 1950s, noting, "No one who attempts to see the contemporary religious situation in the United States in perspective can fail to be struck by the extraordinary pervasiveness of religious identification among present-day Americans."[38] In 1957, when the Census Bureau asked millions of Americans, "What is your religion?" 96 percent of those surveyed responded by naming a specific denomination.[39] More and more Americans joined churches and synagogues, thereby raising the percentage of Americans belonging to religious institutions from 55 percent in 1950 to 69 percent by the end of the decade.[40] Church attendance increased at the same time. In a 1950 Gallup poll regarding religion, 39 percent of respondents reported attending church or synagogue in the previous seven days. By 1957, this number had increased to 51 percent.[41]

Other aspects of American culture also suggested the growing importance of faith. Religious figures such as the Reverend Billy Graham and the Reverend Norman Vincent Peale rose to prominence during the 1950s. Graham's religious revivals drew huge crowds across the country, while his column appeared in 125 newspapers. Peale's self-help books, such as *The Power of Positive Thinking* and *Stay Alive All Your Life*, remained on best-seller lists throughout the decade.[42] Films with religious themes such as *The Ten Commandments* (1956) and *Ben-Hur* (1959) also achieved financial and critical success.

There are a number of explanations as to why religion's importance grew in the 1950s. Some scholars have suggested that the Cold War reinforced the need for Americans to have faith and a belief in God.[43] Many Americans, on moving to the growing suburbs of the 1950s, turned to religious institutions to recreate the sense of community that existed in some older urban neighborhoods.

The American people also seemed to be more tolerant of different religious groups. With regard to Jews in particular, polls demonstrated that the power of traditional stereotypes was fading. The percentage of people who believed that Jews had too much power in the country fell from a high of 58 percent in 1945 to 17 percent in 1962. The number of people who said they would definitely not marry a Jew fell from 57 percent in 1950 to 37 percent in 1962. In 1950, 69 percent of Americans told pollsters that it would not make any difference to them if a Jewish family moved in next door. By 1959, the number increased to 86 percent.[44]

Protestant denominations moved away from a commitment to convert Jews to Christianity. At the World Council of Churches in 1954, American delegates led the opposition to a resolution reiterating the importance of evangelizing, directed at Jews. By the end of the 1950s, some mainline Protestant denominations, such as the Presbyterians, completely eliminated programs aimed at Jewish conversion.[45]

The declining prejudice of the period suggested that doors once closed to non-Protestants might now be open. Former Senator Herbert Lehman of New York, a Jew himself, suggested in 1958, "There's long been a feeling that there couldn't possibly be a Catholic or Jewish president of the United States. Today, prejudice appears to have decreased sufficiently . . . and there is every possibility of a Catholic or Jewish president in the future."[46] Polling data supported Lehman's instincts: 68 percent of those surveyed in 1958 said they would vote for a qualified Catholic to be president, as opposed to 62 percent who had said so in 1940.[47] In 1959, 72 percent of Americans indicated they would vote for a qualified Jewish candidate for president, compared with 49 percent in 1937.[48]

At this time, Americans of all faiths were moving in large numbers to the growing suburbs. Some contemporary observers, in accordance with the idea that a culture of "consensus" prevailed in Eisenhower-era America, believed that these new neighborhoods were homogenous regions where racial, religious, and class divisions weakened or even disappeared. As William Whyte wrote concerning the suburb of Lake Forest, Illinois, "it is classless, or, at least, its people want it to be."[49]

On closer examination, some analysts saw that different religious groups still maintained their distance. Albert Gordon, former executive director of the United Synagogues of America, researched 89 suburban communities in ten states. In his study, he discovered that a single religious group often dominated in a given suburban neighborhood. For instance, Jewish children composed virtually the entire student population in two school districts in Newton, Massachusetts, a suburb of Boston. Similar demographics could be found in numerous other suburbs across the nation.[50]

Gordon's study demonstrated that, even in those communities where religious diversity existed, social segregation prevailed. One Jewish woman commented, "My husband does business with Christians and I see them when I shop. It's always a very pleasant Hello followed by superficial conversation. And that's it." Another said, "We almost never meet Christians socially in our suburb. When we do, it's usually to promote a cause or organization in which the Christians think we may be helpful. Aside from that, no social contacts, no more home visits, no golf club—no nothing."[51] Studies of neighborhoods where Catholics and Protestants mixed revealed much the same dynamic. In general, Protestants and Catholics led separate social lives despite their geographical proximity.[52]

The greatest test of American religious tolerance came at the close of the decade with Massachusetts Senator John F. Kennedy's campaign to become the first Catholic president. Democratic New York Governor Al Smith, nicknamed the "Happy Warrior," had made the first serious attempt in 1928. Smith's campaign occurred during a period of great cultural conflict in American life, as battles over evolution, Prohibition, and the Ku Klux Klan created a climate that strengthened the already potent anti-Catholic sentiment in the country. Shortly after Smith's nomination, one newspaper editorialized, "Governor Smith has a constitutional right to run for President, even though he is a Catholic. . . . And we have a constitutional right to vote against him because he is a Catholic." William Lloyd Clark, editor of the *Rail Splitter* and a longtime opponent of the Catholic Church, went even farther: "Only a mighty campaign of education will whip the Smith-whiskey-Papal gang and save America."[53] Aided by a decade of prosperity under GOP rule, as well as the unpopularity of Smith's support for Prohibition and his roots in New York City's Tammany Hall political machine, Republican Herbert Hoover defeated Smith in a landslide. Still, anti-Catholic prejudice hindered Smith's efforts and contributed to Hoover's wins in five southern states that had been solidly Democratic since Reconstruction. Kennedy's 1960 campaign hoped to prove that times had changed since the "Happy Warrior's" bid for the White House.

In 1956, Kennedy had campaigned for the vice-presidential nomination at the Democratic National Convention. Governor Adlai Stevenson of Illinois garnered the top position on the ticket, just as he had in 1952. At this time, the Democratic Party believed it had begun to lose some of the Catholic vote, a core party constituency, to the GOP. Irish and Italian Catholics, like many Americans, were participating in the economic expansion of the 1950s and moving to the suburbs. Their growing affluence, as well as Eisenhower's personal popularity, were likely responsible for their shift to the

Republican Party.[54] JFK's advisers gave party leaders a memorandum suggesting that a Catholic vice-presidential candidate could help reverse this
trend. In the end, Senator Estes Kefauver of Tennessee defeated Kennedy
for the nomination and lost along with Stevenson in the fall.

Kennedy began his campaign for the 1960 nomination shortly after Stevenson's defeat. In order to win, JFK and his advisers understood they
needed to address many Americans' fears about a Catholic president.
Despite growing tolerance, polls showed that 25 percent of Americans
would not vote for a qualified Catholic for the White House.[55] The forces
that disrupted Al Smith's campaign, though weakened, still remained part
of American life. Many southern evangelicals still believed a Catholic president would take orders from Rome and endanger the separation of church
and state. Groups such as the Protestants and Other Americans United for
the Separation of Church and State (POAU) argued that a Catholic chief
executive would use his power to promote the political agenda of the Catholic Church, including providing federal aid to parochial schools, appoint-
ing an American ambassador to the Vatican, and supporting regimes in
Latin America and other parts of the world that repressed Protestants.
Many liberal intellectuals expressed similar misgivings about these church
policies and what they regarded as the undemocratic nature of the Catholic
hierarchy. Author James Michener recalled a dinner party in early 1960
where many colleagues raised concerns about JFK, observing that American
liberals "had the most serious and deep-seated fears of a Catholic in the
White House."[56]

Ironically, JFK's first significant attempt to allay these fears alienated
many fellow Catholics. In an interview with *Look* magazine in March 1959,
Kennedy strongly expressed his support for separation of church and state
and laid out his positions on a number of contentious issues where he
disagreed with the Catholic hierarchy: among other things, opposition to
federal funding for parochial schools and appointment of an ambassador
to the Vatican.[57]

Leading Catholic journals viewed Kennedy's rejection of certain church
positions as part of an effort to appease anti-Catholic elements in American
society. The *Brooklyn Tablet* editorialized, "Kennedy is sure to get the Catholic vote; he needs the anti and non-Catholic vote to win; he can attract
the latter by showing that he frequently opposed the Hierarchy, Catholic
publications and lay organizations."[58] Gerard E. Sherry agreed, writing in
Catholic Review of Baltimore, "One of the things that bothers me in relation

to Mr. Kennedy is that he appears to have gone overboard, in an effort to placate the bigots."[59]

The next major dispute involved an old story regarding the memorial to the four chaplains in Philadelphia. The Reverend Daniel Poling had invited JFK, along with Senator Herbert Lehman of New York and Charles Taft, president of the Federal Council of Churches, to a dinner in Philadelphia in 1950 to raise money for the memorial. The Catholic hierarchy had opposed building the memorial because it called for Protestant and Jewish ceremonies in the same facilities as Catholic services. JFK accepted the invitation at first but declined shortly before the event. Poling published a book in 1959 that detailed the decade-old incident, alleging that Kennedy had withdrawn at the command of Catholic officials. "One thing in his record is unmistakably clear," Poling told reporters in January 1960, "the church did claim and exercise considerable authority over him while he was in high public office."[60]

Kennedy vehemently rejected the charge, saying he did not attend because he believed Poling invited him as a representative of the Catholic faith rather than as a public official. He added, "I further learned that the memorial was to be located in the sanctuary of a church of a different faith. This is against the precepts of the Catholic Church."[61] Ted Sorensen, a top Kennedy speechwriter and confidant, echoed this message in a speech in February: "When the Congressman learned that the Catholic Church was not participating in the ceremony—because this revolving 3-part altar in a Baptist Church was not in keeping with its practice—Congressman Kennedy—on his own, without any orders from any Cardinal—declared that he had no credential to attend in that capacity."[62]

Kennedy's first major political test during the presidential campaign came in the Wisconsin primary in April 1960, where he faced his main challenger for the nomination, Senator Hubert Humphrey of Minnesota. Humphrey had long been a hero to many in the liberal wing of the Democratic Party because of his staunch support for civil rights and organized labor. Wisconsin's status as a neighbor of Humphrey's Minnesota and traditional supporter of progressives such as Robert LaFollette also made it hospitable territory for Humphrey.

Kennedy's wealth and organization compensated for Humphrey's regional and ideological advantages. JFK opened offices in eight of the state's ten congressional districts, while Humphrey managed to open offices only in two districts. At one point, a frustrated Humphrey complained that his campaign seemed like a "corner grocer" compared with Kennedy's "chain store."[63] Aided by his superior resources and his excellent campaign skills, Kennedy defeated Humphrey in Wisconsin, garnering 56 percent of the popular vote.[64]

The victory, however, generated the kind of negative publicity usually associated with political defeats. Commentators immediately drew attention to the fact that Kennedy's strength came from largely Catholic areas and that many Republican Catholics crossed party lines to support their coreligionist.[65] James Reston of the New York Times wrote that Kennedy's win "demonstrated that there is indeed a 'Catholic vote' in America" and wondered whether "this will create a countermove by the Protestant majority and divide the parties along religious lines."[66] Reston added the following day that Kennedy could not blame others for raising the Catholic issue because his advisers had first introduced the subject at the 1956 convention.[67]

Various publications and individuals echoed Reston's concerns about bloc voting and blamed Kennedy for the dilemma. Time wrote, "Last week Jack Kennedy proved beyond doubt in the Wisconsin primary that an attractive, hard-campaigning Catholic can count on a powerful Catholic vote. . . . By proving it, Kennedy lifted the Catholic issue out of the murk of religious innuendo into the arena of discussion, where it can be debated as a political fact of life." The magazine went on to say that Kennedy's strength created a conundrum for the Democrats; if they rejected JFK, they might lose the support of the Catholic bloc.[68] A Christian Century editorial went even farther: "The magic went out of the Presidential campaign of Senator Kennedy in the Wisconsin Primary Election. . . . His forces managed a bandwagon sweep only in districts where Roman Catholics predominated." The editorial continued:

> The unquestioned fact that Catholics did in large numbers apply a religious test to a candidate for the office of President is bound to have its effect on the remainder of the campaign. Non-Catholics will expect Catholics to follow the example of their fellow churchmen in Wisconsin. It would be wrong for them to ignore this probability in making their own choice of candidates.[69]

Press coverage of the victory frustrated the Kennedys. JFK grew irritated when CBS news anchor Walter Cronkite asked him about the religious question in an interview.[70] When one of the Kennedy sisters asked Robert Kennedy how the media interpretation affected the campaign, he responded, "It means that we have to do it all over again. We have to go through every one and win every one of them—West Virginia and Maryland and Indiana and Oregon, all the way to the Convention."[71] As they realized, the issue was no longer whether Protestants would not vote for someone solely because he was a Catholic. The issue had become whether Catholics *would vote for someone solely because he was Catholic.* Reports noted that Kennedy faced a tougher challenge in the West Virginia primary on May 10, 1960, where Catholics comprised a mere 5 percent of the electorate.

The fear of bloc-voting behavior along religious or ethnic lines was yet another fear with strong roots early in the century. As with the issue of ethnic identity, Teddy Roosevelt and Woodrow Wilson had expressed their strong disapproval of such behavior. "The politician who bids for the Irish or German vote, or the Irishman or German who votes for an Irishman or German," declared Roosevelt, "is despicable."[72] Wilson concurred, "America does not consist of groups. A man who thinks of himself as belonging to a particular national group has not yet become an American."[73] During the debate over the Johnson-Reed Act in 1924, restrictionist representatives had made the same argument and many Americans still held these sentiments in 1960.[74]

In West Virginia, JFK faced Humphrey, the religious issue, and a "stop Kennedy" drive led by hometown senator Robert Byrd. "If you are for Adlai E. Stevenson, Senator Stuart Symington, Senator Johnson or John Doe," Byrd stated, "you better remember that this primary, with all the national attention on it, may be your last chance."[75] Byrd supported Lyndon B. Johnson, who needed a Humphrey victory to slow JFK's momentum toward the nomination. If Kennedy continued to win primaries, LBJ would have little chance of defeating him at the Democratic Convention in the summer.

Those supporting Kennedy advised him to quell fears about his faith by calling attention to the ties between the three major religions and their contributions to the United States. Kenneth Underwood, a professor of social ethics at Wesleyan University, wrote a lengthy memorandum to Kennedy and his staff on the subject. He urged JFK to show "that his own Christian faith is important to him and his life" and that "he shares with

Protestantism and Judaism common concerns without ignoring the diversity in American religions and the contribution it makes to American society." Underwood, among several other suggestions, recommended that Kennedy find a way to demonstrate that he respected religious diversity: "There should be many instances or locales, I am sure, in which the Senator can articulate the ethos or value structure which is part of the Judaic-Christian tradition and which indirectly but importantly informs our public life."[76]

As the fight for West Virginia progressed, Kennedy implied that religious animus motivated his opponents. He said he was battling not only Humphrey but "everybody who doesn't want me for President for one reason or another." Opponents attacked him for suggesting their opposition was rooted in religious intolerance. One of Humphrey's campaign managers said Kennedy "seems to think that everybody who doesn't want him to be President is a bigot." Byrd echoed the charge: "It is regrettable that anyone who happens to be for someone other than Senator Kennedy is immediately attacked as being anti-Catholic."[77] JFK's opponents, in both the primary and general election, continually alleged that Kennedy kept the religious issue in the campaign to win Catholic votes and create the appearance that those opposing him were prejudiced.

On April 21, Kennedy directly responded to these charges in a speech to the American Society of Newspaper Editors: "Nor am I appealing, as it is often claimed, to a so-called Catholic vote. Even if such a vote exists—which I doubt—I want to make one thing clear again: I want no votes solely on account of my religion." He continued, "Neither do I want anyone to support my candidacy merely to prove that this nation is not bigoted—and that a Catholic can be elected President." Kennedy rejected the media interpretation of the Wisconsin results and affirmed that he was not the Catholic candidate for president, that he did not speak for the church, and that the church did not speak for him.[78]

It seemed that his efforts to defuse the religious issue were successful as he won in West Virginia, defeating Humphrey in a landslide.[79] Commentators now argued that Kennedy's Catholicism was no longer an impediment to his presidential aspirations. "On one point there was nearly unanimous agreement. It was that the Senator had proved himself to be what the politicians admiringly call 'a winner' despite his Roman Catholic faith," wrote John D. Morris in the *New York Times*. Morris also noted that "The effect was to demonstrate, at least to the satisfaction of most politicians, that Senator Kennedy's religion could no longer be regarded as a serious obstacle to a victory over the Republican presidential nominee in November."[80]

Kennedy's victories in the primaries proved to the party establishment that he was the strongest candidate to defeat Vice President Richard Nixon in the November election. Despite a last-minute attempt by some liberals to choose Stevenson again, JFK received the nomination at the Democratic National Convention in Los Angeles in July 1960. Kennedy selected Lyndon Johnson as his running mate, in part because many observers believed LBJ's Texas credentials would help in the South, where the religious issue was likely to prove most vexing. In his acceptance speech, JFK acknowledged the risk the party took in making him its nominee: "I am fully aware of the fact that the Democratic Party, by nominating someone of my faith has taken on what many regard as a new and hazardous risk—new, at least, since 1928."[81]

Kennedy held certain advantages at the outset of the campaign against Nixon. Most observers believed that Democratic Party remained the majority party in the country. Nixon did not share Ike's personal popularity, and the economic situation—the country was in the midst of a tentative recovery from a recession—seemed likely to benefit JFK. But Nixon also had strengths. His years as a representative, senator, and Eisenhower's vice-president gave him more experience than Kennedy during a tense period of the Cold War. Finally, no one could be certain how religion would affect Kennedy's fortunes.

As the general election campaign began, many of Kennedy's detractors and supporters alike believed that religion remained an issue. In August, the *Indianapolis Star* criticized JFK for keeping his religious faith in the news: "Jack Kennedy has been shouting and crying persecution, but if anybody else says anything about his religion then that is 'bigotry'. . . . Anybody who uses religion either as a shield or a sword is guilty of bigotry and the greatest offender in the nation at present is Jack Kennedy himself."[82]

Along similar lines, Ted Sorensen still feared anti-Catholicism could derail Kennedy's campaign. In a campaign memorandum in mid-August, he articulated his concerns: "Given the normal Democratic majority, and assuming that his personal appeal, hard work and political organization produce as before, Senator Kennedy *will* win the November election unless defeated by the religious issue. This makes *neutralization* of the issue the key to the election." Sorensen recommended several possible ways of approaching the dilemma, including a "nationwide telecast" during which Kennedy would address the subject.[83]

At this time, a new wave of religiously based opposition to Kennedy emerged. A collection of 150 Protestant clergymen formed a group called Citizens for Religious Freedom to stop Kennedy's presidential bid. Members included Norman Vincent Peale, Billy Graham's father-in-law Nelson Bell, and Poling. Peale declared that "Our American culture is at stake. I don't say it won't survive, but it won't be what it was." The group issued a statement alleging that no Catholic could be independent of Rome, arguing that "It is inconceivable that a Roman Catholic President would not be under extreme pressure by the hierarchy of his church to accede to its policies with respect to foreign relations, including representation to the Vatican."[84]

Nixon did not discuss Kennedy's Catholicism in his public statements and tried to distance himself from those raising it. On *Meet the Press* in September, Nixon rejected the charge, leveled by Peale and other evangelicals, that Kennedy could not maintain his independence from the church, saying, "I have no doubt whatever about Senator Kennedy's loyalty to his country." He added that he would not discuss religion during the campaign and hoped it would not have an effect on the outcome of the election.[85]

In an attempt finally to settle the question, Kennedy addressed the Greater Houston Ministerial Association a few days later. As earlier, he expressed his strong support for the separation of church and state: "I believe in an America where the separation of church and state is absolute—where no Catholic prelate would tell the President (should he be a Catholic) how to act and no Protestant minister would tell his parishioners for whom to vote." He expressed his desire for an America without religious intolerance and where "there is no Catholic vote, no anti-Catholic vote, no bloc voting of any kind." JFK invoked his military service and that of his late brother Joe in World War II: "This is the kind of America I believe in—and this is the kind of America I fought for in the South Pacific and the kind my brother died for in Europe. No one suggested then that we might have a 'divided loyalty'."[86]

Kennedy reiterated that he differed from the church hierarchy on issues such as public funding for parochial schools and appointment of an ambassador to the Vatican. He said he would make any decisions as president based on the national interest. Finally, he stated, "But if the time should

Figure 2. Candidate John F. Kennedy speaks to the Greater Houston Ministerial Association in September 1960, assuring them of his commitment to the separation of church and state. AP, photo by Ted Powers.

ever come—and I do not concede any conflict to be remotely possible—when my office would require me to either violate my conscience, or violate the national interest, then I would resign the office, and I hope any other conscientious public servant would do likewise."[87]

During the question-and-answer period that followed, reporters again queried JFK on his handling of the Four Chaplains dinner. Kennedy gave the same responses as in January: that he had been invited as a representative of the Catholic faith and believed he did not have the credentials to act in such a capacity: "It is not an interfaith chapel. And therefore for me to participate as a spokesman in that sense for the Catholic faith, I think would have given the erroneous impression."

JFK received a rapturous response for the address, even from some of his staunchest critics. Dr. Poling, who made the chaplains controversy a campaign issue, declared the speech "magnificent." Peale recanted his warnings, and the Citizens for Religious Freedom called the statement "the most complete, unequivocal and reassuring statement which could be expected of any person in his position."[88] As with the aftermath of the West Virginia primary, many observers now expected the religious issue to disappear.

Yet the Kennedy campaign continued to receive thousands of letters from citizens concerning the religious issue, even after the Houston speech. Some of them focused on the Chaplains controversy. "If the incident about the banquet is true do you still feel the same way today?" asked a California man. "Do you feel that, if you felt that way ten years ago, that you should now change this theory because of your candidacy for President?"[89] An Indiana man made a similar charge: "You have made statements to the effect that you will not submit to pressure from the Roman Catholic Church if you become President. It looks to me as if your actions and words in relation to the 1950 Chapel of the Four Chaplains banquet contradict your statement. . . . Are you able to explain or defend your refusal to appear in that interfaith meeting?"[90]

Clearly fearing that many Americans still shared the sentiments expressed by those citizens, the Democratic National Committee research division sent materials to its congressional candidates in mid-September to help them deal with Kennedy's religion. These materials included a copy of the Houston address and comments from prominent clergy, as well as editorials that rejected the idea that a Catholic could not be president. The memorandum's conclusion reflected the frustration of many Democrats that Kennedy's faith remained central to the campaign at this late date: "We will, of course, be ready to help you answer any further questions about this matter that may arise, but all future packets will contain materials pertaining to the *real* issues in the campaign."[91]

Kennedy and Nixon addressed the role of religion in their remarks at the Alfred E. Smith Memorial Dinner in New York in mid-October. Candidates traditionally eschew political attacks and controversy at the Smith dinner in favor of compliments and humor.[92] The occasion, however, took on a different resonance because JFK was the first major Catholic candidate since Smith and comparisons between 1928 and 1960 served as a prominent topic of discussion during the evening. Both candidates again declared that religion should not be an issue in the campaign. JFK remarked, "I am confident that whatever their verdict, Republican, or Democrat, myself or Mr. Nixon, that their judgment will be based not on any extraneous issue but on the hard facts that face us, on the convictions of the candidates and their parties, and on their ability to interpret them." Nixon concurred, saying that religion should remain out of the campaign and that he and Kennedy would urge their supporters to do the same.[93] The last comment appeared to be a subtle reminder to JFK not to directly appeal to a Catholic bloc vote or to claim the mantle of victim.

Nixon's comments on faith at the dinner demonstrated the power of the religious message of the 1950s. The vice president elaborated on comments he had made earlier in the year, when he said that religion should be a political issue only if a particular candidate did not adhere to any faith. In Nixon's mind, the nation's battle against communism made a belief in God a requirement for the country's leader: "My point was that in these times whoever is to lead America and the free world must be a man who, in addition to standing for a strong America economically and militarily, is a man of faith—faith in God." Nixon said that the United States needed to extend its hand in charity to the newly independent countries in Asia and Africa to win their support in the Cold War. He cited the traditions of his own faith, Quakerism, as well as of Judaism, in support of this concept "And there is the Hebrew word, seducca. To do justly," said Nixon, "Not to help people because you're doing a favor to them. But to help people because you are doing justly. . . . All of this part of the great Judeo-Christian heritage which is ours."[94] Nixon's remarks reveal how the Cold War and the idea that the major religions are fundamentally the same were central to the public rhetoric concerning religion in the 1950s.

Despite the efforts of both candidates, Kennedy's Catholicism remained in the news even in the last week of the election. A *New York Times* article on October 30 ran under the headline "Issue of Church-State Separation Continues to Plague Both Sides in Presidential Race." In the article, the *Times*' Leo Egan wrote that the Houston speech had pushed the issue into the background for a while "but that recently it has been revived with new vigor."[95] A *Newsweek* headline asked if religion was "The Biggest 'Issue'" in the campaign.[96]

Both sides feared the religious issue could cost them the election. One JFK associate told *Newsweek*, "If we start to fight the anti-Catholic propaganda, we'll get clobbered for 'raising the religious issue.' If we keep our mouths shut, the propaganda really could begin to clobber us." Republicans feared Catholic voters and others dismayed by the bigotry of some Protestants would move into the opposing camp. The *Times* reported that the mother of a Republican officeholder told her son, "I have to vote for Kennedy. I can't be on the same side as those people."[97]

The GOP continued to be angered by what the party perceived to be an attempt by Kennedy and his supporters to make a vote for Nixon appear to be a vote for intolerance. In the weeks before the election, the United Auto Workers distributed a pamphlet with the Statue of Liberty and a Klansman on the cover with a caption asking, "Which do you choose? Liberty or bigotry?"[98] A frustrated Eisenhower declared, "Something's got to be done about this," alleging there were "people who think they can find an advantage in distorting America."[99]

In the end, JFK defeated Nixon in one of the closest elections in the history of the country, becoming the first Catholic president. Kennedy won the popular vote by a mere 120,000 votes, making Al Gore's 500,000 vote margin in 2000 seem like a landslide. JFK earned a more comfortable victory in the Electoral College, garnering 303 votes to Nixon's 219. Nixon and his advisers believed the Democratic political machine of Mayor Richard Daley in Chicago and LBJ's friends in Texas engaged in voting fraud to give Kennedy his margin. Nevertheless, they did not make any serious attempt to challenge the outcome of the election.

Initial media reports suggested that the religious issue did not hinder Kennedy's bid. A *New York Times* headline read, "Protestant and Catholic Votes Found to Offset Each Other."[100] Arthur Krock wrote in the *Times*, "The victory of Senator Kennedy is proof at last that membership in the Catholic Church is not an insuperable bar to the Presidency of the United States," citing Kennedy's ability to retain the Democratic Party's hold on some southern states as additional evidence that the religious issue no longer had the power it had in 1928.[101]

The narrowness of Kennedy's margin, however, disturbed some Democratic Party officials. They had expected JFK to win 53 to 57 percent of the popular vote and defeat Nixon easily because of the strength of the Democratic Party and weakness of the economy in 1960. Harry Truman told Senator William Benton (D) of Connecticut, "Why even our friend Adlai [Stevenson] would have had a landslide running against Nixon." Given the fact that Stevenson ran two desultory campaigns against Eisenhower, Truman's comments dramatize the surprise of many leading Democrats at the closeness of the election.[102]

Academic analysts confirmed Truman's instincts. Writing a few months after the election in *American Political Science Review*, Philip Converse and three coauthors from the University of Michigan provided a thorough examination of the 1960 campaign. They declared, "While the Kennedy victory was initially taken as proof that religion had not been important in the election, all serious students of election statistics have since been impressed by the religious axis visible in the returns." Converse and his coauthors argued that JFK performed poorly compared to other Democratic candidates in 1960 and that he "did not in any sense exceed the 'normal vote' expectations of the generalized anonymous Democratic candidate; rather he fell visibly below expectations." Their analysis demonstrated that Kennedy's Catholicism, when controlling for other issues, helped him garner a net vote gain of 1.6 percent in areas outside the South. In the South, however, the religious issue caused JFK great harm, particularly among regular Protestant churchgoers who historically voted for Democratic candidates. Many of these observant Protestants could not accept a Catholic president, and, as a result, he lost 16.5 percent of the expected vote for a Democrat in the southern states. When accounting for total votes gained and lost nationally due to his Catholicism, Kennedy ran 2 percent behind the vote projected for a "normal" Democrat.[103]

The authors summarized, "Despite his position as majority candidate, Kennedy very nearly lost and ran behind his ticket." They rejected the idea that JFK's victory eliminated Catholicism as a barrier to the presidency:

Not only did Kennedy possess a type of personal appeal which the television debates permitted him to exploit in unusual measure, but he was also the candidate of the party enjoying a fundamental majority in the land. Even the combination of these circumstances was barely sufficient to give him a popular vote majority. Lacking such a strong underlying majority, which Al Smith most certainly lacked in 1928, it is doubtful that the most attractive of Catholic presidential candidates in 1960 would have had much chance of success.

Converse and his coauthors added, "It remains to be seen how far the experience of a Catholic president may diminish the disadvantage another time."[104]

Another study argued that, while Kennedy's faith cost him with regard to the popular vote, it helped him win a larger margin of victory in the Electoral College. Ithiel de Sola Pool, Robert Abelson, and Samuel Popkin's research concluded that Kennedy's exceptionally strong showing among Catholics helped him win six northeastern and midwestern states (with 132 electoral votes) he would have otherwise lost, while the anti-Catholic vote cost him 10 states in the South and Rocky Mountain West (with 110 electoral votes) he would have likely won. In their final tally, Kennedy's religion provided an additional 22 electoral votes.[105] Still, the authors agreed with Converse et al.'s conclusion that JFK's faith cost him popular votes, calculating that he lost 1.5 million votes because of his faith. In the end, they declared "No issue other than religion had a significant net effect on the vote."[106]

During the 1950s, policymakers and intellectuals espoused a message emphasizing the Cold War and the similarities between faiths, while also featuring some elements of contributionism. Though Americans grew increasingly tolerant of different religious groups, Kennedy's election revealed that religious cleavages persisted within American society. The existence of religious or ethnic bloc voting still disturbed many citizens, and, despite his numerous efforts to defuse the question, JFK's Catholicism remained in the national debate until the conclusion of the campaign. At the same time, no candidate or public figure wanted to be associated with intolerance. Though Kennedy's election signaled a turning point in the acceptance of non-Protestant groups in American society, his faith alone still cost him the support of many voters.

Chapter 7

The Triumph of Contributionism

During a congressional debate over immigration reform in September 1965, Robert F. Kennedy, now a senator from New York, decried the spirit of the times that produced the national origins quotas, saying, "the system was imposed during the postwar [World War I] crisis in Europe, when many in the United States feared that a continuance of unlimited immigration would lead to the coming here of tens of millions of unlettered, poverty-stricken refugees—and of hundreds of thousands of revolutionaries." He added, "those fears have proved unfounded. And ever since 1924, we have regretted the excesses of that day." Calling for the passage of legislation to repeal the quotas, Kennedy declared, "It will eliminate from the statute books a form of discrimination totally alien to the spirit of the Constitution. Distinctions based on race or national origin assume what our law, our traditions, and our commonsense deny: that the worth of men can be judged on a group basis."[1]

RFK went on to espouse contributionism, explaining that, "we know, all America knows that our immigrants have built this Nation—the last as well as the first." Kennedy specifically referenced the achievements of immigrants from southern and eastern Europe, declaring that if the national origins system were eliminated, "The children of Pulaski will have the same chance to come to these shores as the children of Lafayette; the descendants of Verrazano and Columbus will have a fair chance to see the shores their ancestors first explored."

On the other hand, Senator Robert Byrd (D) of West Virginia defended the status quo, explaining that the quota framework was the best way to preserve the cultural integrity of the United States. "The original objective of the 1924 act," declared Byrd, "was to maintain the ethnic composition of the American people, on the premise that some nations are far closer to the United States in culture, customs, and standard of living, respect for law, and experience in self-government." He elaborated, "Naturally, those immigrants can best be absorbed into our modern population whose backgrounds and culture are similar." Byrd, however, offered a broader definition of this group than his restrictionist counterparts had offered in the fight over Johnson-Reed in 1924 or during the debate over McCarran-Walter in 1952. The senator from West Virginia seemed to agree with RFK on the subject of newcomers from southern and eastern Europe, expressing his dismay that immigrants from "certain countries, such as Italy and Greece, for example, whose peoples do assimilate readily and easily into American society, have been disadvantaged."[2]

Byrd's rhetoric enlarged the groups considered easily able to assimilate into American culture to include southern and eastern Europeans. This was particularly noteworthy because Byrd was a conservative on racial and ethnic issues and had voted against the Civil Rights Act of 1964 the previous year.[3] His comments reflected the fact that the cultural and economic contributions of southern and eastern Europeans were increasingly included in an emerging image of America as "a nation of immigrants" during the 1960s. Even opponents of immigration reform like Byrd offered tributes to the achievements of immigrants: "I grant that the immigrants who have come to this country have made a magnificent contribution to our development. Anyone who attempts to articulate this contribution is doomed to understatement because, certainly, this Nation was put together by immigrants and would not exist if they had not come here."

But Byrd's rhetoric also revealed that different groups increasingly dominated restrictionist thinking, as he believed Latinos and Asians should remain excluded from acceptance in the "nation of immigrants." He said his major objection to the current system was that "it applies no limitation on immigration from South America and other Western Hemisphere countries and theoretically, any number of persons could emigrate to the United States from the Western Hemisphere immediately." He feared a dramatic increase in immigration from Latin America, and his comments concerning the dangers of Latino migration were echoed by many during summer and fall 1965. No longer fearful of eastern and southern European immigrants, who were now largely seen as "white," Byrd and his colleagues sounded alarms about nonwhite arrivals from Africa and Asia. "It is indubitably clear," he said, "that if the majority of Americans had sprung not from Western, central, and southern Europe, but from central Africa and southern Asia, we would today have a vastly different country."[4]

The immigration debate of 1965 came following the emergence of a more militant civil rights movement, propelled by Martin Luther King, Jr., the sit-ins, and the formation of the Student Nonviolent Coordinating Committee (SNCC) in 1960, that created the momentum for repealing the national origins system and strengthening the forces of contributionism. The movement aimed to eliminate discrimination in all aspects of American law, including employment, public accommodations, and housing. The growing support for civil rights and battles over the integration of education, public accommodations, and voting rights at the University of Mississippi, Birmingham, and Selma further reduced the respectability of an immigration policy that had been supported by the scientific racism of the early part of the century.

The Cold War also strengthened the forces of immigration reform in the 1960s. During the 1950s, both supporters and opponents of the origins system had cited anti-communism as a rationale for their arguments. With the legacy of McCarthyism fading, proponents of the status quo could not as easily draw on fears of Communist subversion to buttress their point of view. In a decolonizing world, opponents of the system drew on powerful arguments that immigration restriction damaged America's international standing in newly independent countries in Asia and Africa.

The growing political power of the Ellis Island immigrants also played a key role in advancing the cause of reform. By the mid-1960s, the second and third generations of newcomers composed a significant share of the nation's population and were concentrated in politically key states in the Northeast and Midwest. The political maturation of these communities played an important role in promoting reform.[5]

At the same time, cultural forces were also laying the groundwork for a greater religious pluralism. President Kennedy's fealty to his campaign promises to maintain the separation of church and state and the reforms of Vatican II reduced the power of traditional anti-Catholicism. Anti-Semitism also continued to fade as a significant part of American life. By the mid-1960s, more and more Americans shared Will Herberg's conviction that Catholicism and Judaism were "American" religions, just like Protestantism.[6]

By the passage of immigration reform in 1965, legislators and intellectuals had developed a clear vision of the "nation of immigrants" and of which groups were included in it. The Ellis Island generation and its descendants were now seen as cultural and economic assets, even by those who wished to restrict immigration. The contributionist view that these immigrants strengthened the American culture and economy while also changing to adapt to American norms had become widely accepted. At the same time, the "nation of immigrants" continued to have very clear limits as nonwhite Asian, Latino, and African immigrants were clearly outside its boundaries, as some policymakers became concerned about a potential rise in immigration from those regions.

☙

John F. Kennedy, who had supported immigration reform in *A Nation of Immigrants* and in the 1960 campaign, faced significant political difficulties with regard to this issue during his presidency.[7] In the first two years of his administration, Kennedy was preoccupied with foreign policy crises like the Bay of Pigs and the Cuban Missile Crisis. On the domestic front, an alliance of conservative southern Democrats and Republicans opposed most of his proposals and prevented passage of major liberal legislation, such as expansion of health care coverage, just as they had since the late 1930s.

Kennedy and his advisers moved to deal with immigration issues when Francis Walter, chairman of the House Immigration Subcommittee and a staunch defender of the quota framework, died in May 1963.[8] Two months later, JFK proposed to eliminate the national origins system and replace it with a system along the lines proposed in *Whom Shall We Welcome*.[9] The bill would abolish quotas and allow immigrants to be admitted on a first-come, first-served basis, with top priority to those with "the greatest ability to add to the national welfare." Family unification would serve as second priority, and the bill called for an overall limit on immigration of 165,000.[10]

In presenting the bill, JFK used the language of tolerance and civil rights, while emphasizing how change would benefit America's international standing. Declaring that the origins system "discriminates among applicants for admission into the United States on the basis of accident of birth," America, he added, should build a policy that "reflects in every detail the principles of equality and human dignity to which our nation subscribes."[11] In that spirit, Kennedy supported the abolition of the Asia-Pacific Triangle, which limited countries in that region to a quota of 100 apiece.[12] JFK added that "many problems of fairness and foreign policy are involved in replacing a system so long entrenched."[13]

Kennedy also suggested that the bill would primarily benefit individuals and families from southern and eastern Europe. To illustrate the inequities in the current quota policy, he explained that "an American citizen with a Greek father or mother must wait at least 18 months to bring his parents here to join him. A citizen whose married son or daughter, or brother or sister, is Italian cannot obtain a quota number for them for an even longer time."[14] News reports echoed his assessment. Tom Wicker wrote in the *New York Times* that "the country that would most be affected would be Italy" and that would-be migrants from Greece and Poland would benefit because these nations had a backlog of people who wanted to emigrate but were unable to because of their small quotas.[15] Like others who spoke on this issue in the next two years, Kennedy stressed that, while the composition of immigration would be altered, "these changes will have little impact on the number of immigrants admitted."[16]

Few expected Kennedy's proposals to be implemented in the near future, and they were correct. Though a dwindling minority were willing to explicitly defend the national origins system, the same political dynamics that hindered the rest of his agenda—the political power of the conservative coalition in Congress—appeared likely to doom immigration reform. Wicker commented, "Congressional approval of these changes, most of them controversial, is not believed likely this year and promises to be difficult at any time in the House of Representatives."[17]

⌒◡

While JFK achieved little in the way of immigration reform, intellectuals increasingly expressed a vision of contributionism that supported the rationale for change. School textbooks of the 1960s, as well, did more to detail the achievements of southern and eastern European immigrants while articulating an image of America as "a nation of immigrants."

Maldwyn Jones's *American Immigration*, published in 1960, offers a subtly different picture from Oscar Handlin's *The Uprooted*, released a decade earlier. Less focused than Handlin on the difficulties of the immigrant experience, Jones depicts the process of adaptation to American culture as a less disruptive and alienating process. Jones is also more effusive than Handlin in his discussion of the benefits of the Ellis Island-era wave of immigrants. Rejecting pejorative comparisons between the "old" and "new" migrants, *American Immigration* hypothesizes that the southern and eastern European immigrants were little different from those who came in the 1840s and 1850s. Furthermore, Jones declares that the 1882–1924 wave of migrants provided essential contributions to the economic growth of America: "The realization of America's vast economic potential has likewise been due in significant measure to the efforts of immigrants. They supplied much of the labor and technical skill needed to tap the underdeveloped resources of a virgin continent."[18]

Jones clearly espouses the contributionist vision when, reflecting the mood of the 1950s and early 60s, he suggests that immigrants have successfully assimilated into American society while maintaining some ties to their home countries. Like Handlin, he describes the immigrants as trying to recreate their native institutions and culture in the U.S., but suggests these institutions ultimately "adopted a common American form."[19] But he also notes that the immigrants continued to celebrate some Old World traditions. "To some observers," Jones commented, "there has been a contradiction in the fact that immigrants assert their patriotism as members of separate groups."[20] He (perhaps unintentionally) rejects Theodore Roosevelt's admonition that newcomers must not observe the patriotic celebrations of their homelands if they are to be become loyal American citizens: "When Polish-Americans observe Pulaski Day, when Irish-Americans parade in honor of St. Patrick . . . they are merely asserting their cultural distinctiveness, merely seeking to make clear their own identity in the larger American community. And even while doing so, they rededicate themselves to the common national ideals that bind them together."[21]

More influential than Jones's work was Nathan Glazer and Daniel Patrick Moynihan's *Beyond the Melting Pot*, a major study of the diversity of New York City that also exemplified the growing appreciation of immigrant contributions. In examining the polyglot cultures that comprised Gotham, they observed that many of the institutions that sustained ethnic identity and offended nativists, such as the ethnic press, ethnic societies, and immigrant neighborhoods, had atrophied in the four decades since the passage of the Johnson-Reed Act in 1924. "The foreign-language press declines rapidly in circulation," they wrote, "the old immigrant quarters now hold only some of the old-timers. The immigrant societies play little role in the city's politics."[22]

Glazer and Moynihan did not maintain, however, that ethnicity had disappeared from American life. While Jones emphasized the "common national ideals" shared by the second and third generations, *Beyond the*

Melting Pot suggested that groups such as the Jews, Italians, and Irish maintained very different worldviews from each other and from native-stock Americans, despite outward appearances to the contrary. Glazer and Moynihan concluded:

> In the third generation, the descendants of the immigrants confronted each other, and knew they were both Americans, in the same dress, with the same language, using the same artifacts, troubled by the same things, but they voted differently, had different ideas about education and sex, and were still, in many ways, as different from one another as their grandfathers had been.[23]

Glazer and Moynihan concluded that Israel Zangwill's melting pot did not describe the America of the early 1960s. Referring to the intellectual climate of the early twentieth century that produced the melting pot concept, they wrote that "It was reasonable to believe that a new American type would emerge, a new nationality in which it would be a matter of indifference whether a man was of Anglo-Saxon or German or Italian or Jewish origin." Glazer and Moynihan believed that was not yet the case: "The initial notion of an American melting pot did not, it seems, quite grasp what would happen in America. At least it did not grasp what would happen in the short run, and since this short run encompasses at least the length of a normal lifetime, it is not something we can ignore."[24]

By the same token, however, Glazer and Moynihan rejected Horace Kallen's "cultural pluralism" as a model for the United States. They noted that native language and culture disappeared in the first two generations, making the vision of "a new Italy or Germany or Ireland in America, a League of Nations established in the New World—as unlikely as the hope of a 'melting pot'." They argued that, while many Old World traditions were lost, ethnic groups maintained a distinct identity that linked them together in ways "the original immigrants would never have recognized as identifying their group, but which nevertheless serve to mark them off, by more than simply name and association, in the third generation and even beyond."[25]

While Glazer and Moynihan rejected the turn-of-the century definition of the melting pot, a new edition of JFK's *A Nation of Immigrants* suggested that a more liberal definition of Zangwill's creation was emerging. Released in 1964 following his assassination, this version of *A Nation of Immigrants* clearly promoted contributionism, suggesting that the 1960s melting pot allowed for greater retention of immigrant traditions: "the ideal of the 'melting pot' symbolized the process of blending many strains into a single nationality, and we have come to realize in modern times that the 'melting pot' need not mean the end of particular ethnic identities or traditions."[26]

Many school textbooks in the 1960s agreed with Glazer and Moynihan concerning the persistence of ethnic identity, as they openly expressed the "nation of immigrants" ideology that had begun to emerge toward the end of the 1950s. *This Is America's Story* (1960), written by Howard Wilder and others, depicted immigrant institutions, such as the ethnic neighborhood and the foreign-language press, in a positive light. Regarding the immigrant community, the authors wrote, "The desire to live with one's fellow countrymen was altogether natural. Not only was the language familiar, but newcomers and earlier immigrants had many other things in common. They shared customs, memories of the old country, experiences in traveling to, and living in, the United States, and perhaps the same religious faith." *This Is America's Story* also praised the role of the immigrant media: "Most of these people speak English well enough to get along, but learning to read another language is not so easy and takes time. Therefore, to keep abreast of the news, these people use newspapers that they can read quickly and easily."[27]

Wilder and his coauthors provided long descriptions of the contributions and achievements of immigrants, similar to those in some earlier textbooks, *Americans . . . All*, and *Whom Shall We Welcome*.[28] Jews, Italians, and other groups from the 1880–1924 period received the same treatment as Germans and Irish migrants. They wrote, "Italians who have come to the United States have made names for themselves in many fields" and mentioned Arturo Toscanini, Fiorello LaGuardia, and Joe DiMaggio. Of Jews, Wilder et al. explained that "they came to escape oppression in other lands. Members of their group, furthermore, have made many important contributions to our nation's progress."[29]

Wilder and his coauthors emphasized above all that the United States was a "nation of immigrants." They wrote, "The record shows, however, that people of almost all races and nations have aided in the successful growth of the United States." The textbook noted that Adolf Hitler had suggested that America's greatest weakness was its ethnic and racial diversity. "To Americans, however, that is one of our strengths, not a weakness," the authors responded, "In our 'melting pot of nations,' America had blended the best features of people from all over the world."[30]

Story of Our Land and People (1964) by Glenn Moon and Don Cline described the role of immigrants in a similar manner. The authors wrote, "It is important to remember that to a great extent it was immigrants who built modern America." They repeated the now-familiar emphasis on the contributions of immigrants from various parts of the world, including southern and eastern Europe. Moon and Cline, like Wilder and his coauthors, rejected the arguments of those who feared immigration, declaring, "Why, you may ask, should any American feel prejudice against immigrants? After all, the United States is a nation of immigrants. All Americans, even the Indians, are either immigrants or descendants of immigrants."[31]

As the 1960s progressed, the contributionist elements seemed to become stronger in history books. *Exploring American History* (1966), by Melvin Schwartz and John O'Connor, maintained that "The United States would not have grown into such a great industrial nation without the help of men and women who came to this country from other lands, the immigrants," adding that "We have always been a nation of immigrants." Describing the contributions of immigrants to the country, the authors said "they brought colorful songs, and dances, different foods, new learning and their own ways of living. . . . Our way of life owes much to these 'newcomers' to our land."[32]

Land of the Free (1966) by John Caughey, John Hope Franklin, and Ernest May went the furthest in expressing the contributionist paradigm. Like Glazer and Moynihan, they rejected the relevance of the melting pot, emphasizing that it was "misleading. It suggests that to become American is to become like all other Americans. In fact, America is unlike other countries, precisely because Americans are not all alike." The authors explained, "A great American historian, Frederick Jackson Turner, once said that the United States ought to be described as a salad bowl rather than a melting pot. Americans, he said, get mixed together like leaves in a salad bowl, but remain distinct. They are not melted into common type."[33] *Land of the Free* praised the accomplishments of immigrants from southern and eastern Europe and strongly rejected the arguments against immigration: "In most cases, however, the hostility of native Americans was not based on reason. It was a reaction against strangeness." Decrying the scientific racism that once gave respectability to some restrictionists, the authors wrote, "We now know that such beliefs are nonsense. Scientists have proved that no color group, race, or nationality is better than any other."[34]

There were very tentative signs of change regarding the portrayal of Asians and Latinos in school texts in the early to mid-1960s. Schwartz and O'Connor provided a small discussion of the contributions of Japanese Americans in *Exploring American History*. "Our government decided to move them from their homes and jobs on the West Coast to inland camps," they wrote, referring to the World War II internment, "even though many had become American soldiers and were fighting bravely for this country." The authors added, "After the war, many families returned to the West Coast. It is to their credit that they have re-entered American life and made many contributions."[35]

Furthermore, the revised edition of JFK's *A Nation of Immigrants* featured a new section on Asian Americans. The book noted how the heroism of the 442nd combat division had changed American attitudes. "It took the extraordinary battlefield accomplishments of the nisei [*sic*], Americans of Japanese descent, fighting in the U.S. Army in Europe, to help restore our perspective," declared Kennedy. "While our attitude toward these citizens has been greatly improved over the years, many inequities in the law regarding Oriental immigration must still be redressed."[36]

The new edition also acknowledged that the composition of immigration was changing again, with more and more Americans arriving from south of the border: "Today many of our newcomers are from Mexico and Puerto Rico . . . they often face the same discriminatory treatment and opprobrium that were faced by other waves of newcomers. The same things are said today of Puerto Ricans and Mexicans that were once said of Irish, Italians, Germans, and Jews."[37] Schwartz and O'Connor also observed that Puerto Ricans faced serious obstacles in America because of the language barrier and scarcity of well-paying jobs, adding, "In spite of these handicaps, Puerto Ricans are producing leaders in government, education, and entertainment."[38]

In general, however, the textbooks continued to give little attention to the contributions of immigrants from Asia and Latin America. Most books, if they mentioned Asians at all, briefly discussed the arrival of workers from China in the nineteenth century and the reaction against them that produced the Chinese Exclusion Act of 1882. Moon and Cline described these events in *Story of Our Land and People*: "In the early 1880's, the public became excited about the immigration of Chinese workers or 'coolies'. . . .

The Chinese accepted very low wages and lived in a way that cost very little. For this reason, other workers feared and hated them. . . . Public opinion forced Congress to pass a law in 1882 that forbade immigration of Chinese laborers."[39]

Like the textbooks and *A Nation of Immigrants*, movies of the early to mid-1960s depict ethnicity in a much more explicit manner than the platoon films and *Gentlemen's Agreement*. In *The Pawnbroker* (1965), Rod Steiger plays Sol Nazerman, a Holocaust survivor so tormented by his experiences that he has lost the ability to feel anything. He simply makes a living running a store in Harlem, shutting the rest of the world out. Departing from the universalist approach that dominated early coverage of the Nazi atrocities, the film portrays the Holocaust as a Jewish phenomenon, as Nazerman repeatedly flashes back to images that would become well known to television and movie viewers over the next half century. Among other things, the film shows Nazerman and his family suffering on the train to Auschwitz and the SS abusing them at the camp.

Unlike the platoon films, *The Pawnbroker* represents Jews as a distinct group with a different culture. The movie also illustrates the growing Hispanic immigration as, reflecting the changing demography of New York City, Nazerman's assistant, Jesus Ortiz, is Puerto Rican. Ortiz asks him, "How come you people come to business so naturally?" Nazerman recounts the history of anti-Semitism and tells Ortiz that, over time, the Jews' lack of land forced them to develop a financial acumen. "Suddenly you make a grand discovery!" Nazerman angrily declares. "You have a mercantile heritage! You are a merchant! You are known as a usurer! A man with secret resources! A witch! A pawnbroker! A sheeny, a mockie, and a kike!"[40]

Similarly, *Exodus* (1960), which retells the Jewish struggle to create the state of Israel, offers a more particularist view of ethnicity. As in *The Pawnbroker*, the Holocaust looms large, and the focus is on Jewish victimhood. Early in the film, which takes place in 1947–48, Zionist leader Ari Ben Caanan (Paul Newman) scoffs at the help offered by American nurse Kitty Fremont (Eva Marie Saint). "You're late. Lady, you're ten years late," Caanan declares. "Almost two million Jewish children were butchered like animals because nobody wanted them. No country would have them. Not your country or any other country. And nobody wants the ones who survived."

The film clearly breaks with the World War II-era cultural universalism that suggested ethnic and religious groups are largely the same. Though he is falling in love with Fremont, a Christian, Caanan shows her the biblical sites in the Holy Land to remind her he is a Jew. Fremont, sounding much like Gregory Peck's Phil Green in *Gentlemen's Agreement*, tells him, "All these differences between people are made up. People are the same no matter what they're called." Caanan responds skeptically, "Don't ever believe it. People are different. They have a right to be different. They like to be different." Reflecting the growing prominence of contributionism, Caanan concludes, "It's no good pretending that differences don't exist. They do. They have to be recognized and respected."[41]

Still, by the mid-1960s, Hollywood increasingly concentrated on the black/white divide in films. Sidney Poitier had become one of the biggest box office draws in the industry as well as the first African American man to win the Oscar for best actor. While *Gentlemen's Agreement* and *Crossfire*, two pictures about the dangers of anti-Semitism, had been nominated for best picture in 1947, these concerns had diminished by the civil rights era. Two decades later, two of Poitier's films focusing on racism, *Guess Who's Coming to Dinner* and *In the Heat of the Night*, were nominated for best picture in 1967, with *In the Heat of the Night* victorious.[42]

∾

Developments in American religion also fostered a climate friendly to contributionism. Kennedy's allegiance to campaign pledges to reject aid to parochial schools and other proposals by the Catholic hierarchy helped him among Protestants. Their fears regarding a Catholic president, so strong in the 1960 campaign, began to fade once JFK proved he would uphold strict separation of church and state. As traditional anti-Catholicism was significantly weakened, even Billy Graham was moved to declare awkwardly that Kennedy had "turned out to be a Baptist President."[43]

In addition, the Second Vatican Council debated and implemented dramatic reforms in the Catholic Church between 1962 and 1965, which laid the groundwork for a greater religious pluralism in the United States. Called into session by Pope John XXIII, the Council, among other things, replaced the Latin mass with the native language of a particular country. Vatican II, as it became known, also opened the way for greater interfaith dialogue between Catholicism and other religions. For the first time, the Church recognized the legitimacy of Protestantism and Judaism and called for removing liturgical references that had sustained anti-Semitism for many generations.[44] Pope Paul VI, under whose term these reforms came to fruition, reached out to other faiths in 1965, declaring, "May our Christian brethren still separated from full communion with the Catholic Church wish to contemplate this new manifestation of its renovated face," adding, "May such contemplation come also from the followers of other religions and, among them, those united by relationship to Abraham, especially the Israelites—certainly not objects of reprobation or distrust but of respect, love, and hope."[45]

For the most part, Protestants reacted favorably to Vatican II, spurring an increase in interfaith activity. The World Council of Churches, an international organization of Protestant and Orthodox churches, opened a dialogue with the Vatican to achieve stronger ties. In America, the National Lutheran Council initiated discussions with the Catholic Church for closer relations based on "an unprecedented desire for mutual understanding and cooperation between Protestants and Catholics throughout the country." Noting that the reforms had lessened tensions between Protestants and Catholics in the United States, Rev. Dr. John Bennett, president of Union Theological Seminary, observed that some Protestants continued to distrust the Church and believed the changes remained "strictly tactical." Bennett rejected this notion, remarking, "those who say this are not Protestants who have really come to know Catholics."[46]

Brotherhood Week in February 1965 reflected the impact of these reforms on American society. Lewis Webster Jones, president of the National Conference of Christians and Jews, commented on Vatican II:

> There are many constructive forces at work. In the realm of religion, we are witnessing great and continuing strides toward reassessment of attitudes among all religions and their relationship to one another. The whole ecumenical spirit and the work of the Vatican Council are indeed prime examples of a reawakening and acknowledgement of plurality in our society.

Mitch Miller, chairman of Brotherhood Week 1965, declared, "We are so many diverse peoples that we might well have become a divided society." Sounding like the school textbooks, he added, "But America's diversity has been America's strength. And both the diversity and the strength must be encouraged."[47]

A few months later, in October 1965, Pope Paul VI journeyed to the United States to speak to the United Nations and meet with President Lyndon Johnson. Paul's trip to the United States was noteworthy for a number of reasons. It continued his break with a century-old papal tradition of remaining ensconced in the Vatican. Most important, the visit was the first by any pontiff to the United States, and his warm reception revealed that anti-Catholicism was a much diminished force in the aftermath of Kennedy's election and Vatican II.

Traditionally, the pope had loomed large in nativist fantasies. In 1928, many suggested that the pope had his bags packed to come to the United States if Al Smith, the Democratic presidential candidate, were elected president. In order to appear independent of the Vatican, JFK, as recently as the 1960 campaign, had pledged not to open diplomatic relations with the papacy. "A visit from the Pope 100 years ago might have caused rioting in the streets," wrote John Cogley in the *New York Times* in 1965, "Certainly there would have been violent protests against it, inspired by religious antagonism."[48]

The pope's visit received overwhelming approval and little resistance. Paul passed through throngs of cheering crowds as he made his way from Kennedy airport through Queens and Upper Manhattan before arriving at St. Patrick's Cathedral. He saw President Johnson before delivering a well-received speech on international peace at the United Nations. Following the address, he met with an interfaith group of Protestants, Eastern Orthodox, and Jews, and concluded with a large mass at Yankee Stadium. Non-Catholics, such as Dr. Eugene Carson of the United Presbyterian Church, praised his performance, saying, "the Pope was at his best in representing the whole Christian community and the whole religious concern for peace."[49]

Over 100 million people in North America watched some of the pope's visit on television. Moreover, the entire city of New York seemed to shut down because of his presence. "For thirteen hours New York was gripped by a drama whose giant audience left parts of the city numb and virtually paralyzed," wrote Bernard Weintraub in the *New York Times*. "It was, in a sense, as if Fifth, Park, and Lenox Avenues and Queens Boulevard had stopped breathing as the frail visitor moved about. Stores were boarded up and some even closed in the morning, appointments were canceled, traffic was rerouted, shoppers were rare and office work was, for many, impossible."[50]

Only a few criticized the pope's visit. *Newsweek* noted that "some ecu-
menically inclined Protestants deplored the display of quasi-monarchial
circumstance that accompanied the papal visit." Protestant theologian Robert McAfee Brown said that "it seemed awfully theatrical."[51] Brown's view,
however, represented an exception to the rule on the subject.

Most commentators observed that the positive response was a dramatic
change from how a papal visit might have been received a mere ten years
earlier. Cogley wrote in the *Times*, "Even a decade ago, with the religious
climate quite different from what it is today, there would have been widespread resentment that the Pope of Rome, with all the emotional feeling
against his position, should be accepted as a spokesman for religion by a
political body as important as the United Nations." He credited the interfaith movement, which included programs like National Brotherhood
Week, for the change: "Relations between Roman Catholics and other
Christians have never been better than they are right now. . . . Nor is the
ecumenical spirit confined to Christians. Pope Paul can count on a warm
reception from Jewish leaders and from many of the unchurched, who
respect his sincerity, however unreceptive they may be to his theology,"
concluded Cogley.[52]

Opinion polls revealed that anti-Semitism, like anti-Catholicism, had
become a much-diminished force in American life.[53] Reflecting this change,
Time published an essay in June 1965 called "The New American Jew." "In
the U.S. today, anti-semitism is at an all-time low," according to the magazine, "and publicly out of fashion." The essay noted that doors in numerous fields had opened to Jews and the remaining vestiges of discrimination
were rapidly diminishing: "Residential and social discrimination remains
considerable, but not nearly so strong as depicted 18 years ago in *Gentlemen's Agreement*. To prep schools and debutante lists, charity boards and
private parties, Jews have an entrée they never had before."[54]

In fact, the piece suggested that the biggest threat to Jewish life in
America was no longer discrimination but assimilation. *Time* described the
myriad influences that Jews were having on American society in fields ranging from popular literature to comedy. With many aspects of Jewish culture
increasingly integrated into the larger American culture, Jewish leaders were
beginning to fear that Jewish identity in America was fading in light of
greater public acceptance. Dartmouth professor Jacob Neusner summarized this point of view, declaring, "The central issue facing Judaism in our

day is whether a long-beleaguered faith can endure the conclusion of its perilous siege."[55]

∽

The growing support for the civil rights movement during the early-to-mid 1960s strengthened the argument for immigration reform. The brutal response of southern authorities to a number of peaceful protests, such as the freedom rides of 1961, fostered public sympathy for the African American cause among whites outside the South. After Birmingham police commissioner Eugene "Bull" Connor unleashed dogs and fire hoses on nonviolent protestors led by Martin Luther King, Jr., in 1963, public opinion rapidly coalesced behind the legal goals of the movement. A year later, President Johnson signed the Civil Rights Act of 1964, which outlawed discrimination based on race, religion, or gender in employment and public accommodations. Increasingly, supporters of immigration reform connected the civil rights movement with the need for abolishing the national origins system. Testifying before Congress a few weeks after the signing of the Civil Rights Act, Attorney General Robert Kennedy, reiterating what his brother had said a year earlier, declared that the system discriminated against southern and eastern Europeans: "It implies that regardless of individual qualifications, a man or women born in Italy or Greece or Poland or Czechoslovakia or the Ukraine is not as good as someone born in Ireland, or England, or Germany, or Sweden." RFK added, "Everywhere else in our national life we have eliminated discrimination based on one's place of birth. Yet this system is still the foundation of our immigration law."[56]

At the same time, President Johnson and advocates of immigration reform were laying the groundwork for the repeal of the national origins system. Drawing on the egalitarian ideas that stemmed from the civil rights movement, they also emphasized Cold War arguments, picking up where JFK had started. In 1964, Secretary of State Dean Rusk, like RFK, testified in favor of change before Congress. Rusk declared that the use of quotas based on race was "indefensible from a foreign policy point of view." He added that the current system was increasingly irrelevant because Congress repeatedly passed special legislation, such as the Displaced Persons Bill of 1948 and the Refugee Relief Act of 1953, to allow immigrants fleeing various crises to enter the United States. At this point, Rusk noted, only one-third of immigrants were actually entering the country under the quota framework.[57]

Immigration was not a major issue in the 1964 presidential campaign, but Johnson's landslide victory over Republican nominee Barry Goldwater, combined with large gains by Democrats in Congress, improved the chances for reform. Johnson now had a mandate for a broad range of liberal initiatives. Moreover, LBJ now had a large block of liberal Democratic representatives that enabled him to break—at last—the power of the conservative coalition that had controlled Congress since 1938.

Representative Michael Feighan (D) of Ohio, who replaced Francis Walter as chairman of the House Immigration Subcommittee, seemed to be one of the few remaining obstacles for reformers. He had opposed repealing the quotas but reconsidered his position after he was nearly defeated by a primary opponent in 1964 who criticized him for his support of the national origins system. As he confronted the possibility of another primary challenge in 1966, the Johnson administration leaked to the press that it was searching for a candidate to run against him. Faced with this pressure, Feighan attacked the status quo as insufficiently restrictive and proposed abolishing the quotas in an address to the American Coalition of Patriotic Societies in February 1965.[58]

Though Samuel Gompers and the AFL had supported the creation of the quotas in 1924, organized labor now backed their abolition. "Forty-one years have elapsed since the national origins quotas were established to regulate immigration into this country," declared the AFL-CIO Executive Council in February 1965, adding, in contributionist language, that "they stand in conflict with the principles of human brotherhood, equality, and justice and with the fact of our ethnic and racial diversity which are the cornerstones of our strength and tradition."[59]

In spring 1965, the House and Senate held hearings on the bill. Freshman Senator Edward Kennedy (D) of Massachusetts chaired the Senate Immigration Subcommittee and discussed the ongoing debate with journalist Russell Black. Kennedy stressed that the abolition of the quotas was essential to any immigration reform and that the new bill would eliminate the Asia-Pacific Triangle, which he called "a blemish on the statute books of the United States." Like his two brothers, he emphasized that reform was necessary because large quotas for northern European countries were routinely undersubscribed, while the small quotas for southern European nations were oversubscribed. With many of the slots therefore unfilled, quota immigration was much lower than the 158,000 maximum allowed. The new legislation, Kennedy said, would relieve these backlogs by allowing immigrants to come on a first-come, first-served basis from countries where there was the greatest demand. According to Kennedy, "Under the new legislation. . . . we can make sure that all those quotas are used." Black asked Kennedy, "Senator, this is not to be interpreted as unlimited immigration into the United States, is it?" Kennedy responded that the new bill maintained an overall ceiling on immigration and that only 6,000 more people would be allowed into the nation under the new system.[60]

Kennedy discussed the differences in philosophy between those backing change and those favoring the quota framework. He said that the law's opponents believed "that those whose cultural patterns and language and customs are closely identified with what would be considered the mainstream of culture in the United States would be more easily assimilated into the United States and therefore, that they ought to be given certain preferences." Kennedy said that the advocates of change believed immigration provided significant benefits to American society. Espousing the contributionist philosophy, he observed that "The proponents of the legislation feel that the great experience of the United States is . . . that we've been able to assimilate people of different groups, different languages, different cultures. . . . This has been the real strength of the United States and that this kind of infusion would be healthy in our society."

The committee hearings revealed some of the major themes of the debate. All those who testified in favor of reform stressed that it would remove a barrier to the nation's foreign relations, allow more skilled workers to enter the country, and unite families, while not significantly increasing immigration. The hearings also illustrated the growing acceptance of eastern and southern Europeans as well as their political power. Representatives from the Greek American and Italian American communities, the two groups with the largest backlogs of people desiring to enter the U.S., eagerly stated the case for abolishing the national origins system.

Representing the American Committee for Italian Migration, Juvenal Marchisio testified about the benefits brought by Italian immigrants. Repeating familiar facts from various films and pamphlets regarding immigration, he noted that the states with the largest Italian populations were among those with the highest incomes. He added that Italian immigrants had among the highest naturalization percentages and rates of service in World War II. "It seems cruel cynicism," declared Marchisio, "to limit to a mere trickle the number of Italians who may annually enter this country and at the same time authorize far greater quotas for nations who either do not have the numbers to migrate or who need them drastically to supplement their own lack of manpower."[61]

Whereas the restrictionists of 1924 were disdainful of political organizing along ethnic lines, Senator Sam Ervin (D) of North Carolina, who was the most vocal opponent of reform on the committee, praised the representatives of the immigrant communities and their organizations. He suggested that the eastern and southern European immigrants were more willing to adapt to American culture than potential newcomers from Latin America and other parts of the world. He noted that groups like the Order of AHEPA, a Greek American organization that backed reform, did a fine job of assimilating immigrants into American society. "I do not know any people more readily assimilated into American life than people of Hellenic descent," Ervin declared, invoking contributionism. "Ahepa is ready, anxious, and willing and does give Greek immigrants training in the fundamentals of our system of government."[62]

The House began floor debate on the bill in August 1965. The legislation, however, differed perceptibly from that proposed by President Kennedy in 1963. JFK's bill made the skills of an individual immigrant the primary criterion for entrance into the United States. As written by Feighan's committee, the House bill abolished the quotas but made family unification the primary criterion for entrance. Feighan urged this change to garner the support of conservatives who were reluctant to discard the quotas.[63] With family unification the main goal of immigration policy, conservatives believed the demographic nature of the country would remain unaltered. As an American Legion representative explained, "nobody is quite so apt to be of the same national origins of our present citizens as are members of their immediate families."[64]

This restrictionists' support of the family unification criterion demonstrated that those unsympathetic to immigration reform were no longer particularly concerned about preserving the America of 1920. Family unification would allow those southern and eastern European immigrants, who now comprised a significant share of the population, to bring their relatives to America as easily as those with roots dating to the Mayflower. A system focused on family connections also appeared designed to forestall a large-scale Asian migration, as Asian Americans were relatively few in number. The criterion also seemed likely to limit African migration because

African Americans, most of whose ancestors had been taken to the United States as slaves centuries earlier, were not likely to have ties to their roots in Africa.

The legislation's proponents emphasized the link between the bill and the Civil Rights Act of 1964 and Voting Rights Act of 1965.[65] Representative Phillip Burton (D) of California declared, "Just as we sought to eliminate discrimination in our land through the Civil Rights Act, today we seek by phasing out the national origins system to eliminate discrimination in immigration to this Nation composed of descendants of immigrants." Representative Leonard Farbstein (D) of New York City agreed with Burton, saying, "In this immigration bill, we express the same belief expressed in the recent Voting Rights Act of 1965. . . . That is the belief that men are to be judged on their own merit, as individuals—and not on the basis of their racial ancestry, their skin color, their religion, or their place of national origin."[66] The New York Times couched its support in similar terms: "The intellectual poison of racism is slow to work its way out of any people's system. . . . As with the passage of the right-to-vote bill for Southern Negroes, the United States is striving to live up to its ideals."[67]

Though the civil rights movement played a central role in advancing the cause of immigration reform, the NAACP did not take a great interest in the battle over the legislation. In fact, Crisis did not feature any articles on the subject during 1965. In all likelihood, the climactic battles of the movement, such as the clash between Alabama state troopers and activists at the Edmund Pettus Bridge in Selma and the ensuing passage of the Voting Rights Act of 1965, understandably crowded out interest in the bill.[68]

As Dean Rusk had done, backers also emphasized that abolishing the quotas would eliminate a hindrance to the nation's foreign policy. Representative Jacob Gilbert (D) of New York City remarked, "It will remove a thorn from the conduct of our foreign relations." Arch Moore (R) of West Virginia agreed, declaring, "Our last four Secretaries of State—Secretary Rusk, Secretary Herter, Secretary Dulles, and Secretary Acheson—have urged that our foreign relations demand a change of the immigration law in this respect."[69]

Members of the House also stressed that the frequent passage of emergency legislation since World War II had already made the national origins system irrelevant. The indefatigable Emanuel Celler of New York City, still endeavoring to eliminate the system he had spoken out against in 1924, listed the numerous refugee bills Congress had passed in the previous two decades, on issues ranging from the displaced persons after World War II to those fleeing the Soviet invasion of Hungary in 1956. Peter Rodino (D) of New Jersey added, "Again and again, emergency legislation has been called for, and Congress has acted painfully and reluctantly. And, of course, each new enactment has taken some of the substance from existing law."[70]

Along these lines, some representatives invoked the nation's failure to allow Jewish refugees from Nazi Germany into the United States in the late 1930s.[71] These references reflected a growing acceptance of the ideological view of World War II as well as greater public knowledge of the Holocaust.[72] Farbstein expressed this perspective in very stark terms: "I believe the 6 million Jews who died under Hitler will rest easier in their reward with the knowledge that never again will this Nation renege on its much-advertised promise of a haven from the gun, the whip, and the gas chamber." Representative Seymour Halpern (D) of New York City echoed the sentiment, suggesting, "Had such legislation as the pending bill been adopted 30 years ago or 25 years ago, many valuable citizens might today be making a contribution to our Nation rather than lying buried in mass graves in Europe at the grim sites of the Nazi death camps."[73]

Advocates of reform also insisted repeatedly that immigration would not grow significantly under the new system. Representative Donald Irwin (D) of Connecticut remarked, "Total immigration will not increase substantially under the newly proposed policy, but will be more fairly apportioned." William Ryan (D) of New York City agreed, saying, "Loudest of all arguments against the enactment of this bill is one which claims that the new bill will 'open the floodgates' for immigration into the United States. This simply is not true."[74]

Finally, many congressmen constantly paid tribute to the achievements of immigrants and referred to America as "a nation of immigrants." Many of their references seemed to come directly from the writings of prominent intellectuals and programs like *Americans . . . All*. Representative Edward Roybal (D) of California declared, "We are, in the words of John F. Kennedy, a 'nation of immigrants'—and no country on earth owes more to immigrants than America." Citing one of FDR's speeches on the contributions of immigrants, Roybal added, "we have always been an outward-looking people, coming as we do from many ethnic and cultural backgrounds—a true melting pot of the strength and diversity that has made America great." Paul Findley (R) of Illinois agreed: "This is indeed a nation of immigrants. The achievements of immigrants of past generations are tremendous."[75] Rodino seemed to draw directly from Louis Adamic's book *A Nation of Nations*, remarking that "The basis of America's greatness has always been a commitment to the value and dignity of the individual and a willingness to admit immigrants of diverse background and talents to our land. . . . We must adhere to this conception and continue to be a nation of nations."[76]

A few congressmen resisting reform argued, as Pat McCarran and others had done in 1952, that communists would take advantage of a more liberal policy. Representative Ovie Fisher (D) of Texas suggested that Asian communists would exploit the new law to infiltrate the country: "I have no doubt that the international Communist conspiracy will avail itself of the opportunity to increase its penetration of our country. The passage of this bill will present an inviting opportunity."[77] Fisher's views, however, were not echoed by many of his colleagues. With the McCarthy era fading into memory, anticommunism, though remaining at the core of American foreign policy, was no longer a major element of the restrictionist argument.

Opponents of the bill emphasized that repealing the quotas would produce an upsurge of relatively poor immigrants at a time when the Johnson administration was implementing its Great Society programs. Representative Maston O'Neal (D) of Georgia said, "You must also consider that this new influx of immigrants from underdeveloped nations will compound our domestic problems. They will compete with the very class our Federal Government is seeking to aid through its war on poverty." Representative Durwood Hall (R) of Missouri stressed that additional immigration did not make sense given the urban riots that had recently occurred in Watts and other cities.[78]

Unlike previous immigration debates, such as the 1939 Wagner-Rogers fight, unemployment fears played a minor role. The economic boom of the Kennedy/Johnson years probably played a key role in diminishing these anxieties. Furthermore, the fact that the legislation's supporters argued that the bill would not significantly increase the number of newcomers no doubt limited the discussion of the impact of the bill on wages and jobs.

Indeed, the bill's foes did not fear the anticipated increase in immigration from southern and eastern Europe. Reflecting the changing concerns of restrictionists, some refused to support the bill because they believed it would produce a dramatic increase in immigration from Asia and Africa. Fisher declared, "My chief objection to this bill is that it very substantially increases the number of immigrants who will be admitted each year, and it shifts the mainstream of immigration from western and northern Europe—the principal source of our present population—to Africa, Asia, and the Orient."[79]

Supporters were very quick to reject the idea that the bill would precipitate an increase in newcomers from these regions. Arch Moore responded, noting that no more than 20,000 immigrants could come from any country in the Eastern Hemisphere: "It does not mean that that number, 20,000, of Chinese, Japanese, or Filipinos are immediately going to come into this country." He added, "People who attack what we are doing today say that it will let millions of orientals come to the United States. I wanted to place in the Record the observation that there is no one who need fear such an event occurring."[80]

By far the most important concern of House opponents of the bill was that it did not include a limit on migration from the Western Hemisphere. Many shared Senator Byrd's concern that a dramatic increase in immigration from Latin America was imminent. Representative William McCulloch (R) of Ohio stated that the bill should place a ceiling on immigration because, "if immigration from the Western Hemisphere should grow sharply, and every sign indicates that it will, we will be faced with great pressures to halt the sudden flow of immigrants." Others suggested that it would be discriminatory to put a cap on immigration from the Eastern Hemisphere while leaving no ceiling on the Western Hemisphere. Representative Clark MacGregor (R) of Minnesota, who was sponsoring the amendment to place a limit of 115,000 on Latin American immigration, made the case:

> To allow unlimited immigration from the Western Hemisphere and the Caribbean while imposing rigid ceilings on the number who would come in from the rest of the world, including our traditional friends and allies across both oceans, and this in the name of ending a quota system labeled as "discriminatory" and "racially prejudicial" is highly contradictory.[81]

The House rejected the MacGregor Amendment by a vote of 218 to 189. It then approved the entire bill by an overwhelming vote of 318 to 95, demonstrating the momentum for reform. Most of the opposition came from southern congressmen, whose forebears had been the strongest proponents of restrictive immigration policies throughout the twentieth century.[82] The legislation eliminated the quotas and replaced them with a

170,000 per year limit on immigration from the Eastern Hemisphere and maintained the nonquota status of the Western Hemisphere.[83]

The Senate passed an immigration bill out of committee a few days later. That version abolished the national origins system as well but added an amendment specifying a limit of 120,000 per year on Western Hemisphere immigration, the current level of immigration from the Americas. Senator Ervin, who still believed that the national origins system was a reasonable way to govern the nation's immigration policy, insisted on this provision in return for supporting the end of the quotas.[84] Revealing the growing concerns about black migration, the New York Times suggested that "another factor, although it has been soft-pedaled in public debate, is a fear of the large number of Negroes who would be admitted as immigrants from the recently independent countries of the Caribbean, such as Jamaica, Trinidad and Tobago."[85]

The Senate debate over immigration reform was similar in many ways to that of the House. Supporters reiterated that abolishing the quotas was the logical conclusion of the civil rights legislation, that refugee legislation had undermined the relevance of the system, and that total immigration would remain largely unchanged. Opponents repeated many of the same arguments as their House counterparts. The Senate opposition, however, even more clearly laid out the boundaries of the "nation of immigrants." They expressed their appreciation for the achievements of immigrants from southern and eastern Europe while making clear their concerns about nonwhite arrivals from Africa, Asia, and Latin America.

The Senate backers also invoked the Cold War and foreign policy considerations. Jacob Javits (R) of New York declared that the quota system "remains today a target for Communist propaganda and making our effort to win over the uncommitted nations more difficult." The abolition of the Asia-Pacific Triangle, he added, would assist America's fight in Vietnam. Javits also feared the "strong propaganda tool which the limitation of 120,000 would give to demagogues, especially Communist demagogues, in Latin America."[86]

Senator Edward Kennedy, managing the bill on the Senate floor, rejected the old arguments against immigration made by restrictionists in 1924 and in following years: "Another fear is that immigrants from nations other than those in northern Europe will not assimilate into our society. The difficulty with this argument is that it comes 40 years too late. Hundreds of thousands of such immigrants have come here in recent years, and their adjustment has been notable." Sounding much like Glazer and Moynihan, Kennedy told his colleagues that the ethnic ghettoes that had traditionally loomed so large in the nativist mindset were a relic of the past: "Let us erase forever today the stereotype of the immigrant in our history. The cities of America no longer have the foreign neighborhoods, the cultural islands, separate, unassimilated, a drag on the Nation. They are gone and the policies based on them are gone."[87]

Senator after senator expressed the belief in the contributionist paradigm. Hiram Fong (R) of Hawaii declared, "There is no part of our society which has not been refined by the contributions of aliens who have come to make their home in United States. This is the essence of our union. It is its strength." Ted Kennedy entered a section of JFK's *A Nation of Immigrants* into the record. Fong added, "As a nation of immigrants, we have developed a racially heterogeneous society in which citizens of many cultures and ethnic origins live and work side by side to make the American dream a reality."[88]

In particular, the senators praised the accomplishments and achievements of immigrants from southern and eastern Europe. John Pastore (D) of Rhode Island insisted that, "If we had followed the logic of those who are opposed to this legislation, we would have handcuffed America." Reminding listeners of the development of the atomic bomb, he exclaimed, "We would not have had an Enrico Fermi. We would not have had a Professor Szilard. We would not have had an Albert Einstein. We would not have had Niels Bohr." From a more personal perspective, Senator Joseph Tydings (D) of Maryland paid tribute to the Italian Americans of his home state: "The Italian community of Baltimore has produced many great Americans. Among them are such outstanding citizens as Thomas J. D'Alessandro, Jr., the former mayor of Baltimore . . . and his son, Thomas J. D'Alessandro, II, the president of the city council of Baltimore."[89]

A few discussed the contributions of Asian Americans to the country. As in 1952, their speeches largely consisted of paeans to the military service of Japanese Americans in the 442nd combat division during World War II. Senator Thomas Kuchel (D) of California declared that among Californians, "none are more highly respected among my fellow citizens than Americans of Japanese extraction. The valor with which many of them distinguished themselves for bravery, wearing proudly the American military uniform in the Second World War, is well-known to our people and to the world." Ted Kennedy agreed: "We have learned that there is no difference between people who participate in the life of our Nation. . . . The Japanese Americans who fought and died in our Armed Forces have taught us this."[90]

Ervin laid out the arguments for the quota on the Western Hemisphere. "The majority of the committee," he explained, "felt that we had reached a point in our Nation's history at which we can no longer have unrestricted immigration from any part of the earth." He cited studies suggesting that a population explosion in Central and South America was fueling an increase in immigration to the United States: "It has been constantly increasing. Immigration from South America alone has increased by 400 percent in the past 10 years. It is necessary, if we are to have restrictions on immigration, that we should have a restriction on immigration from all areas of the world."[91]

Neither the Johnson Administration nor Senate liberals were pleased with the inclusion of the Western Hemisphere quota. In particular, the State Department and Secretary Rusk feared that the provision would harm relations between the United States and Latin America. At one point, Rusk declared that "he could absolutely not live with a numerical ceiling of any kind on the Western Hemisphere."[92] Still, Senate liberals made no significant attempt to remove it from the legislation and seemed to accept the limit as the necessary price for ending the national origins system.[93]

The Southerners who led the opposition were displeased with the bill despite the addition of the Western Hemisphere quota and defended the origins system on cultural grounds. Senator Strom Thurmond (R) of South Carolina claimed, "there is nothing in the national origins quota system which has any connotation of the idea of racial superiority or racial inferiority." Allen Ellender (D) of Louisiana agreed with Thurmond, saying, "It was the purpose and intention of Congress in 1924 to maintain and continue the racial, ethnic and cultural traditions of the United States by admitting immigrants in proportion to their American counterparts."[94]

Though opponents eschewed the racialist arguments made by their predecessors, some elements of the 1924 philosophy influenced their remarks. Ellender and a few others stressed that immigrants congregated in urban centers: "I believe it is almost a certainty that most of the immigrants who have come to this country in the last 20 or 30 years have settled in the large urban areas of the Nation. . . . Changes in our immigration law would only add to the ghettoes which already abound in our great cities." Like Ellender, James Eastland (D) of Mississippi expressed traditional concerns regarding ethnic politics: "It is no secret that both national political parties have 'nationalities' divisions which actively direct the efforts of pursuing the votes of the hyphenated nationalities groups in our population."[95]

Senator John McClellan (D) of Arkansas rejected the foreign policy rationales for immigration reform: "How utterly silly it is to base our immigration policy on the complaint of a few foreign ministers who feel that our policy is discriminatory." McClellan's comments seemed similar to the kind of nationalistic remarks made by supporters of Johnson-Reed. "So the argument about some country feeling it is discriminated against loses its force and persuasion," he continued, "After all, whose country is this? Who has a right?"[96]

The chief concern of the opposition, once the bill included a quota for the Western Hemisphere, was the possibility of increased immigration from Asia and Africa. Senator Spessard Holland (D) of Florida said that "we have not learned anything at all about the difficulties which have arisen from racial admixtures in our country, and, to the contrary, we are going to open the immigration doors equally to the African nations in the same way that we opened doors to the Western European nations." Robert Kennedy and Holland engaged in a verbal sparring match over the issue. RFK declared, "The fact that I might know I came from Ireland does not make me any better than a Negro." Holland responded sharply, "The Senator may not be, but I shall let him be the judge of that."[97]

The Senate opponents did not, however, express much concern over immigration from eastern and southern Europe. In fact, their rhetoric suggested they believed the United States was a "nation of immigrants" that included those who had arrived between the 1880s and 1924 and their descendants. Ellender commented, "It has been said that we are a nation of immigrants. This is, of course, true with the exception of the American Indian." He suggested that this generation of newcomers had been able to assimilate into American society, adding, "Today only the politicians are aware of the hyphenated Americans. The great mass of American people consider themselves only American and this is true whether their name is 'Jones' or 'Janowsky'."[98] Even the most hardened opponents suggested that there was a marked difference between the Eastern European descendants of Ellis Island-era immigrants and Latinos, Asians, and Africans. Holland declared, "We have many people whose ancestors were Irish. We have many whose ancestors were Polish. We have many whose ancestors were Italian. We have many whose ancestors were Greek. We are proud and happy to have them." Senator Donald Russell (D) of South Carolina said much the same: "In my State, many Greek and Italian families are making great contributions to the progress of South Carolina. They are outstanding citizens."[99]

The Senate approved the bill, officially called the Hart-Celler Act, by an overwhelming margin of 76 to 18.[100] The final draft allowed 170,000 per year to enter the country on a first-come, first-served basis from the Eastern Hemisphere, with a ceiling of 20,000 on immigration from any individual nation. The bill also featured a 120,000 per year cap on Western Hemisphere immigration without a limit per country. Though the bill is usually hailed as an example of liberal reform, some have noted that it did not have salutary consequences for every ethnic group. While the abolition of quotas expanded opportunities for eastern Europeans and Asians, the new caps on the Western Hemisphere created new barriers for immigrants from Latin America.[101]

Hart-Celler also created seven preference categories under which visas would be allocated: 84 percent of the quotas were to be distributed based on family unification, including preferences for adult sons and daughters of U.S. citizens, spouses and children of legal aliens, and brothers and sisters of U.S citizens; 10 percent of the remaining slots were to be based on skills and 6 percent on refugee status. The bill allowed parents of U.S. citizens to enter the country outside the hemisphere caps.[102]

The *New York Times* praised the bill for abolishing quotas and aiding those who wanted to emigrate from southern and eastern Europe: "it will sweep away the national origins system which historically has favored immigrants from northwest Europe as against those from eastern and southern Europe." Reflecting the boundaries of the "nation of immigrants," the *Times* also editorialized in support of the new limits on immigration from the Western Hemisphere, saying "a good case exists for placing immigration from all countries throughout the world on essentially the same basis." The editorial added that population growth in Latin America could precipitate an immigration wave and a dilemma for policymakers in the future. "It would be an act of prudence and foresight," the *Times* concluded, "to stabilize hemisphere immigration at its present level on a nondiscriminatory, first-come, first-served basis."[103]

President Johnson planned an elaborate signing ceremony at the Statue of Liberty in early October, one day before his meeting with Pope Paul VI. In doing so, Johnson became the first president to go to the statue since President Franklin Roosevelt delivered his speech paying tribute to immigrants on Lady Liberty's fiftieth anniversary in 1936.[104] In that time, the

Statue of Liberty had become a major tourist attraction and a central symbol of the "nation of immigrants."[105]

Johnson's speech downplayed the numerical impact of the Hart-Celler Act. LBJ declared that the bill swept away the origins system but that this would not mean a dramatic increase in immigration: "This Bill is not a revolutionary Bill. It does not affect the lives of millions. It will not reshape the structure of our daily lives, or add importantly to our wealth and power." Later, he added, "The days of unlimited immigration are past. But those who come will come because of what they are—not because of the land from which they sprung."[106]

Johnson reiterated the major themes of the congressional debates, as well as the public celebrations surrounding immigration in the years preceding the bill's passage. Expressing a contributionist vision that encompassed those from eastern and southern Europe, LBJ said, "Men of needed skill and talent were denied entrance because they came from southern and eastern Europe or from one of the developing continents." He proclaimed,

America was built by a nation of strangers. From a hundred different places they have poured forth into an empty land—joining and blending in one mighty and irresistible tide. The land flourished because it was nourished and fed from so many sources—because it was nourished by so many cultures and traditions and peoples.

∿

Ellis Island's fate clearly illustrates the growing appreciation for the benefits brought by eastern and southern European immigration and the acceptance of contributionism.[107] Closed by the government in 1954, the facility had fallen into disrepair. While debating the island's future, Congress received several suggestions, ranging from turning the site into a liberal arts college to using the buildings as housing for the elderly. In its report evaluating the recommendations, the National Park Service wrote of the importance of Ellis Island in the minds of eastern and southern European immigrants: "To these huddled masses and their descendants Ellis Island has been as important in fact as Plymouth Rock has become in fancy for the descendants of those who came in the first colonization wave."[108] The Park Service suggested turning the island into a national historical monument because the system had not paid sufficient attention to the

Figure 3. President Lyndon B. Johnson signs the Hart-Celler Act of 1965, eliminating
the national origins quotas that had excluded southern and eastern Europeans
since 1924, with the Statue of Liberty, symbol of the "nation of immigrants," in the
background. LBJ Library, photo by Yoichi Okamato.

immigrant experience. "Proper balance in presenting our history to the
millions of American families who travel widely," the report concluded,
"fully justifies an Ellis Island National Historic Museum."[109]

In his speech at the Statue of Liberty, President Johnson affectionately
referred to the island where millions of southern and eastern Europeans
had first entered the United States: "Over my shoulder you can see Ellis
Island, whose vacant corridors echo today the joyous sounds of long-ago
voices."[110] Reflecting the incorporation of these groups into the "nation of
immigrants," Ellis Island gained renewed stature in 1965 when the Park
Service incorporated it as part of the Statue of Liberty National Monument.
Still, the references to Ellis Island made it very clear that Asians and Latinos,
most of whom did not arrive through New York Harbor, remained outside
the "nation of immigrants."

Epilogue

"How great to be an American and something else as well"

By the mid-1960s, contributionism had emerged as a central theme in public discourse regarding immigration in the United States. The acceptance of contributionism, the idea that newcomers strengthened the American economy and culture while also accepting certain American norms, represented a significant shift from the mentality of the early years of the century, when the benefits of immigration were hardly appreciated. Though contributionism borrowed elements from Horace Kallen, Randolph Bourne, and Israel Zangwill, it did not completely replicate any of these ideologies. A series of international events, starting with World War II and continuing through the Cold War, created a climate where policymakers contrasted the diversity of America with its totalitarian enemies. The civil rights movement helped the contributionist idea gradually gain acceptance during the 1950s and 1960s, and by the passage of the Immigration Act of 1965, intellectuals and policymakers routinely spoke of a "nation of immigrants" that included eastern and southern Europeans. Asians and Latinos, though, remained firmly outside the broader definition of American identity.

In the decades after reform, immigration remained a controversial issue, in large part due to changes in immigration sparked by the reform itself. Though the supporters of the Immigration Act of 1965 said it would hold the level of immigration constant, the number of newcomers grew significantly after the law went into effect in 1968. Indeed, the total migration to the United States grew from a mere 3.3 million during the 1960s to 4.5 million in the 1970s to roughly 7.5 million in each of the next two decades.[1] The percentage of foreign-born Americans grew from a low of 4.7 percent in 1970 to 13 percent in 2010, the highest level since the Ellis Island-era immigration.[2]

Initially, immigration grew from southern and eastern European countries like Italy, which had long backlogs of people who desired to come to America. Over time, though, significant immigration from Europe diminished. Most eastern Europeans were unable to enter the country before 1989 because of the restrictions imposed by the Iron Curtain. Furthermore, the family unification measures embodied in the 1965 bill limited the arrival of immigrants from the older sources of American immigration. For instance, few Irish emigrated because the family ties of Irish Americans had diminished over the years. This led some supporters of Hart-Celler, such as Ted Kennedy, to call for reforms to rectify this situation.

Rather than hailing from Europe, the majority of this new wave of immigrants came from Asia and Latin America. This influx of racially diverse migrants altered the demographic face of the nation. Immigration from Latin America grew from 1.3 million during the 1960s to 1.8 million in the 1970s to almost 3.5 million by the 1980s.[3] Immigration from Asia rose from a mere 400,000 in the 1960s to 1.6 million in the 1970s, reaching 2.7 million in the 1980s.[4] By 2000, Latinos composed half the foreign-born population, from 10 percent in 1960. Asians grew from 5 to 25 percent over the same period.[5]

Why did this unexpected result occur? Congress did not foresee how cheaper transportation, along with advancements in jet travel, would enable Asians, free from the restrictive quotas of the pre-1965 era, to enter the United States in large numbers under the Eastern Hemisphere caps. Policymakers also did not anticipate how the family unification provisions would facilitate Latin American immigration. For instance, a legal immigrant from Mexico could bring his or her spouse and unmarried children under the second preference, become a citizen, and bring his or her brother and sister under the fourth preference. This process repeated itself in a series of chain migrations. Furthermore, the new citizens could bring their spouses, minor children, and parents outside the quota framework, causing immigration levels to exceed the hemispheric caps. Finally, administrations of both parties implemented measures admitting additional refugees during crises, such as the fall of South Vietnam in 1975 and the Mariel boatlift from Cuba in 1980.

Illegal immigration also rose significantly in the post-1965 period and became a persistent source of controversy. The tremendous demand for immigration from Latin America overwhelmed the slots available under the Immigration Act of 1965 as the Western Hemispheric caps caused more and more newcomers to try to enter the country illegally. In 1976, Congress extended the 20,000 per nation limit, which was already in place for the Eastern Hemisphere, to the Western Hemisphere as well. This adjustment increased illegal migration from high demand countries like Mexico and elsewhere as 1.8 million illegal immigrants arrived in the 1980s, with the number growing to almost 5 million in the 1990s.[6]

∾

Amid these demographic changes, contributionism continued to be a primary element in the discussion of immigration in the United States in the last third of the twentieth century. From the late 1960s onward, the concept of America as a "nation of immigrants" became a staple of the nation's political discourse. A new generation of restrictionists, however, emerged in the late twentieth and early twenty-first centuries who sought to limit both legal and illegal immigration. As debates over immigration developed in these years, the Ellis Island generation became more firmly accepted as integral to the "nation of immigrants," while Asians and Latinos remained clearly on the periphery. Though contributionism became further cemented into the American mainstream in the post-1965 period, it faced assaults from those who considered it too assimilationist.

In the late 1960s, elements of the Student Non-Violent Coordinating Committee (SNCC) and the Congress of Racial Equality (CORE) rejected integrationism in favor of the black power ideology of Malcolm X. Though the majority of African Americans remained committed to Martin Luther King, Jr.,'s integrationist philosophy, black leaders such as Stokely Carmichael, the leader of SNCC, embraced identity politics and rejected contributionism. "The goal of black people," Carmichael declared in *Black Power* (1967), "must not be to assimilate into middle class America." Every ethnic group of Americans, he suggested, organized as a political entity to advance in American society and continued to do so: "Studies of voting behavior specifically and political behavior generally have made it clear that politically the American pot has not melted," observed the SNCC leader. "Italians vote for Rubino over O'Brien; Irish for Murphy over Goldberg, etc."[7]

As part of the "white ethnic revival" of the 1970s, which emphasized the different cultural traditions of the Ellis Island-era immigrants, some intellectuals from an eastern and southern European background agreed with Carmichael. Michael Novak, a college professor and the child of Slovak immigrants, published *The Rise of the Unmeltable Ethnics* in 1971, in which he argued that the costs of Americanization had been too high for ethnic Americans. He bemoaned the loss of native traditions and believed the melting pot was nothing more than a synonym for Anglo-conformity. "Whereas the Anglo-Saxon model appears to be a system of atomic individuals and high mobility, our model has tended to stress communities of our own, attachment to family, stability, and roots," wrote Novak. "The melting pot is a kind of a homogenized soup," he added, "and its mores only partly appeal to ethnics: to some, yes, to others, no."[8]

Films of the 1970s, in the spirit of the ethnic revival, portrayed the distinct cultural life of the second- and third-generation immigrants. Movies like the *Godfather* series and the *Rocky* films depicted a world like Nathan Glazer and Daniel Patrick Moynihan described, where old traditions did not simply fade away and various ethnic groups held different values. In the *Godfather* films, Michael Corleone, played by the young Al Pacino, begins as a character straight out of the World War II films—a clearly ethnic but assimilated veteran who identifies with "American" traditions. At a family dinner shortly after Pearl Harbor, his older brother Sonny (James Caan) calls the thousands of men enlisting in the military "saps." Michael asks, "Why are they saps?" "They're saps," Sonny replies, "because they risk their lives for strangers." Michael sharply disagrees, "That's pop talking. . . . They risk their lives for their country." "Your country ain't your blood," Sonny lashes back, "you remember that!" Michael says he does not feel that way, and Sonny challenges him: "Why don't you just quit college and go to join the army!" Much to the family's dismay, Michael responds, "I did. I enlisted in the Marines."[9]

Following the war, Michael attends his sister's wedding wearing his military uniform and brings his Protestant girlfriend, Kay Adams (Diane Keaton). After telling her the story of how his mobster father helped a friend out by threatening violence, Michael famously declares, "That's my family, Kay; that's not me," indicating his desire to stay out of the family business and enter the legitimate American mainstream.[10] But Michael's story, of course, takes a very different turn. Instead of continuing the journey toward Anglo norms, Michael adopts the values of his father, becomes the godfather himself, holding loyalty to the "family" and Italian traditions, above all things, including country. "The movie revealed aspects of American life never before glimpsed by the public," remarked Novak, "and it revealed, incidentally, some of the ways in which Anglo-American systems of justice and power excluded other ethnic groups and led some of them to fall back on their own resources."[11]

While the ethnic revival challenged contributionism, it still remained the dominant message regarding immigration. Around the same time, the ABC program *Schoolhouse Rock* exposed the children of the 1970s to the contributionist version of the melting pot that was gaining acceptance. The show, watched by millions of young members of Generation X on Saturday mornings, featured a series of cartoons accompanied by songs educating children about government, grammar, and other subjects. One tune, titled "The Great American Melting Pot," clearly refers to the 1882–1924 wave of migrants, beginning, "My grandmother came from Russia, / a satchel on her knee. My grandfather had his father's cap / he brought from Italy. . . . They paid the fare to America / and there they melted in." Showing the Statue of Liberty, the song's chorus airs: "Lovely Lady Liberty / with her book of recipes / and the finest one she's got / is the Great American Melting Pot," as the audience sees people of various ethnicities jumping into a pot. Like many of the programs from the 1930s and 1940s, the song goes on to describe how the nineteenth-century immigrants brought their native cultural traditions and built the American economy. Finally, "The Great American Melting Pot" declares that immigrants need not surrender their heritage to become "real" Americans, concluding, "Go on and ask your grandma / hear what she has to tell / how great to be an American / and something else as well," as "grandma" reveals a pin saying "Kiss Me, I'm Polish."[12]

Many public events celebrating immigration after 1965 prominently featured contributionism. In 1976, the nation's Bicentennial festivities included a number of paeans to immigration. In the tradition of I Am an American Day, the government held naturalization ceremonies across the country on Fourth of July weekend.[13] President Gerald Ford addressed one such gathering at Monticello, home of Thomas Jefferson. Sounding much like Zangwill, Ford praised the accomplishments and contributions of immigrants: "Such transfusions of traditions and cultures, as well as of blood, have made America unique among nations and Americans a new kind of people." Ford placed his argument in a Cold War framework: "The wealth we have of culture and ethnic, and religious and racial traditions are valuable counterbalances to the overpowering sameness and subordination of totalitarian societies," reiterating that message in his conclusion: "And remember, as well, the rich treasures you brought from whence you came, and let us share your pride in them. This is the way we keep our independence as exciting as the day it was declared and keep the United States of America even more beautiful than Joseph's coat."[14]

The Statue of Liberty Centennial on Fourth of July weekend in 1986 also highlighted contributionism. The four-day celebration of the nation's foremost symbol of immigration joined together all the characteristics of the public holidays, school textbooks, and political debates about immigration since World War II. Organizers held naturalization ceremonies in 44 sites across the country as Chief Justice Warren Burger himself swore in 200 citizens on Ellis Island.[15] In the spirit of National Brotherhood Week, John Cardinal O'Connor led an ecumenical service at Saint Patrick's Cathedral in New York City, where he declared, "All of us are here as refugees, all exiles, all pilgrims, and unless we understand this reality, we cannot understand ourselves as people or why we need the Statue of Liberty at all."[16]

President Ronald Reagan, a conservative Republican whose intellectual predecessors had resisted the immigration from southern and eastern Europe, expressed contributionist sentiments at the celebration. Relating how the French workers who joined with Americans in preparing Lady Liberty for its reopening were struck by the cooperation between different ethnic groups in America, the president echoed Zangwill, "Well, it's how we like to think of America. And it's good to know that Miss Liberty is still giving life to the dream of a new world where old antagonisms could be cast aside and people of every nation could become one." At the ceremonial relighting of the torch on July 3, Reagan articulated the contributionist ideal clearly to the entire country via national television: "While we applaud the immigrants who stand out, whose contributions are easily discerned, we know that America's heroes are all those whose names are remembered by only a few. . . . They worked in our factories, on ships and railroads, in stores, and on road construction crews. . . . They came from every land."[17]

While some debated whether the new immigrants from Asia and Latin America could assimilate, the incorporation of eastern and southern European immigrants into the "nation of immigrants" became more evident. By the 1980s, politicians such as 1988 Democratic presidential nominee Michael Dukakis, the Greek American governor of Massachusetts, made their immigrant roots a central part of their political personas. Dukakis repeatedly declared that he was the "son of Greek immigrants" to appeal to voters from immigrant backgrounds and to combat the charge that he was a liberal elitist with little understanding of the concerns of ordinary Americans. Though Dukakis lost the general election to Vice President George H. W. Bush, immigrant roots, at least of the Ellis Island-era variety, were now often seen as a sign of Americanism rather than as a sign of alien status.[18] "The lore of the late 19th and early 20th century immigrant—Ellis Island, pushcarts, slums—has become the East Coast equivalent of the log cabin, poor farm-boy upbringing and the rest of that Americana unavailable to so many people with exotic surnames," observed *Newsweek* columnist Meg Greenfield.[19]

Reflecting this sentiment, a refurbished Ellis Island opened as a museum in 1990, albeit without the fanfare of the neighboring Statue of Liberty. The museum, which restored the facility where so many immigrants entered the country between 1892 and 1924, clearly placed eastern and southern European immigration at the center of the American experience. As Vincent Cannato, author of a history of the island, put it, "Ellis Island was the new Plymouth Rock and the immigrants who passed through it were the Pilgrims of a modern, multicultural America."[20]

◠

While public celebrations often cheered the contributions of eastern and southern European immigrants and politicians invoked their Ellis Island roots, more and more Americans were becoming aware that a new wave of migration from Asia and Latin America was reshaping the nation's demography The unanticipated consequences of immigration reform provoked a whole new series of debates about American identity as many policymakers began to make arguments similar to the restrictionists of the 1920s, albeit bereft of the explicit racism of that time. Though the "new" immigrants of the post-1965 era were mostly nonwhite, the civil rights movement, as well as the discrediting of scientific racism, made public racism unacceptable to most Americans. Still, the fact that Latinos and Asians were nonwhite obviously influenced public attitudes toward the newcomers.

As in the early part of the century, many observers feared that immigrants lacked the work ethic of native-born Americans or earlier waves of immigrants. Economist George Borjas wrote that immigrants who arrived in the 1970s had higher unemployment rates and were more likely to use welfare than those who arrived in the 1950s and 1960s: "Not only are the new immigrants more likely to be welfare recipients than the old, but also the welfare participation rate of a particular cohort increases the longer the cohort has been in the United States."[21]

Restrictionists of the 1980s and 1990s, like their 1920s counterparts, also feared that recent arrivals were fracturing the common American culture. The threat of "multiculturalism," which became a major issue in the late 1980s and early 1990s, loomed large in their minds. Like the advocates of the white ethnic revival, supporters of multiculturalism challenged contributionism, urging ethnic minorities to retain their unique cultures as well as advocating educational programs to teach students about the histories of particular groups. Such efforts, however, were now focused on Hispanics, Asians, and African Americans, rather than southern and eastern Europeans. "Various groups are pressing for things like bilingual education, not, as it was originally intended, to help foreign children to learn English, but to maintain their native languages and cultures," wrote Richard Bernstein in the *New York Times* before the opening of the Ellis Island museum. "Across the country," he added, "there are ever more ethnic studies programs, more demands that history texts be rewritten, more protests urging the hiring of minority faculty members."[22]

Some liberal supporters of immigration, like historian Arthur Schlesinger, Jr., a longtime activist in Democratic politics, also expressed concern about these policies. To Schlesinger, multiculturalism posed a serious threat to national unity in a period of growing ethnic conflict around the world following the end of the Cold War. Describing his fears, Schlesinger wrote, "The impact of ethnic and racial pressures on our public schools is more troubling. The bonds of national cohesion are fragile already. . . . If separatist tendencies go on unchecked, the result can only be the fragmentation, resegregation, and tribalization of American life."[23]

Restrictionists also feared that the new immigrants could not assimilate. Conservative commentator Pat Buchanan, twice a challenger for the Republican presidential nomination, declared that America could not assimilate the new migration from Asia and Latin America and maintained that it was dividing America:

The Melting Pot is in need of repair. . . . If America is to survive as "one nation . . . one people" we need to call a "time-out" on immigration, to assimilate the tens of millions who have lately arrived.

We need to get to know one another, to live together, to learn together America's language, history, culture, and traditions of tolerance, to become a new national family, before we add a hundred million more.[24]

Harvard political scientist Samuel P. Huntington echoed these concerns in his book *Who Are We?* (2005). Like Buchanan and Borjas, Huntington believed that recent immigrants, particularly Hispanics, posed different challenges from the Ellis Island generation. The previous waves of immigrants spoke a multitude of languages, Huntington suggested, whereas an overwhelming majority of the post-1965 migration spoke Spanish. Hispanic newcomers, particularly Mexicans, were heavily concentrated in areas like the Southwest, where they remained close to their native cultures. Finally, the emergence of multiculturalism hindered assimilation because it meant that the "Americanization" programs of the early twentieth century were now considered xenophobic. All these forces led to the potential fracturing of what Huntington saw as the Anglo-Protestant national identity that had traditionally held the nation together. "In the past, assimilation was greatly facilitated because both waves substantially tapered off due to the Civil War, World War I, and the laws limiting immigration," he declared. "The erosion of other national loyalties and the assimilation of recent immigrants could be much slower and more problematic than assimilation has been in the past."[25]

A portion of the environmental movement represented a new part of the restrictionist coalition. Concerned about a growing population, some advocates believed large-scale immigration harmed the nation's ecology. Colorado Governor Richard Lamm summarized the environmental case for lower immigration, declaring, "Do we really want an America of 500 million people," adding, "immigration will decide whether we stabilize or we continue to grow." The movement remained divided on the issue, as the Sierra Club, a leading environmental lobby, narrowly rejected a measure to make immigration restriction part of the organization's mission.[26]

From the 1980s onward, immigration would emerge as a hot-button political issue every few years. After a long debate, Congress passed and President Reagan signed the Immigration Reform and Control Act (IRCA) in 1986, which was designed to address the problem of illegal immigration. The bill, often referred to as Simpson-Mazzoli, provided amnesty for illegal immigrants who had entered the country before 1982 and imposed sanctions against employers who hired undocumented workers.[27] The bill also included "diversity visas" for legal immigration from nations like Ireland that had been disadvantaged by the family unification provisions of the Immigration Act of 1965.[28]

While President Reagan hailed the bill as "the most comprehensive reform of our immigration laws since 1952," Representative Charles Schumer (D) of New York, a supporter of IRCA, cautioned that "The bill is a gamble, a riverboat gamble. There is no guarantee that employer sanctions will work or that amnesty will work. We are headed into uncharted waters."[29] Schumer proved prophetic as the law achieved mixed results. Three million illegal immigrants would eventually gain citizenship, but employer sanctions turned out to be ineffective, as a cottage industry for fraudulent documents emerged and the federal bureaucracy lacked the apparatus to enforce the law.[30] Illegal immigration remained a serious problem throughout the 1990s and into the twenty-first century.

Congress enacted additional reforms regarding legal immigration in 1990. This bill took small steps to move the system away from family unification and toward employment skills. Like IRCA, the 1990 legislation expanded opportunities for European immigrants, adding 40,000 "diversity visas."[31] In the end, while the law increased the percentage of visas for those with skills, it did little to change the general composition of the post-1965 immigration.[32]

The most serious attempt to undo the 1965 reforms came during the mid-1990s. As the nation's economy recovered slowly from the recession of the early 1990s, support for immigration restriction grew dramatically. The percentage of Americans who wanted fewer immigrants grew from 49 percent in 1986 to 65 percent by 1993.[33] The sentiment grew significantly in California, which was among the regions hardest hit by the economic slowdown. The 1992 Los Angeles riots, a major earthquake, brushfires, and downsizing in the defense industry brought about by the end of the Cold War combined to hinder the state's growth. The post-1965 immigration had significantly changed the demography of the Golden State, and the state's tough economic circumstances intensified existing resentments toward recent arrivals.[34]

Faced with a difficult fight for reelection in 1994, California Republican Governor Pete Wilson seized on Proposition 187, a ballot initiative to deny social service benefits to illegal immigrants, as the centerpiece of his campaign. Down by double digits in the polls, Wilson ran commercials showing the migration of Mexicans across the southern border while a narrator intoned, "They keep coming."[35] In the end, Wilson and Proposition 187 both won easily in fall 1994, with many crediting Wilson's embrace of the initiative as the primary reason for his comeback victory. At the same time, Republicans, some of whom had campaigned for tougher restraints on immigration, gained control of both houses of Congress for the first time in forty years.

Emboldened by these two victories, supporters of more restrictive policies and their congressional allies pressed for tougher action on both illegal and *legal* immigration during the 1995–96 congressional term. They called for stiffer border controls, stronger deportation policies, and the denial of government aid to legal immigrants. *New York Times* columnist A. M. Rosenthal observed, "The nation is face to face with questions that involve its character and purpose. Are immigrants an essential part of American strength and identity? Or have they become one more American problem, a blister that gets increasingly annoying?"[36]

It was not only the conservative Republican congressional majority that supported stronger limits with regard to legal immigration. In the summer of 1995, a federal advisory commission chaired by Barbara Jordan, a Democrat and the first African American woman elected to Congress from the Deep South, recommended reducing legal migration by one-third. President Bill Clinton, still recovering from the poor Democratic showing in the 1994 midterm elections, endorsed the commission's report to prevent the GOP from using immigration as a wedge issue in the 1996 presidential campaign.[37]

In this debate, there were tentative signs that policymakers were slowly incorporating Asians and Latinos into the "nation of immigrants." Though calls for lowering immigration were aimed at these groups, Jordan and Clinton both employed contributionist rhetoric. Jordan declared, "the United States has been and should continue to be a nation of immigrants. A well-regulated system of legal immigration is in our national interest."[38] Clinton remarked in a speech in California, "We've done what we could to close the borders and send people back. But you know what? This is a nation of immigrants. Most of us do not have ancestors who were born here."[39]

In 1995, the House passed legislation out of committee that would, among other things, reduce the number of newcomers allowed to enter the country by tightening the all-important family unification provisions. Under this proposal, foreign-born siblings and adult children of legal residents and American citizens would no longer receive preference for obtaining visas. Representative Lamar Smith (R) of Texas, a leading advocate of restrictive policies, declared, "I think the debate over whether legal immigration reform should occur is over. The question is no longer whether legal immigration should be reformed, but how it should be reformed."[40]

Despite Smith's confidence, a powerful and diverse coalition emerged to combat this plan. "As Congress today considers some of the most severe anti-immigration measures since the 1920's, it is facing resistance from a surprising alliance of high-technology manufacturers, religious leaders, conservative think tanks, civil liberties organizations, and tiny-grass-root immigrant groups," wrote Matthew Purdy in the *New York Times*.[41] Some of the opposition came from within the GOP itself, as many high-tech businesses, as well as small enterprises, needed immigrant workers to alleviate labor shortages or to provide inexpensive labor. Free-market Republicans such as 1996 vice presidential candidate Jack Kemp and House Majority Leader Dick Armey also opposed the measures. Stephen Moore, an economist at the libertarian Cato Institute, made the conservative case for liberal immigration, calling the measures "anti-business, anti-family, anti-freedom."[42]

Just as they had in the past, ethnic organizations lobbied on behalf of their compatriots. The immigrant population's continued growth, along with its concentration in politically pivotal states such as California, Texas, and New York, strengthened the influence of these groups.[43] Finally, liberal intellectuals opposed the new proposals on humanitarian and civil libertarian grounds. "It is time for the President and Congress to return to the constitutional tradition," declared columnist Anthony Lewis, "equal treatment of immigrants in a nation of immigrants."[44]

This coalition, assisted by the divisions within the GOP, defeated the measures reducing legal immigration. Instead, Congress enacted and President Clinton signed legislation in 1996 that strengthened border controls and made it easier to deport criminal aliens.[45] In addition, the backlash against Wilson and Proposition 187 eventually drove Hispanics away from the California GOP, nearly destroying the party in the Golden State. The strong economy of the 1990s weakened anti-immigration feeling as the number of Americans who wanted lower immigration declined from 65 percent at the height of the debate in 1995 to a mere 38 percent by the turn of the century.[46] In 2000, national GOP leaders sought out Texas Governor George W. Bush, an opponent of Proposition 187, as their presidential candidate, in part because of his strong support among Latino voters. While advocates of restriction achieved a few of their goals, the basic structure of the 1965 reforms remained intact, and few sought to challenge the status quo in the late 1990s.

Broad support for the contributionist perspective also played a role in these debates as legislators repeatedly paid tribute to the "nation of immigrants" ideology during the immigration battles of the 1990s.[47] This view had a strong hold on Americans outside the Beltway as well. While researching popular attitudes on cultural issues during the late 1990s, sociologist Alan Wolfe found mixed views regarding the value of recent immigrants. He noted, however, that many of the people he interviewed repeatedly expressed their support for the "nation of immigrants" ideology. "The cliché that America is a nation of immigrants has remarkable staying power in middle-class America; it was repeated over and over again by those with whom we talked," Wolfe observed, adding, "It is not an exaggeration to say that open borders, rather than having the effect of diluting what it means to be an American, define for a sizable portion of the American middle class, what America is all about."[48]

The security fears raised by the attacks of September 11, 2001, and an increase in illegal immigration brought the debate back to the center of American politics during the George W. Bush years. Growing at a rate of 500,000 a year in the first decade of the twenty-first century, the number of undocumented workers rose from 8.4 million in 2000 to 11.1 million in 2005, 56 percent of them coming from Mexico.[49] As more illegal immigrants entered the country, they moved beyond traditional entry states such as California and New York and into southern states like Georgia and North Carolina that did not have long traditions of immigration.[50] This contributed to a rise in restrictionist sentiment which, while not reaching the levels of the mid-1990s, grew to a majority viewpoint again after 9/11.[51]

The fight over the nation's border again dominated American politics in 2006–7, when, despite support from many Democrats as well as President Bush, an effort to create a path to citizenship for undocumented workers failed. Some in Congress cited the perceived failure of IRCA as a reason to oppose what they viewed as "amnesty" for illegal immigrants.[52] Many

Americans demanded that the government secure the border first and believed that giving such workers citizenship rewarded unlawful behavior.

Like his predecessor, President Barack Obama pledged comprehensive immigration reform during his campaign. Despite entreaties from the Latino community and the Congressional Hispanic Caucus, legislative action was delayed during his first two years in office as Obama focused on health care as well as measures to combat the Great Recession. The Republican victory in the 2010 midterm elections added another obstacle to reform and the status quo remained in place as of the 2012 presidential election.

∾

Despite the failure of immigration reform, many policymakers and intellectuals in the early twenty-first century spoke of a "nation of immigrants" encompassing the descendants of southern and eastern European immigrants. Contributionism, the belief that the achievements of these immigrants strengthened the nation's economy and its culture, has become a routine part of public dialogue about immigration in the United States. Still, the new wave of immigration from Latin America and Asia has created heated debates regarding the benefits of immigration, just as the Ellis Island immigrants did in the early years of the twentieth century. While efforts to restrict this new wave of immigration have largely failed, it remains to be seen if Asians and Latinos will eventually be fully incorporated into the "nation of immigrants."

Notes

Introduction

1. William Jefferson Clinton, *Public Papers of the Presidents of the United States: William Jefferson Clinton*, vol. 1, *1998* (Washington, D.C., 1999), 956.

2. J. Hector St. John de Crevecoeur, *Letters from an American Farmer* (New York, 1981 ed.), 68.

3. Ibid., 70.

4. Herman Melville, *Redburn: His First Voyage* (New York, 1924), 190.

5. John Higham, *Strangers in the Land: Patterns of American Nativism* (New Brunswick, N.J., 1955), 21.

6. The government did place some limits on prostitutes entering the U.S. in 1875, but Chinese exclusion was the first major restriction.

7. The bill included provisions allowing for some Chinese students and merchants to enter the country. See Roger Daniels, *Asian America: The Chinese and Japanese in the United States Since 1850* (Seattle, 1988), 91.

8. U.S. Department of Homeland Security, Office of Immigration Statistics, *2003 Yearbook of Immigration Statistics* (Washington, D.C., 2004), 12–13.

9. U.S. Department of Commerce, Bureau of the Census, *Historical Statistics of the United States: Colonial Times to 1970, Part 1* (Washington, D.C., 1976), 12, 14.

10. Alan M. Kraut, *The Huddled Masses: The Immigrant in American Society, 1880–1921* (Arlington Heights, Va., 1982), 77.

11. Higham, *Strangers in the Land*, 3–12. Higham lists anti-Catholicism, anti-radicalism, and racial nativism as the three components of American nativism.

12. *Watson's Magazine* 20, 66 (April 1915): 338, Thomas E. Watson Papers, University of North Carolina, Digital Archive.

13. Leonard Dinnerstein, *Anti-Semitism in America* (Oxford, 1994), 42.

14. *Century* 35, 2 (March 1888): 798, Cornell University Library, Making of America Project.

15. Samuel Gompers, "Immigration—Up to Congress," *American Federationist*, January 1911, 1, RG 98–002, Ser. 1, Subject Vertical Files I, 1882–1990, Box 23, Folder 16, George Meany Memorial Archives, National Labor College, Silver Spring, Md.

16. Madison Grant, *The Passing of the Great Race; or, The Racial Basis of European History* (New York, 1916), 228.

17. For more on Boas, see Marshall Hyatt, *Franz Boas Social Activist: The Dynamics of Ethnicity* (New York, 1990).

18. Theodore Roosevelt, *The Works of Teddy Roosevelt*, vol. 13 (New York, 1926), 24.

19. Woodrow Wilson, *The Public Papers of Woodrow Wilson, the New Democracy: Presidential Messages, Addresses and Other Papers*, vol. 1, ed. Ray Stannard Baker and William E. Dodd (New York, 1926), 319.

20. Theodore Roosevelt, "True Americanism," *Forum Magazine*, April 1894.

21. Ibid., 319.

22. Ibid., 318

23. For a thorough look at Americanization programs, see Higham, *Strangers in the Land*, 234–63; Desmond King, *Making Americans: Immigration, Race, and the Origins of the Diverse Democracy* (Cambridge, 2000), 86–126.

24. Ibid., 113–14.

25. Ibid., 98.

26. Peter C. Marzio, ed., *A Nation of Nations: The People Who Came to America as Seen Through Objects and Documents Exhibited at the Smithsonian Institution* (New York, 1976), 372.

27. Israel Zangwill, *The Melting Pot: Drama in Four Acts* (New York, 1975), 33.

28. Ibid., 185.

29. Kraut, *Huddled Masses*, 146–47; David Hollinger, *Postethnic America: Beyond Multiculturalism* (New York, 1995), 91–92.

30. Michael Lind, *The Next American Nation: The New Nationalism and the Next American Revolution* (New York, 1995), 238.

31. Higham, *Strangers in the Land*, 248

32. Hollinger, *Postethnic America*, 91–92.

33. Randolph Bourne, *History of a Literary Radical and Other Essays* (New York, 1969), 270.

34. Ibid., 278, 278, 280.

35. Ibid., 282, 283, 297.

36. Horace Kallen, "Democracy vs. the Melting Pot," *The Nation*, February 25, 1915, 217.

37. Ibid., 219, 20.

38. National Archives, RG 12, Records of the Office of Education (ROE), Records of the Office of the Commissioner, Historical File, 1870–1950, File 106: Council of National Defense, Entry 6, Box 7, NACP.

39. Higham, *Strangers in the Land*, 306.

40. See Gary Gerstle, *American Crucible: Race and Nation in the Twentieth Century* (Princeton, N.J., 2001), Mathew Frye Jacobson, *Roots Too: White Ethnic Revival in Post-Civil Rights America* (Cambridge, 2006); Peter Novick, *The Holocaust in American Life* (Boston, 1999).

41. *Gentlemen's Agreement*, dir. Elia Kazan (Fox, 1947).

42. Michael Novak, *The Rise of the Unmeltable Ethnics: Politics and Culture in the Seventies* (New York, 1971), 72.

43. Diana Selig, *Americans All: The Cultural Gifts Movement* (Cambridge, 2008); Wendy Wall, *Inventing the "American Way": The Politics of Consensus from the New Deal to the Civil Rights Movement* (Oxford, 2008).

44. Jeffrey Mirel, *Patriotic Pluralism: Americanization Education and European Immigrants* (Cambridge, Mass., 2010).

45. Jacobson, *Roots Too*.

46. To some extent, contributionism resembles the "Pennsylvania Model" developed by Lawrence Fuchs in *American Kaleidoscope: Race, Class, and Civic Culture* (Hanover, N.H., 1990) and elaborated on by Susan Martin in her book, *A Nation of Immigrants* (Cambridge, Mass., 2011). The model refers to the Pennsylvania colony's openness to newcomers during the seventeenth and eighteenth centuries. Martin writes, "Pennsylvania is thus the locus of origins of two traditions that go hand in hand throughout U.S. history. On the one hand, it is the birthplace of a robust pluralism that celebrates the contributions of immigrants from throughout the world (or at least from the European world in the seventeenth and eighteenth centuries)" (59). On the other hand, she adds that "the very pluralism that Pennsylvania represented yielded harsh criticism of the immigrants about their ability to integrate into what was largely an English environment."

47. *Exodus*, dir. Otto Preminger (MGM, 1960).

48. See, e.g., David Roediger, *Wages of Whiteness: Race and the Making of the American Working Class* (London, 1991); Matthew Frye Jacobson, *Whiteness of a Different Color: European Immigrants and the Alchemy of Race* (Cambridge, 1998); Matt Guterl, *The Color of Race in America, 1900–1940* (Cambridge, 2001); Roediger, *Working Toward Whiteness: How America's Immigrants Became White* (Cambridge, 2005). For a critical perspective, see Eric Arnessen, "Whiteness and the Historians' Imagination," *International Labor and Working-Class History* 60 (Fall 2001): 3–32; Ronald H. Bayor, "Another Look at 'Whiteness': The Persistence of Ethnicity in American Life," *Journal of American Ethnic History* 29, 1 (Fall 2009): 13–30.

Chapter 1. The Beginning of the Era of Restriction

1. *Congressional Record.*, 68th Cong., 1st Sess., April 8, 1924, 5922, 5823.

2. "Department of the Interior, Bureau of Education, *Slogans for the National Campaign of Americanization*," Records of the Office of Education (ROE), Records of the Office of the Commissioner (ROC), Historical File, 1870–1950, File 106, Record Group (RG) 12, Entry 6, Box 7, National Archives at College Park [Maryland] (NACP).

3. "To the Superintendent of City Public Schools," September 9, 1918, ROE, ROC, Historical File, 1870–1950, File 106, RG 12, Entry 6, Box 7, NACP.

4. "The Syracuse Plan for Americanization," ROE, ROC, Historical File, 1870–1950, File 106. Child Health Organization—Americanization War Work, RG 12, Entry 6, Box 11, NACP.

5. "Co-ordination of Americanization Work in Massachusetts," ROE, ROC, Historical File, 1870–1950, File 106, Council of National Defense, RG 12, Entry 6, Box 7, NACP.

6. "The Syracuse Plan for Americanization."

7. "U.S. Army—Chautauqua American Legion," ROE, ROC, Historical File, 1870–1950, File 106, Child Health Organization—Americanization War Work, unnamed folder, RG 12, Entry 6, Box 11, NACP.

8. "Seeks to Show 'All-American' Exhibit to U.S.," *Chicago Daily Tribune*, April 27, 1919.

9. "Project," 1, ROE, ROC, Historical File, 1870–1950, File 106, Council of National Defense, RG 12, Entry 6, Box 7, NACP.

10. "A New Word in Americanization," ROE, ROC, Historical File, 1870–1950, File 106, Council of National Defense, RG 12, Entry 6, Box 7, NACP.

11. "Project," 4.

12. "Seeks to Show 'All-American' Exhibit to U.S."

13. "All American Show Is Near Split on Hyphen," *Chicago Daily Tribune*, August 26, 1919.

14. Ibid.

15. "Ask Receiver for Exposition at Coliseum," *Chicago Daily Tribune*, September 13, 1919.

16. "All American Show Fills Date Despite Debts," *Chicago Daily Tribune*, September 15, 1919.

17. *Cong. Rec.*, 68th Cong., 1st Sess., April 8, 1924, 5865, 5868.

18. Ibid., 5922, 5909.

19. Ibid., 5848.

20. Ibid., 5824.

21. Ibid., 5919.

22. Ibid., 5922.

23. Ibid., 5872.

24. "Legion and Labor Would Bar Aliens," *New York Times*, March 24, 1924.

25. James Gregory, *The Southern Diaspora: How the Great Migrations of Black and White Southerners Transformed America* (Chapel Hill, N.C., 2005), 50. Two-thirds of the *Defender*'s circulation was from outside Chicago.

26. "Immigration Law Is Help to Our Race," *Chicago Defender*, November 1, 1924.

27. W. E. B. Du Bois, "The Negro Mind Reaches Out," in *The New Negro: An Interpretation*, ed. Alain Locke (New York, 1925), 412. Booker T. Washington expressed similar misgivings regarding immigration. For more on black attitudes toward immigration, see Arnold Shankman, *Ambivalent Friends: Afro Americans View the Immigrant* (Westport, Conn., 1983) and Lawrence Fuchs, "The Reactions of Black Americans to Immigration," in *Immigration Reconsidered: History, Sociology, and Politics*, ed. Virginia Yans-McLaughlin (New York, 1990).

28. *Cong. Rec.*, 68th Cong., 1st Sess., April 8, 1924, 5899, 5911.

29. Ibid., 5920, 5897.

30. Ibid., 5912.

31. Ibid., 5858, 5893.

32. Ibid., 5923, 5870.

33. *Ozawa v. United States*, 160 U.S. 178 (1922); *United States v. Thind*, 261 U.S. 204.

34. *Cong. Rec.*, 68th Cong., 1st Sess., April 5, 1924, 5681; April 8, 1924, 5927.

35. Ibid. April 8, 1924, 5927.

36. Ibid., April 5, 1924, 5681. I also have to credit Gary Gerstle, *American Crucible: Race and Nation in the Twentieth Century* (Princeton, N.J., 2001), 120, for this point.

37. "Excluding Japanese," *Chicago Defender*, April 19, 1924.

38. *Cong. Rec.*, 68th Cong., 1st Sess., April 18, 1924, 6628.

39. Ibid., 6621, 6626.

40. Ibid., 6630, 6628.

41. Ibid., 6624.

42. Ibid., 6623, 6630.

43. Robert Divine, *American Immigration Policy, 1924–1952* (New Haven, Conn., 1957), 17. In the House, the Northeast voted against the bill 56–53, with the Midwest in favor by 125–15, the South 115–0, and the Far West 30–0. In the Senate, the Northeast supported the bill 10–5, the Midwest 13–0, the South 21–0, and the Far West 18–1.

44. See Mae Ngai, *Impossible Subjects: Illegal Aliens and the Making of America* (Princeton, N.J., 2004), 25–37, for more on how the national origins criteria were determined.

45. *Cong. Rec.*, 70th Cong., 2nd Sess., February 14, 1929, 3476; June 5, 1929, 2378.

46. *Cong. Rec.*, 70th Cong., 1st Sess., June 6, 1929, 2428; June 5, 1929, 2382; 2382.

47. Ibid., 70th Cong., 2nd Sess., March 3, 1929, 5190.

48. Ibid., June 6, 1929, 2428.

49. Ibid.

50. After agitation to reduce the number of Filipinos, Congress eventually limited immigration from the Philippines in 1934, giving the U.S. colony a quota of 50, the lowest of any nation. See Ngai, *Impossible Subjects*, 96–126.

51. *Whom Shall We Welcome: Report of the President's Commission on Immigration and Naturalization* (Washington, D.C., 1953), 99–101. I will discuss this report, initiated by President Truman, in greater detail in Chapter 5. Among other things, *Whom Shall We Welcome* detailed the history of the quota system.

52. Desmond King, *Making Americans: Immigration, Race, and the Origins of the Diverse Democracy* (Cambridge, Mass., 2000), 228.

53. Ngai, *Impossible Subjects*, 25

54. See Matt Guterl, *The Color of Race in America, 1900–1940* (Cambridge, Mass., 2001), 14–67.

55. Ngai, *Impossible Subjects*, 56–89.

56. House Committee on Immigration and Naturalization, *Immigration from Countries of the Western Hemisphere*, Report, 71st Cong., 2nd Sess., March 13, 1930 (Washington, D.C., 1930), 7.

57. Ibid., 2.

58. House Committee on Immigration and Naturalization, *Immigration from Countries of the Western Hemisphere*, Minority Report, 71st Cong., 2nd Sess., March 13, 1930 (Washington, D.C., 1930), 2.

59. Lothrop Stoddard, *Re-Forging America: The Story of Our Nationhood* (New York, 1927), 256–57.

60. Jonathan Zimmerman, *Whose America? Culture Wars in the Public Schools* (Cambridge, Mass., 2002). Zimmerman notes that ethnic groups and patriotic societies actually agreed on preserving traditional approaches to the American Revolution during the 1920s. For widely different reasons, both sides believed that questioning the motives of the nation's founders undermined the country.

61. U. S. Department of Commerce, Bureau of the Census, "Educational Attainment of the Population 25 Years Old and Over in the United States: 1940," April 25, 1942, http://www.uscensus.gov/, accessed August 13, 2011. See also Suzanne Mettler, *Soldiers to Citizens: The G.I. Bill and the Making of the Greatest Generation* (Oxford, 2005), 15–58; and Glenn C. Altschuler and Stuart M. Blumin, *The G.I. Bill: A New Deal for Veterans* (Oxford, 2009), 86–116.

62. The textbooks I have chosen to use are largely junior high school and high school textbooks.. Since there is no true "typical" sample of textbooks, I have relied on Frances Fitzgerald's bibliography from *America Revised: History Textbooks in the Twentieth Century* (Boston, 1979), to provide a respectable and established map to the most important books of the period. In each chronological period, I examined four to six books.

63. George Stephenson, *A History of American Immigration, 1820–1924* (Boston, 1926), 191–92.

64. Charles Beard and Mary Beard, *History of the United States* (New York, 1925), 411.

65. Rolla M. Tryon and Charles R. Lingley, *The American People and Nation* (Boston, 1927), 497, emphasis original.

66. Carl Russell Fish, *History of America* (New York, 1925), 466.

67. Henry Eldridge Bourne and Elbert Jay Benton, *A History of the United States* (Boston, 1925), 460.

68. Charles Beard and William C. Bagley, *History of the American People* (New York, 1928), 527, 529.

69. Tryon and Lingley, *The American People and Nation*, 498.

70. George Cohen, *The Jews in the Making of America* (Boston, 1924), 259.

Chapter 2. Contributionism in the Prewar Period

1. U.S. Department of Homeland Security, Office of Immigration Statistics, *2003 Yearbook of Immigration Statistics* (Washington, D.C., 2004), 13.

2. Diana Selig, *Americans All: The Cultural Gifts Movement* (Cambridge, Mass., 2008), 6: "It was *because* of the success of nativist efforts that the notion of cultural gifts gained widespread acceptance."

3. Arthur Hertzberg, *The Jews in America: Four Centuries of an Uneasy Encounter: A History* (New York, 1989), 285.

4. Ronald Bayor, *Neighbors in Conflict: The Irish, Germans, Jews, and Italians of New York City, 1929–1941* (Baltimore, 1978), 147. Roosevelt's appointments also helped incorporate these groups into American life: among other gestures, he nominated the first Italian American judge to the federal bench; Samuel Lubell, *The Future of American Politics* (New York, 1952), 79.

5. Franklin D. Roosevelt, *Nothing to Fear: The Selected Addresses of Franklin Roosevelt, 1932–1945* (Boston, 1946), 70, 71.

6. Franklin D. Roosevelt, *The Public Papers and Addresses of Franklin Roosevelt*, vol. 5, *The People Approve—1936* (New York, 1938), 545.

7. See James Pitt, *Adventures in Brotherhood* (New York, 1955), 40–62.

8. "Brotherhood Day," Brotherhood Day 1934, National Conference of Christians and Jews Collection, Social Welfare History Archives (SWHA), Elmer L. Andersen Library, University of Minnesota, Minneapolis.

9. Roosevelt, *Public Papers and Addresses*, vol. 3, *The Advance of Recovery and Reform, 1934*, 186.

10. Nicholas V. Montalto, *A History of the Intercultural Education Movement, 1924–1941* (New York, 1982), 110–15.

11. Ibid., 122.

12. Ibid., 68.

13. Louis Adamic, "Thirty Million New Americans," *Harper's Weekly*, November 1934, 685–86.

14. Ibid., 691–92.

15. Ibid., 693.

16. Ibid., 694.

17. Leo Ribuffo, *The Old Christian Right: The Protestant Far Right from the Great Depression to the Cold War* (Philadelphia, 1983); Leonard Dinnerstein, *Anti-Semitism in America* (New York, 1994), 105–31.

18. Philip Gleason, "Americans All," in *Speaking of Diversity: Language and Ethnicity in Twentieth-Century America* (Baltimore, 1992), 153–88; Richard Steele, "The War Against Intolerance: The Reformulation of American Nationalism," *Journal of American Ethnic History* 9 (Fall 1989): 9–35; Richard Weiss, "Ethnicity and Reform: Minorities and the Ambience of the Depression Years," *Journal of American History* 66 (December 1979): 566–85.

19. Montalto, *A History of the Intercultural Education Movement*, 149–70.

20. First program of *Americans All . . . Immigrants All*, November 13, 1938; Sound Recording of Educational Radio Programs, 1937–1951, ROE, RG 12, NACP.

21. Press release, February 1, 1939; Americans All, Promotion and Follow-Up; Special Programs and Projects; Records Relating to Radio Programs, 1935–1941, Americans . . . All, Immigrants . . . All-Brave New World; ROE, RG 12, NACP.

22. "What the Recordings Are About," Promotion and Follow-Up; Special Programs and Projects; Records Relating to Radio Programs; ROE, RG 12, NACP.

23. Press release, February 20, 1939; Promotion and Follow-Up; Special Programs and Projects; Records Relating to Radio Programs; ROE, RG 12, NACP.

24. Internal document, Promotion and Follow-Up; Special Programs and Projects; Records Relating to Radio Programs; ROE, RG 12, NACP.

25. Minutes of Meeting, September 28, 1928, Americans All; Special Programs and Projects; Records Relating to Radio Programs; ROE, RG 12, NACP.

26. Dorothea Seelye to William Boutwell (no date on document), Promotion and Follow-Up; Special Programs and Projects; Records Relating to Radio Programs, ROE, RG 12, NACP.

27. Chester S. Williams to Dr. Studebaker, February 3, 1939; Planning; Records of Special Programs and Projects; Records Relating to Radio Programs; ROE, RG 12, NACP.

28. Boutwell to Studebaker, February 9, 1939; Planning; Records of Special Programs and Projects; Records Relating to Radio Programs; ROE, RG 12, NACP.

29. Montalto, *History of the Intercultural Education Movement*, 165.

30. Though the celebration became a week in 1939, many materials still refer to Brotherhood Day. "Plans and Programs for Brotherhood Day," 1, NCCJ, Box 5, Brotherhood Day/Week 1939, SWHA.

31. Ibid., 1, 5.

32. Ibid., 1.

33. Ibid., 7–8.

34. Ibid., 1, 34, 4.

35. Eric Foner, *Story of American Freedom* (New York, 1998), 212. According to Foner, the Popular Front suggested, "ethnic and racial diversity was the glory of American society," adding that "Museum exhibitions, murals sponsored by the Works Progress Administration, the federally sponsored 'people's theater,' and Hollywood films all rediscovered the American people and expanded its definition to include the new immigrants and their children, and even non-whites." For more on the Popular Front, see Michael Denning, *The Cultural Front: The Laboring of American Culture in the Twentieth Century* (London, 1996).

36. David Kennedy, *Freedom from Fear: The American People in Depression and War* (New York, 1999), 761.

37. "Radio: Bravos," *Time*, November 20, 1939, 59.

38. "American Common," July 30, 1940, "World Fair's Bulletin, # 1" Century of Progress World Exposition Collection, Group 820, Box 38, Folder 1, Yale University Library, Manuscripts and Archives, New Haven, Connecticut.

39. Robert Rydell, *World of Fairs: The Century-of-Progress Expositions* (Chicago, 1993), 185–86.

40. "World's Fair's Bulletin, #1."

41. "American Common," *Common Ground* 1, 1 (Autumn 1940): 78.

42. "Teaching the New York World's Fair, No. 1," Century of Progress World Exposition Collection.

43. "Gala Program Set For Week At Fair," *New York Times*, October 5, 1940.

44. Milton Bracker, "Jinx of Weather at Fair Broken," *New York Times*, July 7, 1940.

45. "Cut-Rate Tickets Jump Fair Crowds," *New York Times*, October 7, 1940.

46. "Negro Week on the American Common," 4, Century of Progress World Exposition Collection, Group 820, Box 38, Folder 1.

47. "NAACP Press Release" and "Letter to Gardner Cobb," NAACP Papers, Part I, Box C418, Folder 9, Library of Congress (LOC).

48. "Job Discrimination at N.Y. World's Fair Hit by N.A.A.C.P.," NAACP Papers, Part I, Box C418, Folder 9, LOC.

49. "Letter to Thomas Dewey," NAACP Papers, Part I, Box 418, Folder 9, LOC.

50. Montalto, *A History of the Intercultural Education Movement*, 62–67.

51. Louis Adamic, "The St. Paul Festival of Nations," *Common Ground* 1, 4 (Summer 1941): 103–4.

52. Montalto, *A History of the Intercultural Education Movement*, 66.

53. Adamic, "The St. Paul Festival of Nations," 106, 108.

54. *Gateway to Citizenship*, 1948, 41; Citizenship Through the Use of Class Materials; Citizenship Training Textbooks, 1918–55; Educational and Americanization Files; Records of INS, RG 85; National Archives Building (NAB), Washington, D.C.

55. Press release, April 30, 1941; AJC Records, RG 347.17.10 Gen-10, Box 98, Holidays and Holydays, 1941–1954, I'm An American Day, YIVO Archives, American Jewish Historical Society (AJHS), New York.

56. NBC, *I'm an American*, August 3, 1940, Museum of TV and Radio (MTR).

57. Ibid., June 8, 1940, MTR.

58. Ibid., February 2, 1941, MTR.

59. Ibid., August 3, 1940, MTR.

60. Ibid., June 8, 1940, MTR.

61. Ibid., March 3, 1941, MTR.

62. Ibid., February 2, 1941, MTR.

63. Nathan Glazer, *We Are All Multiculturalists Now* (New York, 1997), 87.

64. George Earl Freeland and James Truslow Adams, *America and the New Frontier* (New York, 1936), 449, 445, 457.

65. John Holladay Latane, *The History of the American People* (Boston, 1938), 615.

66. Leon H. Canfield, Howard Wilder, Frederic L. Paxson, Ellis Merton Coulter, and Nelson P. Mead, *The United States in the Making* (Boston, 1937), 607.

67. Ibid., 608. The authors also note that Californians were displeased with the small immigration of Filipinos to their state in the 1920s and 1930s, 671.

68. Ralph Volney Harlow, *Story of America* (New York, 1937), 736.

69. Latane, *The History of the American People*, 614.

70. *Federal Textbook on Citizenship Training, Part III: Our Nation*, 207; Department of Labor Textbooks; Citizenship Training Textbooks, 1918–55; Education and Americanization Files; Records of the INS, RG 85, NAB.

71. "Out of the Many—One: A Plan for Intercultural Education," 4; Sec Series Service Bureau Cole; Special Programs and Projects; Records Relating to Radio Programs; ROE, RG 12, NACP. The pamphlet contained no exact date.

72. Ibid., 10–11.

73. Selig, *Americans All*, 151.

74. Deborah Dash Moore, *At Home in America: Second Generation New York Jews* (New York, 1991), 120: "By the late 1930s, with the overt anti-Semitism of the Christian Front spreading from the city's streets to its schools, the Board of Education needed to define the public school as a bastion of tolerance."

75. Eugene C. Barker, William E. Dodd, and Henry Steele Commager, *Our Nation's Development* (Evanston, Ill., 1934), 627.

76. Eugene C. Barker and Henry Steele Commager, *Our Nation* (Evanston, Ill., 1941), 606, 614, 617.

77. Ibid., 621, 625.

78. Marcus Lee Hansen, *The Atlantic Migration, 1607–1860* (Cambridge, Mass., 1940).

79. Ibid., 12.

80. Marcus Lee Hansen, *The Immigrant in American History* (New York, 1940), 151.

81. Ibid., 152.

82. Carl Wittke, *We Who Built America: The Saga of the Immigrant* (New York, 1939), 362.

83. Ibid., 471.

84. Ibid., 456.

85. Ibid., 406–7.

86. Ibid., 438.

87. E. P. Hutchinson, *Legislative History of American Immigration Policy* (Philadelphia, 1981), 214–50: "On the whole, however, there was notably little legislative reaction in the form of immigration bills to the domestic and international problems of the time, compared with the amount of legislative activity in preceding and following periods." Referring to the Great Depression and the international situation, he adds, "there were other and much more pressing problems to occupy Congress' attention."

88. Martin Dies, "The Immigration Crisis," *Saturday Evening Post*, April 20, 1935, 105.

89. For a summary of Wagner-Rogers fight, see Robert Divine, *American Immigration Policy* (New Haven, Conn., 1957), 92–109.

90. J. Joseph Huthmacher, *Senator Robert F. Wagner and the Rise of Urban Liberalism* (New York, 1968), 249.

91. In their minds, FDR's unwillingness to support the bill was simply a response to overwhelming public opposition. Leonard Dinnerstein wrote, "Roosevelt . . . was unwilling to alienate significant segments of the public or the Congress for what he considered a divisive issue. Only overwhelming encouragement from a broad segment of the population and/or Congress would move him to reconsider his stance." While suggesting that FDR sympathized with the plight of European Jews, Doris Kearns Goodwin agreed with Dinnerstein, adding, "it was one thing to sympathize with the plight of the Jewish refugees and quite another to pit his presidency against the xenophobic, anti-Semitic climate of the country in the late 1930s and early '40s. This Roosevelt was unwilling to do." Dinnerstein, *Anti-Semitism in America*, 143; Doris Kearns Goodwin, *No Ordinary Time: Franklin and Eleanor Roosevelt: The Home Front in World War Two* (New York, 1994), 102.

92. *Fortune*, April 1939, 102; July 1938, 80.

93. Joint Hearings Before a Subcommittee of the Committee on Immigration, Senate and a Subcommittee of the Committee on Immigration and Naturalization, House, 76th Cong., 1st Sess., *Admission of German Refugee Children* (Joint Hearings) (Washington, D.C., 1939), 17, 21.

94. Ibid., 20.

95. Hearings Before the Committee on Immigration and Naturalization, House, 76th Cong., 1st Sess., *Admission of German Refugee Children* (House Hearings) (Washington, D.C., 1939), 92.

96. House Hearings, 11.

97. Joint Hearings, 198; House Hearings, 133.

98. House Hearings, 227; Joint Hearings, 227.

99. "Let's Keep Our Immigration Law," *Chicago Defender*, May 27, 1939.

100. Joint Hearings, 208, 135.

101. Ibid., 232, 228.

102. House Hearings, 233; Joint Hearings, 187.

103. Summary of Divine, *American Immigration Policy*, 102.

Chapter 3. The Quest for Tolerance and Unity

1. Louis Adamic, "No 'Hyphens' This Time," *New York Times Magazine*, November 1, 1942, 18.

2. David Kennedy, *Over Here: The First World War and American Society* (New York, 1980), 45–92.

3. U.S. Department of Commerce, Bureau of the Census, *Historical Statistics of the United States: Colonial Times to 1970, Part 1* (Washington, 1976), 14.

4. Adamic, "No 'Hyphens,'" 18, 38.

5. Ibid., 38.

6. David Bennett, *Party of Fear: From Nativist Movements to the New Right in American History* (New York, 1995), 285: "By war's end, nativism was all but finished." John Blum discussed the greater acceptance of Jews and Italians in *V Was for Victory: Politics and American Culture During World War II* (New York, 1976), 154, 175: "More important, the President's order [ending the enemy alien status of Italians] marked the beginning of the end of Italian-American separatism. As in the past, Italian-Americans, like Irish or Polish or Scandinavian Americans, preserved much of their ethnicity, but henceforth, increasingly, they did so from choice rather than necessity." About Jews, he echoed this sentiment: "Nevertheless, wartime prosperity, the increasing geographic mobility of Americans, the homogenizing effects of shared dangers in battle, the essential contributions of Jewish refugee scientists, and the stunned reactions to the Nazi gas chambers, continued to facilitate for American Jews acceptance by the society in which they lived." These works and others like them have influenced books that synthesize long periods of American history. Eric Foner concurred in *The Story of American Freedom* (New York, 1998), 237: "By the end of the war, the new immigrant groups had been fully accepted as ethnic Americans, rather than members of distinctive and inferior 'races'." See also Desmond King, *The Liberty of Strangers: Making the American Nation* (Oxford, 2005), 83–109.

7. Richard Polenberg, *One Nation Divisible: Class, Race, and Ethnicity in the United States Since 1938* (New York, 1980), 54.

8. Louis Adamic, *A Nation of Nations* (New York, 1944), 5–6.

9. *New York Evening Post*, March 25, 1943.

10. Polenberg, *One Nation Divisible*, 55.

11. Matthew Frye Jacobson, *Whiteness of a Different Color: European Immigrants and the Alchemy of Race* (Cambridge, Mass, 1998), 91–135.

12. Werner Sollors, *Beyond Ethnicity: Consent and Descent in American Culture* (New York, 1986), 23.

13. Ibid., 56.

14. *INS Monthly Review*, May 1944, 11; Speech Materials; Public Relations Files, 1940–54; Education and Americanization Files; Records of the INS, RG 85, NAB.

15. Polenberg, *One Nation Divisible*, 72–73.

16. Thomas Sugrue, *The Origins of the Urban Crisis: Race and Inequality in Postwar Detroit* (Princeton, N.J., 1996), 34–88; Arnold Hirsch, *The Making of the Second Ghetto: Race and Housing in Chicago, 1940–1960* (New York, 1983).

17. Studs Terkel, *"The Good War": An Oral History of World War Two* (New York, 1984), 138.

18. *The Life of Hank Greenberg*, dir. Aviva Kempner (Fox, 1999).

19. John Dower, *War Without Mercy: Race and Power in the Pacific War* (New York, 1986), 3–32.

20. Scholars of Asian Americans believe that, despite the Japanese American internment, the war had some liberalizing impact. Roger Daniels wrote, "None of this should be forgotten; at the same time, none of this should be allowed to obscure the fact that, despite its degradations, World War II marks a positive turning point in the Asian American experience." Daniels, *Asian America: The Chinese and Japanese in the United States Since 1850* (Seattle, 1988), 282.

21. *Time*, December 22, 1941, 33.

22. Reed Ueda, "The Changing Path to Citizenship: Ethnicity and Naturalization During World War II," in *The War and American Culture*, ed. Lewis Erenberg and Susan Hirsch (Chicago, 1996), 208–12.

23. Franklin D. Roosevelt, *The Public Papers and Addresses of Franklin D. Roosevelt*, vol. 12, *The Tide Turns, 1943* (New York, 1950), 548.

24. Allan M. Winkler, *The Politics of Propaganda: The Office of War Information, 1942–1945* (New Haven, Conn.,1978), 1–6.

25. Polenberg, *One Nation Divisible*, 46.

26. Roosevelt, *Public Papers and Addresses*, vol. 11, *Humanity on the Defensive*, 6.

27. Franklin D. Roosevelt, *Nothing to Fear: The Selected Addresses of Franklin Delano Roosevelt* (New York, 1946), 321.

28. Roosevelt, *The Tide Turns*, 27.

29. Ibid., 103.

30. Roosevelt, *Nothing to Fear*, 431–32.

31. OWI poster, 44-PA-1869, Records of the Office of Government Reports, RG 44; NACP.

32. Ibid., 44-PA-414A, 2151.

33. Ibid., 44-PA-2219.

34. Ibid., 44-PA-1477, 660.

35. Ibid., 44- PA-352.

36. Ibid., 44-PA-2049, 165.

37. Ibid., 44-PA-660.

38. Ibid., 179-WP-50.

39. http://digital.library.northwestern.edu/wwii-posters/img/ww1647-43.jpg, accessed August 22, 2011.

40. Address by Alan Cranston, Chief, Foreign Language Division, Office of War Information, Before the Editors and Publishers of Foreign Language Newspapers in New York City, August 25, 1942; Speech Materials; Public Relations Files, 1940–54; Education and Americanization Files; Records of the INS, RG 85, NAB.

41. Ibid.

42. *Why We Fight*, dir. Frank Capra (Special Service Division, Army Service Forces, 1942–44), episode 7.

43. *The House I Live In*, dir. Mervyn LeRoy (RKO, 1945).

44. Ibid.

45. African American singer Paul Robeson often performed this version of the song. It is not exactly clear when he began, but he must have started sometime after summer 1942, as the lyrics contain references to the Battle of Midway (June 1942); *Paul Robeson: The Original Recording of Ballad for Americans and Great Songs of Faith, Love and Patriotism* (Vanguard, 1989 ed.).

46. See Thomas Doherty, *Projections of War: Hollywood, American Culture, and World War II* (New York, 1999), 139–48, and Gary Gerstle, *American Crucible: Race and Nation in the Twentieth Century* (Princeton, 2001), 204–10, for a thorough look at these films.

47. "Letter from Walter White to Elmer Davis," NAACP Papers, Part II, Box A462, Folder 5, LOC. The OWI worked closely with Hollywood on the content of these films during the war.

48. *Gung Ho*, dir. Ray Enright (Republic, 1943).

49. *Guadalcanal Diary*, dir. Lewis Seller (Fox, 1943).

50. "America's Big Idea," 2, NCCJ, Brotherhood Week 1943, Box 5, Social Welfare History Archives (SWHA), Elmer L. Andersen Library, University of Minnesota, Minneapolis.

51. "A Call to the Churches of America," NCCJ, Box 5, Brotherhood Week 1943, SWHA.

52. "Brotherhood Week Broadcast #1," 5, NCCJ, Box 5, Brotherhood Week 1943, SWHA.

53. "America's Big Idea," 5.

54. "Brief Suggestions on Citizenship Recognition Ceremonies for 'I'm an American Day Committees'," INS, Holidays and Holydays, I'm an American Day, 1941–54, YIVO Institute for Jewish Research (YIVO), AJHS, New York.

55. "I'm an American Day," 5/1/43, AJC Records, RG 347.17.10, Gen-10, Box 98, Holidays and Holydays, 1941–54, I'm an American Day, YIVO, AJHS. There were speeches and editorials in the same folders, and it was not always possible to differentiate one from the other.

56. "I'm an American Day," 1944, 4, AJC Records, RG 347.17.10, Gen-10, Box 98, Holidays and Holydays, 1942–50, I'm an American Day, Articles, Editorials, and Speeches, YIVO, AJHS.

57. Ibid., 1.

58. "Suggested Spot Announcements for I Am an American Day, Sunday, May 20, 1945," 2, AJC Records, RG 347.17.10, Gen-10, Box 98, Holidays and Holydays, 1945–49, I'm an American Day, Radio and Television, YIVO, AJHS.

59. Papers of the NAACP, Part II, General Office File, 1940–55, Box A319, Folder 3, "I'm an American Day," 1941–49, LOC.

60. Gunnar Myrdal, *An American Dilemma: The Negro Problem and Modern Democracy* (New York, 1944), 997, 1004.

61. K. Scott Wong, *Americans First: Chinese Americans and the Second World War* (Cambridge, Mass., 2005), 87–88.

62. Stuart Svonkin, *Jews Against Prejudice: American Jews and the Fight for Civil Liberties* (New York, 1997), 64: "Whereas the Service Bureau under DuBois (1934–1941) had stressed the distinctive cultural contributions of particular racial and ethnic groups . . . the reconstituted bureau emphasized 'unity and understanding among all cultural groups,' a message specifically designed to fit wartime demands for social cohesion."

63. *AJC Reporter*, April 1944, 6.

64. Ibid., May 1944, 6.

65. Ibid., April 1944, 6.

66. "Prejudice!—Roadblock to Progress," *Common Ground* 6, 1 (Autumn 1945): 24.

67. Ibid., 25, 28.

68. Ibid., 27, 30.

69. Deborah Dash Moore, *GI Jews: How World War II Changed a Generation* (Cambridge, Mass., 2004), 118–55.

70. *Anti-Defamation League Bulletin*, October 1952, 3.

71. Samuel H. Flowerman, speech at Waldorf Towers, November 30, 1945, AJC Records, RG 16, DIS-15, Scientific Research Subject Files, General Subject Files, 1945–48, Blaustein Library (BL), New York.

72. "Details of Plan," 1945, 2, AJC Records, RG 347.17.10, Gen-10, Box 168, Mass Media, 1944–48, Intergroup Relations, YIVO, AJHS.

73. Ibid., 4.

74. *AJC Reporter*, November 1945, 2.

75. "Brotherhood Week Is a Fighting Week," January 9, 1945, AJC Records, RG 347.17.10, Gen-10, Box 97, Holidays and Holydays, 1946–60, National Brotherhood Week, YIVO, AJHS.

76. Ibid.

77. "Prejudice Is Bad Business," 4, AJC Records, RG 347.17.10, Gen-10, Mass Media, Bigotry and Prejudice, Educational Kit-WWB, YIVO, AJHS.

78. Ibid., 4.

79. *Pride of the Marines*, dir. Delmer Daves (Warner Brothers, 1945).

80. "Program Information Exchange: Recommendation for an Advertising Campaign on American Unity," 1946, 1, AJC Records, RG 347.17, Gen-10, Box 14, Mass Media, Bigotry and Prejudice, Advertising and Public Relations, 1946–1951, YIVO, AJHS.

81. Ibid.

82. Flowerman speech, 16, BL.

83. "Brotherhood Week in 1946," 1, NCCJ, Box 5, Brotherhood Week 1946, SWHA.

84. "Problem No.1 for Americans," NCCJ, Box 5, Brotherhood Week 1946, SWHA.

85. "Brotherhood Week in 1946," 4.

86. "The Good World of the Future," 2, 11/14//45, AJC Records, RG 347.17.10, Gen-10, Box 97, Holidays and Holydays, 1945–59, Brotherhood Week, Radio and Television, YIVO, AJHS.

87. "Problem No.1 for Americans."

88. Ibid.

89. "U.S. Justices Plead for Tolerance," February 14, 1946, Universal Newsreels, RG 200, 19–47, NACP.

90. "Problem No. 1 for Americans."

91. "Letter from Truman to Clinchy," NCCJ, Box 5, Brotherhood Week 1946, SWHA.

92. "'I'm an American Day,' a Fact Sheet for the Use of I'm an American Day Committees," INS, 1, AJC Records, RG 347.17.10, Gen-10, Box 98, Holidays and Holydays, 1941–54, I'm an American Day, YIVO, AJHS.

93. Ibid., 3

94. Papers of the NAACP, Part II, General Office File, 1940–45, Box A319, Folder 3, "I'm an American Day," 1941–49, LOC.

95. "Memo from Minnesota Jewish Council," May 29, 1947, AJC Records, RG 347.17.10, Gen-10, Box 98, Holidays and Holydays, 1941–54, I'm an American Day, YIVO, AJHS.

96. Ibid.

97. "Eighth Annual Welcome to New Citizens," May 18, 1947, AJC Records, RG 347.17, Gen-10, Box 98, Holidays and Holydays, 1941–54, I'm an American Day, YIVO, AJHS.

98. Many of the editorials were identified as "suggested" editorials. "The Watchword Is Vigilance," 1, May 18, 1947, AJC Records, RG 347.17.10, Gen-10, Box 98, Holidays and Holydays, 1942–50, I'm an American Day, Articles, Editorials, and Speeches, YIVO, AJHS.

99. I found a copy of this play, written by Lynn Rhodes, in the AJC files for I'm an American Day 1948. I am assuming they used it as a tool for that day. *Do You Know the Score?* 1948, AJC Records, RG 347.17.10, Gen-10, Box 98, Holidays and Holydays, 1945–49, I'm an American Day, Radio and Television, YIVO, AJHS.

100. Ibid., 12.

101. Ibid., 16.

102. "Dress Parade," *Common Ground* 9, 3 (Spring 1949): 52.

103. "Memo on Exhibit on Superstition, Fear, and Prejudice," October 5, 1946, 5, AJC Records, RG 347.17.10, Gen-10, Box 14, Exhibits, Bigotry, and Prejudice, 49–61, YIVO, AJHS.

104. *AJC Reporter*, September 1948, 5.

105. The Brooklyn Dodgers, who ended Jim Crow in baseball by signing Jackie Robinson, played in the National League.

106. "Textual Sequence for Exhibit on Superstition, Fear, and Prejudice," 10–8-48, 3, AJC Records, RG 347.17.10, Gen-10, Box 14, Exhibits, Bigotry, and Prejudice, 49–61, YIVO, AJHS.

107. *AJC Reporter*, September 1948, 5.

108. K. R. M. Short, "Hollywood Fights Anti-Semitism," in *Feature Films as History*, ed. Short (Knoxville, Tenn., 1981), 157–89.

109. *Crossfire*, dir. Ed Dmytryk (RKO, 1947).

110. *Gentlemen's Agreement*, dir. Elia Kazan (Fox, 1947).

111. *Crossfire*.

112. *Gentlemen's Agreement*.

113. Ibid.; Gerald L. K. Smith was a populist, anti-Semitic demagogue in the 1930s and 1940s.

114. Ibid.

115. *Crossfire*.

116. For more on cooperation between Jewish and African American groups, see Cheryl Greenberg, *Troubling the Waters: Black-Jewish Relations in the American Century* (Princeton, N. J., 2006).

117. "Resolutions Adopted by the National Conference of the NAACP, Washington, D.C., June 28, 1947," Papers of the NAACP, Part I, 1909–1950, Reel 12, Group II/Series A/Box 40, 1947 Annual Convention, File: Resolutions, 0119, "Resolutions Adopted," Rhode Island College, Providence.

118. "Address by Rabbi Irving Miller to the 41st Annual Convention of the National Association for the Advancement of Colored People, Boston, Massachusetts, July 21, 1950," Papers of the NAACP, Part I, 1909–1950, "Address of Rabbi Irving Miler."

119. "1946–1947 Ad Council Annual Report," Ad Council Annual Reports, 1942–2000, Record Series (RS) 13/2/202, Box 1, Folder: Ad Council Annual Report, 1946–47, University of Illinois Archives (UIA), Urbana. In 1949, the AD Council noted in an introduction to proofs of these ads that "In the past few years newspapers in the United States have run thousands of ads which are especially prepared by volunteer advertising agencies."

120. Wendy Wall, *Inventing the "American Way": The Politics of Consensus from the New Deal to the Civil Rights Movement* (Oxford, 2008), 172–87.

121. "Proof of Ad Council Ads," Ad Council Historical File, 1942–97, RS 12/2//207, Box 7, United America (Anti-Prejudice, 1949), UIA.

122. "Do You Know a Rumor?—When You Hear One," Ad Council Historical File, 1942–97, RS 12/2//207, Box 7, United America (Anti-Prejudice, 1949), UIA.

123. "How to Commit Suicide," Ad Council Historical File, 1942–97, RS 12/2//207.

124. See Mary L. Dudziak, *Cold War Civil Rights: Race and the Image of American Democracy* (Princeton, N.J., 2000); Thomas Bortelsmann, *The Cold War and the Color Line: American Race Relations in the Global Arena* (Cambridge, Mass., 2001).

125. "Do You Know the Score?" 11, YIVO, AJHS.

126. "I'm an American Day, 30 Second Spot," AJC Records, RG 347.17.10, Gen-10, Holidays and Holydays, 1945–49, I'm an American Day Radio and Television, YIVO, AJHS.

127. "Letter from Mark Kinsey to Joseph J. Wolfson," January 12, 1949, AJC Records, RG 347.17.10, Gen-10, Holidays and Holydays, 1945–57.

128. Ibid.

Chapter 4. How Much Did the War Change America?

1. Joe McCarthy, "GI Vision of a Better America," *New York Times Magazine*, August 5, 1945, 10.

2. Anthony Chen, *The Fifth Freedom: Jobs, Politics, and Civil Rights in the United States, 1941–1972* (Princeton, N.J., 2009), 118. Though some states passed fair employment laws, the combination of a divided public opinion and organized campaigns by conservative and business organizations prevented many others from passing such measures (115–69).

3. Charles Herbert Stember, *Jews in the Mind of America* (New York, 1966), 131.

4. Roger Daniels, *Asian America: Chinese and Japanese in the United States Since 1850* (Seattle, 1988), 293–316.

5. Alan Brinkley, *Voices of Protest: Huey Long, Father Coughlin, and the Great Depression* (New York, 1982), 219.

6. Chester M. Morgan, *Redneck Liberal: Theodore G. Bilbo and the New Deal* (Baton Rouge, 1985).

7. "Footnotes on Headliners," *New York Times*, September 1, 1940,

8. *Cong. Rec.*, 79th Cong., 1st Sess., June 27, 1945, 6809, 6812. Walter Winchell was a prominent radio commentator at the time.

9. *The Nation*, July 7, 1945, 2.

10. *Cong. Rec.*, 79th Cong., 1st Sess., June 27, 1945, 7995.

11. *New York Post*, July 27, 1945.

12. *Cong. Rec.*, 79th Cong., 1st Sess., appendix, August 1, 1945, 3702–3.

13. "Mississippi Mud," *Newsweek*, August 6, 1945, 39.

14. "'Dear Dago,'" *Commonweal*, August 10, 1945, 397.

15. *The Nation*, August 4, 1945, 101.

16. "Senator Bilbo Assailed," *New York Times*, August 10, 1945.

17. "Senators Praise O'Dwyer," *New York Times*, August 11, 1945.

18. "Full Veterans' Aid Asked by O'Dwyer," *New York Times*, August 17, 1945.

19. "Bill Mauldin Says . . . ," AJC Records, RG 347.17.10, Gen-10, Box 14, Mass Media, Bigotry and Prejudice: Cartoons, 45–62, YIVO, AJHS.

20. *ADL Bulletin*, November 1948, 5.

21. Aristide Zohlberg, *A Nation by Design: Immigration Policy and the Fashioning of America* (Cambridge, 2006), 302. The Truman figures are for 1945 to summer 1951.

22. James Patterson, *Grand Expectations: The United States, 1945–1974* (New York, 1996), 4–5.

23. Ibid., 71.

24. *The Gallup Poll: Public Opinion 1935–1971*, vol. 1 (New York, 1972), 555.

25. "Immigration: At the Bars," *Newsweek*, December 30, 1946, 23.

26. "Congressmen Found Cool to Truman's Plan for Admission of More European Refugees," *New York Times*, August 18, 1946.

27. Ibid.

28. Leonard Dinnerstein, *America and the Survivors of the Holocaust* (New York, 1982), 118.

29. Immigration: At the Bars."

30. "Revercomb Urges Quota Retention," *New York Times*, December 31, 1946.

31. Dinnerstein, *America and the Survivors of the Holocaust*, 115.

32. "Revercomb Urges Quota Retention."

33. Dinnerstein, *America and the Survivors of the Holocaust*, 117–36.

34. Ibid., 129.

35. "Talk and the Closed Door," *Newsweek*, May 10, 1948, 23.

36. *Cong. Rec.*, 80th Cong., 2nd Sess., May 20, 1948, 6182; June 2, 1948, 6900.

37. *Cong. Rec.*, 80th Cong., 2nd Sess., June 2, 1948, 6892, 6893.

38. *Cong. Rec.*, 80th Cong., 2nd Sess., June 2, 1948, 6894.

39. *ADL Bulletin*, June–July 1948, 2.

40. *Cong. Rec.*, 80th Cong., 2nd Sess., May 27, 1948, 6585.

41. *ADL Bulletin*, June–July 1948, 2.

42. Half the DPs who entered from an individual country were counted against the future quota for that nation. Under this "mortgaging," some country's quotas were technically used up until the next century.

43. "DP Discrimination," *New Republic*, June 14, 1948, 7.

44. *The Public Papers of the Presidents of the United States: Harry S. Truman, 1948* (Washington, D.C., 1964), 383.

45. Dinnerstein, *America and the Survivors of the Holocaust*, 176.

46. *Cong. Rec.*, 80th Cong., 2nd Sess., May 20, 1948, 6187.

47. John Holladay Latane, *The History of the American People* (Boston, 1948), 613–17; Leon H. Canfield, Howard B. Wilder, Frederic L. Paxson, Ellis Merton Coulter, and Nelson P. Mead, *The United States in the Making* (Boston, 1946).

48. George Freeland and James Thurlow Adams, *America's Progress in Civilization* (New York, 1949), 519. Harold Underwood Faulkner, Tyler Kepner, and Edward H. Merrill, *History of the American Way* (New York, 1950) noted that "The largest immigration from the South, however, has been from Mexico. . . . With few exceptions they are unskilled workers, laborers on railroads, in the mines, or on farms and ranches" (33).

49. Ralph Volney Harlow, *Story of America* (New York, 1947), 414, 416.

50. Ibid., 736.

51. Ibid., 416.

52. Glenn Moon, *Story of Our Land and People* (New York, 1949), 454.

53. Faulkner et al., *History of the American Way*, 36.

54. This is an excerpt of the speech that appeared in the January 1950 *AJC Reporter*, 6.

55. Louis Adamic, "American History as a Record and a Process," *Common Ground* 8, 4 (Summer 1948): 21.

56. Samuel H. Flowerman, speech at Waldorf Towers, November 30, 1945, AJC Records, RG 16, DIS-15, Scientific Research Subject Files, General Subject Files, 1945–48, Blaustein Library (BL), New York, 9. Studies during the war revealed a similar phenomenon: 65 percent of soldiers surveyed in 1942 agreed with the statement "We are in the war to fight until we can guarantee democratic liberties to all the world." But when a cross-section of American soldiers in July 1943 were asked to provide their own rationale for what the conflict was about, only 15 percent expressed "relatively idealistic concepts," while 36 percent had no response, 24 percent said "relatively defensive concepts," and 16 percent offered brief slogans such as "peace," "freedom," or "victory." Samuel Stouffer et al., *The American Soldier: Adjustment During Army Life*, vol. 1 (New York, 1949), 432, 436.

57. Flowerman speech, 10–11.

58. "Summary of the Chicago Veteran Study," 1–2, AJC Records, RG 16, DIS-15, Scientific Research Study Files, Studies and Polls, Summary of Studies—1948, BL.

59. Leonard Dinnerstein, *Anti-Semitism in America* (New York, 1994), 152: "To what extent the knowledge of Hitler's slaughter of six million Jews contributed to the desire to curb bigotry is impossible to state but after 1945 millions of Christian Americans became more cautious in expressing negative reactions to Jews." Steve Lawson, *Running for Freedom: Civil Rights and Black Politics in America Since 1941* (New York, 1991), 10: "Fighting Hitler's atrocities abroad shifted the focus of racism at home from an economic to a moral issue, prompting liberals to try to prove that their society did not behave like Nazi Germany."

60. Deborah Lipstadt touches on this theme in *Beyond Belief: The American Press and the Coming of the Holocaust, 1933–1945* (New York, 1986), 262. "Both the Allies and the American press repeatedly depicted the Jewish victims simply as nationals of countries. This helped cloud the public's perceptions of the Nazi war against the Jews." Peter Novick agreed in *The Holocaust in American Life* (Boston, 1999), 64–65.

61. Edward R. Murrow, *In Search of Light: The Broadcasts of Edward R. Murrow, 1938–1961* (New York, 1967) 91, 92, 94.

62. Ibid., 92.

63. Gene Currivan, "Nazi Death Factory Shocks Germans on a Forced Tour," *New York Times*, April 18, 1945.

64. "Nazi Atrocities," Universal Newsreels, RG 200, Vol. 18–393, NACP.

65. "To Look at Horror," *Newsweek,* April 28, 1945, 34–35.

66. "Germany," *Time,* April 30, 1945, 38.

67. "Nazi Atrocities," *New Republic,* April 30, 1945, 572.

68. Harold Denny, "'The World Must Not Forget,'" *New York Times Magazine,* May 6, 1945.

69. C. L. Sulzberger, "Oswiecim Killings Placed at 4,000,000," *New York Times,* May 8, 1945.

70. "U.S. Editors Back, Urge Harsh Peace," *New York Times,* May 9, 1945.

71. Novick, *The Holocaust in American Life,* 66.

72. Stember, *Jews in the Mind of America,* 143, 144.

Chapter 5. The Reemergence of Contributionism

1. James T. Patterson, *Grand Expectations: The United States, 1945–1974* (New York, 1996), 70, 72, 77.

2. Ellen Schrecker, *Many Are the Crimes: McCarthyism in America* (Boston, 1998); Stephen J. Whitfield, *The Culture of the Cold War* (Baltimore, 1991).

3. David Caute, *The Great Fear: The Anti-Communist Purge Under Truman and Eisenhower* (New York, 1979), 11: "It was indeed a desperate time, a time when the words 'democracy' and 'freedom' resembled gaudy advertising slogans suspended above an intersection where panic, prejudice, suspicion, cowardice, and demagogic ambition constantly collided in a bedlam of recriminations."

4. Alan Brinkley, "The Illusion of Unity in Cold War Culture," in *Rethinking Cold War Culture,* ed. Peter Kuznick and James Gilbert (Washington, D.C., 2001), 72. Brinkley diminishes the Cold War's impact on American culture, suggesting that "American society and culture would likely have looked much the same in the 1940s and 1950s with or without the Cold War."

5. Peter Filene, "'Cold War Culture' Doesn't Say It All," in *Rethinking Cold War Culture,* 169.

6. See, among others, Gil Loescher and John Scanlan, *Calculated Kindness: Refugees and America's Half-Open Door, 1945 to the Present* (New York, 1986).

7. "Robert Montgomery Speech for Brotherhood Week" 5, 1, National Conference of Christians and Jews Collection (NCCJ), Box 5, Brotherhood Week 1952, SWHA, Elmer L. Andersen Library, University of Minnesota, Minneapolis.

8. Sample Editorial, "Brotherhood: An Imminent Necessity for Survival," NCCJ, Box 5, Brotherhood Week 1952, SWHA.

9. "Quotable Material," NCCJ, Box 5, Brotherhood Week 1950, SWHA.

10. Mary Dudziak, *Cold War Civil Rights: Race and the Image of American Democracy* (Princeton, 2000); Thomas Borstelmann, *The Cold War and the Color Line: American Race Relations in the Global Arena* (Cambridge, Mass., 2001).

11. "Remarks by Eric Johnston," 7, NCCJ, Box 5, Brotherhood Week 1950, SWHA.

12. *Sands of Iwo Jima,* dir. Allan Dwan (Republic, 1949).

13. *Go for Broke!*, dir. Robert Pirosh (MGM, 1951). See Chapter 3 for more on *Crossfire* and *Gentlemen's Agreement.*

14. Stanley S. Jacobs, *ADL Bulletin*, "The Nisei Making the Grade," October 1956, 4–5.

15. "58-second spots for Brotherhood Week," AJC Records, RG 347.17.10, Gen-10, Holidays and Holydays, 1945–59, Brotherhood Week, Radio and Television, YIVO (AJHS from now on).

16. Ibid.

17. "That's My Boy," Ad Council Historical File, 1942–1997, RS 13/2/207, Box 8, 528: Group Prejudice Campaign, February 1951, University of Illinois Archives, Urbana.

18. Bureau of the Census, *Historical Statistics of the United States: Colonial Times to 1970, Part 1* (Washington, D.C., 1976), 12, 14.

19. *Whom Shall We Welcome: Report of the President's Commission on Immigration and Naturalization* (Washington, D.C., 1953), 104.

20. Robert Divine, *American Immigration Policy, 1924–1952* (New Haven, Conn., 1957), 165–66.

21. U.S. Senate Committee on the Judiciary, *The Immigration Systems of the United States*, 81st Cong., 2nd Sess., 1950, Senate Report 1515, 455.

22. Ibid., 212.

23. Ibid., 252.

24. Michael Ybarra, *Washington Gone Crazy: Senator Pat McCarran and the Great American Communist Hunt* (Hanover, N.H., 2004), 228.

25. Ibid., 759, 758. Ybarra wrote, "McCarthy spoke of twenty years of treason. McCarran spoke of treason for twenty years. The difference is that McCarran did something about it. McCarthy left no legislative legacy. . . . McCarran did not create American anti-Communism alone, but his role was bigger and more important that that of his colleague."

26. Ibid, 7.

27. Oscar Handlin, "The Immigration Fight Has Only Begun," *Commentary*, July 1952, 3.

28. Stephen Thomas Wagner, "The Lingering Death of the National Origins Quota System: A Political History of United States Immigration Policy, 1952–1965," Ph.D. dissertation, Harvard University, 1986, 250–51.

29. C.P. Trussell, "Congress Passes Immigration Bill," *New York Times*, June 12, 1952. This provision retained certain racialist elements. The ceiling on immigration from the Asia-Pacific Triangle also included Asians who were citizens of another country. For instance, an immigrant of Chinese ancestry from a country other than China was included under these limits.

30. *Cong. Rec.*, 82th Cong., 1st Sess., April 23, 1952, 4314.

31. Ibid., 4316; *Cong. Rec.*, 82th Cong., 2nd Sess., June 26, 1952, 8215.

32. *Cong. Rec.*, 82th Cong., 2nd Sess., May 13, 1952, 5094.

33. Ibid., 5095.

34. Ibid., May 14, 1952, 5094, 5167.

35. Ibid., May 16, 1952, 5330.

36. Ibid., May 13, 1952, 5089.

37. Ibid., April 25, 1952, 4440.

38. Ibid., May 13, 1952, 5102.

39. Samuel Lubell, *The Future of American Politics* (New York, 1952).

40. *Cong. Rec.*, 82 Cong., 2nd Sess., May 14, 1952, 5162; June 27, 1952, 8256.

41. Ibid., April 23, 1952, 4310; May 14, 1952, 5157.

42. Ibid., May 14, 1952, 5162; April 23, 1952, 4310.

43. Ibid., April 23, 1952, 4305; May 14, 1952, 5158.

44. Ibid., April 25, 1952, 4441.

45. "Veto Wanted," *New York Times*, June 13, 1952.

46. *Cong. Rec.*, 82 Cong., 2nd Sess., April 25, 1952, 4435, 4439.

47. *Crisis*, April 1952, 235.

48. Matthew Frye Jacobson, *Whiteness of a Different Color: European Immigrants and the Alchemy of Race* (Cambridge, Mass., 1998), 116–17.

49. *Cong. Rec.*, 82 Cong., 2nd Sess., May 13, 1952, 5102; May 14, 1952, 5170.

50. Divine, *American Immigration Policy*, 183. The House passed the measure by a vote of 205–68. The Senate passed the bill by voice vote because the opponents wanted to save their resources for a fight over the president's veto.

51. *The Public Papers of the President of the United States: Harry S. Truman, 1952–53* (Washington, D.C., 1966), 443.

52. Ibid.

53. Anthony Leviero, "President Vetoes Immigration Policy as Discriminatory," *New York Times*, June 26, 1952.

54. *Cong. Rec.*, 82th Cong., 2nd Sess., June 27, 1952, 8254.

55. Divine, *American Immigration Policy*, 185. In the Senate, the South supported the bill by a margin of 18–3, the Far West 15–5, and the Midwest 15–8. The margins in the House were basically the same: 91–3 in the South, 35–12 in the Far West, and 96–32 in the Midwest.

56. "Victory for a Bad Bill," *New York Times*, June 28, 1952.

57. *Whom Shall We Welcome*, xii.

58. David McCullough, *Truman* (New York, 1992), 770–71.

59. Anthony Leviero, "Truman Says GOP Backs Racial Bias," *New York Times*, October 10, 1952.

60. Ibid.

61. Anthony Leviero, "Truman Asserts Eisenhower Endorses 'Reign of Terror': In Boston Speech, He Says the Republican Crusade Thrives on Slander," *New York Times*, October 18, 1952. For more on the DP bill, see Chapter 4.

62. Richard H. Parke, "Memorial Diners Hear Eisenhower"; "Text of Eisenhower's Addresses at Waldorf-Astoria Dinner and in Patterson Armory," *New York Times*, October 17, 1952.

63. "Text of Eisenhower's Address on the Boston Common," *New York Times*, October 22, 1952.

64. "Text of General Eisenhower's Address at Madison Square Garden Last Night," *New York Times*, October 31, 1952.

65. Kalman Siegel, "Sparkman Puts Blame for Inflation on Republican 'High Price Boys,'" *New York Times*, October 2, 1952; "Text of Address by Governor Stevenson in Chicago," *New York Times*, October 22, 1952.

66. W. H. Lawrence, "Stevenson Says GOP Hurts Effort to Gain Korea Peace," *New York Times*, October 30, 1952.

67. Oscar Handlin, "We Need More Immigrants," *Atlantic Monthly*, May 1953, 27.

68. "Text of Address by Governor Stevenson in Chicago," *New York Times*, October 22, 1952.

69. Though he probably does not remember, I credit Eric Foner for this analogy. He made it during a discussion of a paper by Professor Aristide Zolberg at Columbia University in fall 2001.

70. *Whom Shall We Welcome*, 23, 24.

71. Ibid., 26.

72. Ibid., 96.

73. Ibid., 97.

74. Ibid., 118–23.

75. *The Public Papers of the President of the United States: Dwight D. Eisenhower, 1953* (Washington, D.C., 1960), 12.

76. "Eisenhower Urges U.S. Admit 240,000 Above Alien Quota," *New York Times*, April 23, 1953.

77. "Senate, 63–30, Votes to Let 209,000 Refugees into U.S.," *New York Times*, July 30, 1953. Two-thirds of the senators voting against the bill came from the South.

78. See Chapters 2 and 3 for more on I Am an American Day.

79. "The American Legion Constitution Day-Citizenship Day Program," AJC Records, RG 347.17.10, Gen-10, Box 98, Holidays and Holydays, 1948–1968, YIVO, AJHS.

80. Milton Bracker, "16,000 Take Oaths as Citizens Here," *New York Times*, November 12, 1954. Included were 41 former Nazi rocket scientists who became citizens in Birmingham, Alabama. See "41 Pledge Allegiance," *New York Times*, November 12, 1954.

81. "Show Of New Hands," *Life*, November 22, 1954, 49.

82. "Text of U.S. Attorney General's Talk to New Citizens," *New York Times*, November 12, 1954.

83. Oscar Handlin, *The Uprooted: The Epic Story of the Great Migrations That Made the American People* (New York, 1951), 170.

84. Ibid.

85. Ibid., 200.

86. Nathan Glazer, "The Integration of American Immigrants," *Law and Contemporary Problems* 21, 2 (Spring 1956): 267.

87. Ibid., 268.

88. Ibid., 269.

89. Louis L. Jaffe, "The Philosophy of Our Immigration Law," *Law and Contemporary Problems* 21, 2 (Spring 1956): 359.

90. Ibid., 360.

91. Everett Augspurger and Richard McLemore, *Our Nation's Story* (Chicago, 1954), 520.

92. Ralph Volney Harlow, *Story of America* (New York, 1953), 283 (emphasis added).

93. Henry Bragdon and Samuel McCutchen, *History of a Free People* (New York, 1954), 541.

94. Center for Migration Studies of New York, ACIM General Record, Miscellaneous Speeches, 1934–66, CMA Archive, Staten Island, N.Y.

95. "Make Freedom's Birthday Count," AJC Records, RG 347.17.10, Gen-10, Box 98, Holidays and Holydays, 1941–56, Independence Day, YIVO, AJHS.

96. "The Fence," AJC Records, RG 347.17.10, Gen-10, Box 147, The Fence, YIVO, AJHS.

97. "In Quest of Freedom," AJC Records, RG 347.17.10, Gen-10, Box 147, In Quest of Freedom, YIVO, AJHS.

98. Ibid.

99. *The Public Papers of the President of the United States: Dwight D. Eisenhower*, 240.

100. Francis Walter, "The War Against Our Immigration Law," *Human Events*, April 20, 1957.

101. *Blackboard Jungle*, dir. Richard Brooks (MGM, 1955).

102. Mae Ngai, *Impossible Subjects: Illegal Aliens and the Making of Modern America* (Princeton, N.J., 2004), 54–55.

103. See Camille Guerrin-Gonzales, *Mexican Workers, American Dreams: Immigration, Repatriation, and California Farm Labor, 1900–1939* (New Brunswick, N.J., 1994), 77–96.

104. Juan Ramon Garcia, *Operation Wetback: The Mass Deportation of Mexican Undocumented Workers in 1954* (Westport, Conn., 1980), 43.

105. Ibid., 36.

106. Eleanor Hadley, "A Critical Analysis of the Wetback Problem," *Law and Contemporary Problems* 21, 2 (Spring 1956): 334.

107. Garcia, *Operation Wetback*, 143–44.

108. Gladwin Hill, "Two Every Minute Across the Border," *New York Times Magazine*, January 31, 1954.

109. "Statement of J. Walter Mason, National Legislative Representative, American Federation of Labor, Before the Senate Judiciary Committee on S. 3660, 3661,

Concerning Illegal Immigration into the United States, July 13, 1954," 1, RG 21, AFL-CIO, Department of Legislation Records, 1906–1978, Box 27, Folder 14, George Meany Memorial Archives, National Labor College, Silver Spring, Md.

110. Garcia, *Operation Wetback*, 116, 125.

111. Ibid., 157–68.

112. Ibid., 169–223.

113. Ibid., 226.

114. *Cong. Rec.*, 84th Cong., 2nd Sess., June 4, 1956, 9465.

115. *Gallup Poll: Public Opinion 1935–1971*, vol. 2, *1949–58* (New York, 1972), 1340.

116. "Statement of Hyman Bookbinder," 7, 9, NAACP Papers, Part IX, Box 107, Folder 6, LOC.

117. Harry N. Rosenfield, "The Prospects for Immigration Amendments," *Law and Contemporary Problems* 21, 2 (Spring 1956): 405–6, 426.

118. Walter, "The War Against Our Immigration Law."

119. "'National Orgins' Should Be Kept in Immigration Law," *Saturday Evening Post*, April 20, 1957, 10.

120. Robert C. Alexander, "Our National Origins System: The Mirror for America," *American Legion Magazine*, September 1956, excerpted in *Debating American Immigration, 1882–Present*, ed. Roger Daniel and Otis L. Graham (Lanham, Md., 2001), 198–99. One AJC member conceded that Alexander's charge was "a tough one to answer": Otis Graham, "Regulating Immigration in the National Interest," in *Debating American Immigration, 1882–Present*, 142.

121. Graham, "Regulating Immigration in the National Interest," 143–44.

122. John Kennedy, *A Nation of Immigrants* (New York, 1958), 6.

123. Ibid., 11–15, 20–21.

124. Ibid., 35.

125. Ibid., 37.

Chapter 6. The Cold War and Religious Unity

1. Will Herberg, *Protestant, Catholic, Jew: An Essay in American Religious Sociology* (Garden City, N.Y., 1955), 258.

2. "The Message of the Four Chaplains," December 9, 1949, AJC Records, RG 347.17.10, Gen-10, Box 98, Holidays and Holydays, 1944–1957, Four Chaplains Day, YIVO, AJHS.

3. "Text of Truman Dedicating Chapel," *New York Times*, February 4, 1951.

4. Ibid.; "Four Chaplains," February 7, 1951, Universal Newsreels, RG 200, Vol. 24, No. 428, NACP.

5. Ibid., newsreel.

6. "Four Chaplains Honored," *New York Times*, May 26, 1952.

7. "Legion to Honor Four Chaplains," *New York Times*, January 27, 1952.

8. *Cong. Rec.*, 83rd Cong., 2nd Sess., June 7, 1954, 7758.

9. *Cong. Rec.*, 83rd Cong., 1st Sess., Appendix, February 16, 1953, A668.

10. Ibid. I could not find a record of whether this resolution passed.

11. See Chapter 5 for more on McCarthy and the impact of the Cold War.

12. Mark Silk, *Spiritual Politics: Religion and America Since World War II* (New York, 1988), 96–99.

13. *Cong. Rec.*, 83rd Cong., 2nd Sess., June 7, 1954, 7758, 7764.

14. Ibid., 7765, 7764.

15. "'Faith' Stamp Issued," April 18, 1954, Universal Newsreels, RG 200, Vol. 27, No. 559, NACP.

16. *Cong. Rec.*, 84th Cong., 2nd Sess., June 7, 1955, 7798.

17. "The Church and the Synagogue Teach the Meaning of GOOD NEIGHBOR," NCCJ, Box 5, Brotherhood Week 1955, SWHA, Elmer L. Andersen Library, University of Minnesota, Minneapolis.

18. "Brotherhood—A Dynamic Force," NCCJ, Box 5, Brotherhood Week 1955, SWHA.

19. "Suggestions for Speakers and Discussion Leaders," 1, NCCJ, Box 5, Brotherhood Week 1955, SWHA.

20. Ibid., 4.

21. "Suggestions for Programming Brotherhood Week," 1, NCCJ, Box 5, Brotherhood Week 1955, SWHA.

22. "Live Copy for . . . STATION BREAKS, Brotherhood Week Spots, February 20–27, 1955," NCCJ, Box 5, Brotherhood Week 1955, SWHA.

23. Ibid.

24. For a full-length examination of this concept, see Kevin Schultz, *Tri-Faith America: How Catholics and Jews Held Postwar America to Its Protestant Promise* (New York, 2011).

25. Silk, *Spiritual Politics*, 41.

26. Ibid., 40–53

27. Ibid., 44.

28. "Text of Eisenhower Speech," *New York Times*, December 23, 1952.

29. Silk, *Spiritual Politics*, 49.

30. Theodore Roosevelt, *The Works of Teddy Roosevelt*, vol. 13 (New York, 1926), 25; Woodrow Wilson, *The Public Papers of Woodrow Wilson, the New Democracy: Presidential Messages, Addresses and Other Papers*, vol. 1, ed. Ray Standard Baker and William E. Dodd (New York, 1926), 319.

31. See Introduction for more on Roosevelt's and Wilson's views and Chapter 1 for more on the debate over immigration restriction in 1924.

32. Herberg, *Protestant, Catholic, Jew*, 50.

33. Ibid., 91 92.

34. Ibid., 52.

35. Louis Hartz, *The Liberal Tradition in America: An Interpretation of American Political Thought Since the Revolution* (New York, 1955); Daniel Bell, *The End of Ideology: On The Exhaustion of Political Ideas in the Fifties* (Glencoe, Ill., 1960).

36. Herberg, *Protestant, Catholic, Jew*, 96.

37. Ibid., 73.

38. Ibid., 59.

39. Stephen Whitfield, *The Culture of the Cold War* (Baltimore, 1991), 87.

40. Ibid., 83.

41. *Gallup Poll: 1935–1971*, vol. 2, *1949–58* (New York, 1972), 902, 1479.

42. Whitfield, *The Culture of the Cold War*, 78–79, 84.

43. Ibid., 83. Whitfield wrote that, during the 1950s, "certain traits reasserted themselves, such as the tendency to equate faith with individual success and prosperity, and the assumption that national well-being was a sign of divine approval. What intensified such beliefs was the need to combat a political system [Communism] that was above all, defined as godless."

44. Charles Stember, *Jews in the Mind of America* (New York, 1966), 121, 106, 96.

45. Alan Petigny, *The Permissive Society: America, 1941–1965* (Cambridge, Mass., 2009), 82–86.

46. *ADL Bulletin*, December 1958, 4.

47. Fletcher Knebel, "Democratic Forecast: A Catholic in 1960," *Look*, March 3, 1959, 15.

48. Stember, *Jews in the Mind of America*, 126.

49. Quoted in Richard Polenberg, *One Nation Divisible: Class, Race, and Ethnicity in the United States Since 1938* (New York, 1980), 139.

50. Albert Gordon, "Suburbia: 'Just a Pleasant Hello,'" *ADL Bulletin*, October 1959, 3.

51. Ibid.

52. Polenberg, *One Nation Divisible*, 147. See also Joshua Michael Zeitz, *White Ethnic New York: Jews and Catholics and the Shaping of Postwar Politics* (Chapel Hill, N.C., 2007).

53. Christopher Finan, *Alfred E. Smith: The Happy Warrior* (New York, 2002), 210, 211.

54. Writing in *American Political Science Review* in June 1961, Philip Converse and three coauthors from the University of Michigan declared, "most of what attracted attention as a Republican trend among Catholics during the 1950's finds little support in our data, at least as a trend peculiar to Catholics." They noted that, while some Democratic Catholics defected to vote for Eisenhower in 1952 and 1956, they did so at lower rates than Democratic Protestants. Though their analysis argues that there was no long-term shift of Catholics to the GOP, Converse and his coauthors still show there was at least a minor shift to Ike during the 1950s. Even if later analysts found no such trend, Democrats of the late 1950s certainly believed it at the time. Philip E. Converse, Angus Campbell, Warren E. Miller, and Donald E. Stokes, "Stability and Change in 1960: A Reinstating Election," *American Political Science Review* 55, 2 (June 1961): 275.

55. *Gallup Poll*, vol. 2, 1574.

56. Thomas Carty, *A Catholic in the White House? Religion, Politics, and John F. Kennedy's Presidential Campaign* (New York, 2004), 67.

57. Knebel, "Democratic Forecast: A Catholic in 1960," *Look*, March 3, 1959, 17.

58. "More Catholic Papers Comment on Remarks of Sen. Kennedy," Theodore E. Sorensen Papers, Campaign Files 1959–60, Box 24, Religious Issues, Articles and Clippings, Folder 1, JFK Library (JFK), Boston.

59. "Senator Kennedy and His Critics," *Commonweal*, Sorensen Papers, Campaign Files 1959–60, Box 24, Religious Issues, Articles and Clippings, Folder 3, JFK.

60. William Weart, "Dispute Clouded Chapel At Start," *New York Times*, January 17, 1960.

61. John D. Morris, "Kennedy Pledges a Firm Presidency," *New York Times*, January 15, 1960.

62. "Excerpts from Remarks of Theodore C. Sorensen, February 1960, The Catholic Issue in American Politics," Sorensen Papers, Campaign Files 1959–60, Box 25, Campaign Material, Folder 1, JFK.

63. Theodore White, *The Making of the President 1960* (New York, 1961), 92–93. White's *The Making of the President* is the classic examination of the 1960 campaign. For an updated look, see W. J. Rohrbaugh, *The Real Making of the President: Kennedy, Nixon, and the 1960 Election* (Lawrence, Kan., 2009).

64. Ibid, 95.

65. The Wisconsin Democratic primary allowed Republicans and independents to participate alongside Democrats.

66. James Reston, "Wisconsin Wins Again," *New York Times*, April 7, 1960.

67. James Reston, "Washington: Kennedy at Critical Point in Campaign," *New York Times*, April 8, 1960.

68. "Politics: The Catholic Issue," *Time*, April 18, 1960, 16.

69. "Religion Plays Part in Wisconsin Vote," *Christian Century*, April 20, 1960, Sorensen Papers, Campaign Files 1959–60, Box 24, Religious Issues, Articles and Clippings, Folder 1, JFK.

70. Robert Dallek, *An Unfinished Life: John F. Kennedy, 1917–1963* (Boston, 2003), 251.

71. White, *The Making of the President 1960*, 94.

72. Roosevelt, *The Works of Theodore Roosevelt*, vol. 13, 25.

73. Wilson, *Public Papers of Woodrow Wilson*, 319.

74. For more on the Johnson-Reed Act, see Chapter 1.

75. W. H. Lawrence, " 'Stop Kennedy' Drive Led by Byrd of West Virginia," *New York Times*, April 11, 1960.

76. "Memorandum to: Senator Kennedy and Staff on the Relation of Protestantism to the West Virginia Primary," Sorensen Papers, Campaign Files 1959–60, Box 24, Religion Issue, General Folder 3, JFK.

77. W. H. Lawrence, "Kennedy Charges 'Gang-Up' by Foes," *New York Times*, April 19, 1960.

78. "Text of Speeches by Kennedy, Symington, and Humphrey at Editors' Convention," *New York Times*, April 22, 1960.

79. Kennedy won with 60 percent to Humphrey's 40 percent.

80. John D. Morris, "Triumph Is Hailed: Experts Say Religion Is No Bar—Johnson Cites Party Appeal," *New York Times*, May 12, 1960.

81. "Texts of Kennedy and Johnson Speeches Accepting Democratic Nomination," *New York Times*, July 16, 1960.

82. "You Can't Buy the White House," *Indianapolis Star*, August 14, 1960, Sorensen Papers, Campaign Files 1959–60, Box 24, Religious Issues, Articles and Clippings, Folder 3, JFK.

83. "Memorandum on the Religious Issue," emphasis original, August 15, 1960, Sorensen Papers, Campaign Files 1959–60, Box 25, Religious Issue, Campaign Material, Folder 1, JFK.

84. "The Campaign: The Power of Negative Thinking," *Time*, September 19, 1960, 21.

85. Stephen Ambrose, *Nixon: The Education of a Politician, 1913–1962* (New York, 1987), 564–67.

86. "Transcript of Kennedy Talk to Ministers and Questions and Answers," *New York Times*, September 13, 1960.

87. Ibid.

88. "Test of Religion," *Time*, September 26, 1960, 21.

89. D. E. Crimmins to Senator John F. Kennedy, October 6, 1960, Papers of President Kennedy, Pre-Presidential Papers, '60 Campaign, Issues, Religious Issue Files of James Wine 1960, Correspondence C-D, Box 1003, Folder C-1, JFK.

90. Walter J. Claeys to Senator John F. Kennedy, October 19, 1960, Papers of President Kennedy, Pre-Presidential Papers, '60 Campaign, Issues, Religious Issue Files of James Wine 1960, Correspondence C-D, Box 1003, Folder C-1, JFK.

91. Memo, "TO: Congressional Candidates, FROM: Research Division, Democratic National Committee," Papers of President Kennedy, Pre-Presidential Papers, '60 Campaign, Press and Publicity, DNC Press Releases 1958–60, Box 1034, Religious Answer Kits, 8/28/60–9/13/60, JFK.

92. The two major party presidential candidates still attend the memorial dinner every four years.

93. "Text of Speeches by Kennedy and Nixon at Al Smith Dinner Here," *New York Times*, October 20, 1960.

94. Ibid.

95. Leo Egan, "Issue of Church-State Separation Continues to Plague Both Sides in Presidential Race," *New York Times*, October 30, 1960.

96. "The Biggest 'Issue,'" *Newsweek*, November 7, 1960, 36.

97. Egan, "Issue of Church-State Separation," *New York Times*, October 30, 1960.

98. "Ike—Warming Up," *Newsweek*, October 31, 1960, 21.

99. "Sticky 'Issue,'" *Newsweek*, October 31, 1960, 20.

100. John Wicklein, "Religious Effect Not Nation-Wide," *New York Times*, November 11, 1960.

101. Arthur Krock, "In The Nation: Among the Most Important Electoral Consequences," *New York Times*, November 11, 1960.

102. This section from Dallek, *An Unfinished Life*, 296.

103. Converse et al., "Stability and Change," 270, 273, 278.

104. Ibid., 279.

105. Ithiel Sola Pool, Robert P. Abelson, and Samuel L. Popkin, *Candidate, Issues, and Strategies: A Computer Simulation of the 1960 Presidential Election* (Cambridge, Mass., 1964), 115–18.

106. Ibid., 118.

Chapter 7. The Triumph of Contributionism

1. *Cong. Rec.*, 89th Cong., 1st Sess., September 20, 1965, 24482–83.

2. Ibid., September 14, 1965, 23793.

3. Byrd had also admitted to briefly being a member of the Ku Klux Klan in the 1940s.

4. *Cong. Rec.*, 89th Cong., 1st Sess., September 14, 1965, 23793.

5. David Reimers, *Still the Golden Door: The Third World Comes to America* (New York, 1985), 63–90.

6. See Chapter 6 for more on Herberg.

7. For more on JFK and *A Nation of Immigrants*, see Chapter 5.

8. Steven Gillon, *"That's Not What We Meant to Do": Reform and Its Unintended Consequences in Twentieth Century America* (New York, 2000), 166.

9. See Chapter 5 for more on *Whom Shall We Welcome*.

10. Tom Wicker, "President Urges Repeal of Quotas for Immigration," *New York Times*, October 24, 1963.

11. *Public Papers of the President of the United States: John F. Kennedy, 1961* (Washington, D.C., 1962), 595.

12. Ibid., 596. The triangle also hurt America's international standing because it embodied racialist principles. For instance, a person of Indian descent who was a British citizen was counted under the India quota, not the British one.

13. Ibid., 595.

14. Ibid.

15. Wicker, "President Urges Repeal of Quotas for Immigration," *New York Times*, July 24, 1963.

16. *Public Papers of the President of the United States: John F. Kennedy*, 596.

17. Wicker, "President Urges Repeal of Quotas for Immigration," *New York Times*, July 24, 1963.

18. Maldwyn Allen Jones, *American Immigration* (Chicago, 1960), 309.

19. Ibid., 317.

20. Ibid., 319.

21. Ibid.

22. Nathan Glazer and Daniel Patrick Moynihan, *Beyond the Melting Pot: The Negroes, Puerto Ricans, Jews, Italians, and Irish of New York City* (Cambridge, Mass., 1963), 12.

23. Ibid., 14.

24. Ibid., 13.

25. Ibid.

26. John F. Kennedy, *A Nation of Immigrants* (New York, 1964), 67. I have not been able to determine precisely who made the revisions. It is possible that John Roche, who wrote a foreword to an edition released in the 1980s, was responsible.

27. Howard Wilder, Robert P. Ludlum, and Harriet McCune Brown, *This Is America's Story* (Boston, 1960), 501–2, 509.

28. See Chapter 2 for more on *Americans . . . All* and Chapter 5 for more on *Whom Shall We Welcome*

29. Wilder et al., *This Is America's Story*, 505, 507.

30. Ibid., 509.

31. Glenn W. Moon and Don C. Cline, *Story of Our Land and People* (New York, 1964), 558, 557.

32. Melvin Schwartz and John O'Connor, *Exploring America's History* (New York, 1966), 326–27.

33. John W. Caughey, John Hope Franklin, and Ernest E. May, *Land of the Free: A History of the United States* (New York, 1966), 413.

34. Ibid., 416–17.

35. Schwartz and O'Connor, *Exploring American History*, 327.

36. Kennedy, *A Nation of Immigrants*, 63.

37. Ibid.

38. Schwartz and O'Connor, *Exploring American History*, 327.

39. Moon and Cline, *Story of Our Land and People*, 557–58. Caughey et al., *Land of the Free*, 418–19: "In the 1870s workingmen in California became aroused against all Chinese. Chinese had then come by the thousands and were willing to take work of any kind and any wages offered. . . . Meanwhile, the national government was persuaded to take action. In 1882, Congress passed a Chinese Exclusion Act which put a stop to immigration from China."

40. *The Pawnbroker*, dir. Sidney Lumet (Republic, 1965)

41. *Exodus*, dir. Otto Preminger (MGM, 1960).

42. For more on these films, see Mark Harris, *Pictures at a Revolution: Five Movies and the Birth of the New Hollywood* (New York, 2008); Aram Goudsouzian, *Sidney Poitier: Man, Actor, Icon* (Chapel Hill, N.C., 2004).

43. See Mark Noll, *American Evangelical Christianity: An Introduction* (Malden, Mass., 2001), 122–32. Graham quote, 123.

44. Andrew Greeley, *The Catholic Revolution: New Wine, Old Wineskins, and the Second Vatican Council* (Berkeley, Calif., 2004), 54.

45. Robert Doty, "Pope Paul Promulgates Five Council Documents, One Absolving the Jews," *New York Times*, October 29, 1965.

46. Lloyd Garrison, "Church Council Votes Unity Talk," *New York Times*, January 20, 1965; Gladwin Hill, "Lutherans in U.S. Vote to Meet Catholics in Ecumenical Talks," February 10, 1965; George Dugan, "Protestant Sees Less Fear of Rome," May 9, 1965.

47. "1965 Brotherhood Week Statements," NCCJ, Box 6, Brotherhood Week 1965, SWHA, Elmer L. Andersen Library, University of Minnesota, Minneapolis.

48. John Cogley, "Pope's Trip Seen as Sign of Church's New Link with Secular World," *New York Times*, October 5, 1965.

49. "The Pope: 'Live and Help Live'," *Newsweek*, October 18, 1965, 41.

50. Bernard Weintraub, "A Transfixed City," *New York Times*, October 5, 1965.

51. "The Pope: 'Live and Help Live'."

52. Cogley, "Pope's Trip Seen as Sign of Church's New Link with Secular World."

53. The percentage of Americans who said they would never marry a Jew declined from 57 percent in 1950 to 37 percent in 1962; 95 percent of respondents in 1962 declared that it "wouldn't make any difference" if their neighbor was Jewish, up from 69 percent in 1950. Traditional fears about excessive Jewish political influence had also lost much of their power. In 1945, 58 percent of respondents said yes when asked, "Do you think the Jews have too much power in the United States?" By 1962, this percentage had declined to 17 percent. See Charles Stember, *Jews in the Mind of America* (New York, 1966), 106, 96, 121.

54. "The New American Jew," *Time*, June 25, 1965, 24.

55. Ibid.

56. C. P. Trussell, "New Alien Quotas Urged by Kennedy," *New York Times*, July 23, 1964.

57. "Quota Immigration Criticized by Rusk," *New York Times*, July 3, 1964.

58. Gillon, *"That's Not What We Meant to Do"*, 169–70.

59. *Minutes of Meetings, Executive Council, AFL-CIO, February, April, May, September, October, December 1965*, vol. 10, 62, George Meany Memorial Archives, National Labor College, Silver Spring, Md.

60. Radio Interview, "Senator Edward Kennedy on New Immigration Bill," April 11, 1965; Records of the U.S. Information Agency, 1900–1988, RG 306, NACP.

61. Hearings Before the Subcommittees on Immigration and Naturalization of the Committee on the Judiciary, United States Senate, 89th Cong., 1st Sess. (Washington, D.C., 1965), 496.

62. Ibid., 383.

63. Gillon, *"That's Not What We Meant to Do"*, 173.

64. Ibid, 173.

65. The Voting Rights Act, signed by President Johnson in the summer of 1965, guaranteed African Americans in the South the right to vote.

66. *Cong. Rec.*, 89th Cong., 1st Sess., August 25, 1965, 21783, 21784.

67. "Farewell to Quotas," *New York Times*, August 5, 1965.

68. I examined all *Crisis* issues for 1965. See also Ira Berlin, *The Making of African America: The Four Great Migrations* (New York, 2010), 5–6. Berlin observed that "the black press hardly noted the occasion."

69. *Cong. Rec.*, 89th Cong., 1st Sess., August 25, 1965, 21771, 21590.

70. Ibid., 21594, 21590.

71. See Chapters 3 and 4 for more on the acceptance of the ideological view of the war.

72. Peter Novick, *The Holocaust in American Life* (Boston, 1999), 127–44. See also Hasia R. Diner, *We Remember with Reverence and Love: American Jews and the Myth of Silence After the Holocaust, 1945–1962* (New York, 2009) for more on Holocaust memory during the 1950s and early 1960s.

73. *Cong. Rec.*, 89th Cong., 1st Sess., August 25, 1965, 21784, 21779.

74. Ibid., August 24, 1965, 21597; August 25, 1965, 21781.

75. Ibid., 21799, 21783.

76. Ibid., 21784.

77. Ibid., 21774.

78. Ibid., 21775, 21786.

79. Ibid., 21774.

80. *Cong. Rec.*, 89th Cong., 1st Sess., August 24, 1965, 21591.

81. Ibid., August 25, 1965, 21759, 21760.

82. Cabell Phiillips, "The House Approves Bill for Reform of Immigration," *New York Times*, August 26, 1965. Southern Democrats opposed the legislation by a margin of 62–30 and accounted for two-thirds of the no votes. Stephen Thomas Wagner, "The Lingering Death of the National Origins Quota System: A Political History of United States Immigration Policy, 1952–1965," Ph.D. dissertation, Harvard University, 1986, 438.

83. Cabell Phiilips, "The House Approves Bill for Reform of Immigration."

84. Cabell Phillips, "Senators Weigh Immigrant Curb," *New York Times*, August 28, 1965.

85. Cabell Phillips, "Immigration Bill Gains in Senate," *New York Times*, August 27, 1965.

86. *Cong Rec.*, 89th Cong., 1st Sess., September 20, 1965, 24469–70.

87. Ibid., September 17, 1965, 24228; September 22, 1965, 24777.

88. Ibid., September 20, 1965, 24467, 24485, 24467.

89. Ibid., September 21, 1965, 24563; September 20, 1965, 24501. D'Alessandro, Jr., is the father of former speaker of the House Nancy Pelosi (D) of California.

90. *Cong. Rec.*, 89th Cong., 1st Sess., September 20, 1965, 24502; September 22, 1965, 24777.

91. Ibid., September 22, 1965, 24776.

92. Gillon, *"That's Not What We Meant to Do"*, 171.

93. The *New York Times* published a UPI article on September 22 which reported that Senator Javits "introduced an amendment yesterday to eliminate the hemispheric ceiling, but he indicated that it was doubtful he would call it up for a vote." "Immigration Change Backed," *New York Times*, September 22, 1965.

94. *Cong. Rec.*, 89th Cong., 1st Sess., September 17, 1965, 24237; September 22, 1965, 24769.

95. Ibid., September 22, 1965, 24772; September 21, 1965, 24544.

96. Ibid., September 21, 1965, 24554.

97. Ibid., September 22, 1965, 24776, 24778.

98. Ibid., 24669, 24770.

99. Ibid., 24779, 24757.

100. "Hart" refers to Senator Philip Hart (D) of Michigan.

101. Mae Ngai, *Impossible Subjects: Illegal Aliens and the Making of Modern America* (Princeton, N.J., 2003), 263. "By extending the system of formal equality in admissions to all countries, the new law affected immigration from the Third World differently—creating greater opportunities for migration from Asia and Africa, but severely restricting it from Mexico, the Caribbean, and Latin America."

102. Pub. Law 89–236, 79 Stat. 911. Previously, only spouses and unmarried minor children could enter outside the quota system.

103. "A New Day in Immigration," *New York Times*, September 24, 1965.

104. Phillips, "Congress Sends Immigration Bill to White House," *New York Times*, October 1, 1965. For more on FDR's 1936 speech, see Chapter 2.

105. John Higham, "The Transformation of the Statue of Liberty," in Higham, *Send These to Me: Immigrants in Urban America* (Baltimore, 1975), 71–80.

106. "Text of President's Speech on Immigration," *New York Times*, October 4, 1965.

107. For more on Ellis Island's history, see Vincent Cannato, *American Passage: The History of Ellis Island* (New York, 2009).

108. National Park Service, *A Study Report on Ellis Island* (Washington, D.C., 1964), 7.

109. Ibid., 16.

110. "Text of President's Speech on Immigration."

Epilogue: "How great to be an American and something else as well"

1. U.S. Department of Homeland Security, Office of Immigration Statistics, *2003 Yearbook of Immigration Statistics* (Washington, D.C., 2004), 13–14.

2. U.S. Census Bureau, "Profile of the Foreign-Born Population in the United States: 2000," December 2001, 9; "The Foreign-Born Population in the United States: 2010," May 4, 2012, http://www.census.gov/prod/2012pubs/acs-19.pdf.

3. *2003 Yearbook of Immigration Statistics*, 13–14.

4. Ibid.

5. Census, "Profile of the Foreign-Born Population in the United States: 2000," 9.

6. Jeffrey Passel, "The Size and Characteristics of the Unauthorized Migrant Population in the U.S.," Research Report, Pew Hispanic Center, Washington, D.C., March 7, 2006, 2.

7. Stokely Carmichael and Charles Hamilton, *Black Power: The Politics of Liberation in America* (New York, 1967), 40, 44–45.

8. Michael Novak, *The Rise of the Unmeltable Ethnics: Politics and Culture in the Seventies* (New York, 1971), 72.

9. *The Godfather: Part II*, dir. Francis Ford Coppola (Paramount, 1974). While this scene is from the second film, it is a flashback to the beginning of Michael Corleone's story.

10. *The Godfather*, dir. Francis Ford Coppola (Paramount, 1972).

11. Michael Novak, *The Rise of the Unmeltable Ethnics*, paperback ed. (New York, 1973), xiv. The discussion of *The Godfather* came in the preface to the paperback edition.

12. *School House Rock: Special Thirtieth Anniversary Edition*, music and lyrics by Lynn Ahrens (Buena Vista Home Entertainment, 2002).

13. "The Big 200th Bash," *Time*, July 5, 1976, 14.

14. *The Public Papers of the Presidents of the United States: Gerald R. Ford, 1976–77*, Book 2 (Washington, D.C., 1979), 1975, 1976.

15. Sara Rimer, "Across U.S., a Ceremony for History," *New York Times*, July 4, 1986.

16. Ibid.

17. *The Public Papers of the Presidents of the United States: Ronald Reagan, 1986*, Book 2 (Washington, D.C., 1989), 918, 920.

18. Matthew Frye Jacobson, *Roots Too: White Ethnic Revival in Post-Civil Rights America* (Cambridge, Mass., 1998), 321–36.

19. Meg Greenfield, "The Immigrant Mystique," *Newsweek*, August 8, 1988, 76.

20. Vincent Cannato, *American Passage: The History of Ellis Island* (New York, 2009), 396.

21. George Borjas, *Friends or Strangers: The Impact of Immigrants on the U.S. Economy* (New York, 1990), 134–35, 150.

22. Richard Bernstein, "Immigrant Celebration: Is the Experience Still Relevant?" *New York Times*, September 11, 1990.

23. Arthur Schlesinger, Jr., *The Disuniting of America: Reflections on a Multicultural Society* (New York, 1998), 23.

24. Patrick J. Buchanan, "Immigration Time-Out," *Washington Times*, October 31, 1994.

25. Samuel P. Huntington, *Who Are We? The Challenges to American Identity* (New York, 2004), 18.

26. Otis Graham, "Regulating Immigration in the National Interest," in *Debating American Immigration, 1882–Present*, ed. Roger Daniels and Otis L. Graham (Lanham, Md., 2001), 174–75.

27. Robert Pear, "President Signs Landmark Bill on Immigration," *New York Times*, November 7, 1986.

28. Aristide Zolberg, *A Nation by Design: Immigration Policy in the Fashioning of America* (Cambridge, Mass., 2006), 369.

29. Pear, "President Signs Landmark Bill on Immigration."

30. Zolberg, *A Nation by Design*, 373.

31. Philip Hilts, "Landmark Accord Promises to Ease Immigration Curbs," *New York Times*, October 26, 1990.

32. Ibid.; Roger Daniels, *Guarding the Golden Door: American Immigration Policy and Immigrants Since 1882* (New York, 2004), 238. For more on the 1990 bill, see Daniel Tichenor, *Dividing Lines: The Politics of Immigration Control* (Princeton, N.J., 2002), 267–74.

33. "Immigration," *Gallup.Com*, http://www.gallup.com/poll/1660/Immigration .aspx.

34. The state's share of foreign born grew from 9 percent in 1960 to 22 percent by 1990; Steven Gillon, *"That's Not What We Meant to Do": Reform and Its Unintended Consequences in Twentieth-Century America* (New York, 2000), 190.

35. R. Drummond Ayres, "A Ballot Proposition Gives Voters the Opportunity to Influence National Immigration Policy," *New York Times*, September 25, 1994.

36. A. M. Rosenthal, "As California Goes," *New York Times*, February 17, 1995.

37. Assessing Clinton's immigration record, Eric Schmitt wrote, "Still reeling from the devastating election results, Mr. Clinton vowed not to let Republicans out-flank him." "Milestones and Missteps on Immigration," *New York Times*, October 26, 1996.

38. Barbara Jordan, "The Americanization Ideal," *New York Times*, September 11, 1995.

39. Alison Mitchell, "President Rebuts Some G.O.P. Themes on Economic Woes," *New York Times*, September 5, 1995.

40. Steven A. Holmes, "Congress Plans Stiff New Curb on Immigration," *New York Times*, September 25, 1995.

41. Matthew Purdy, "Unlikely Allies Battle Congress over Anti-Immigration Plans," *New York Times*, October 11, 1995.

42. Ibid.

43. In 1996, two-thirds of the immigrants entering the country intended to live in California, Texas, New Jersey, Illinois, New York, and Florida. U.S. Department of Justice, Immigration and Naturalization Service, *1996 Statistical Yearbook of the Immigration and Naturalization Service* (Washington, D.C., 1997), 11.

44. Anthony Lewis, "Some Are Less Equal," *New York Times*, November 17, 1995.

45. Eric Schmitt, "Bill Tries to Balance Concerns on Immigration," *New York Times*, September 29, 1996.

46. "Immigration," *Gallup.Com*.

47. David Reimers, *Unwelcome Strangers: American Identity and the Turn Against Immigration* (New York, 1998), 145–46.

48. Alan Wolfe, *One Nation After All: What Middle-Class Americans Really Think About: God, Country, Family, Racism, Welfare, Immigration, Homosexuality, Work, the Right, the Left, and Each Other* (New York, 1998), 133–63, 142.

49. Passel, "The Size and Characteristics of the Unauthorized Migrant Population," i, 4.

50. Jeffrey Passel and D'Vera Cohn, "A Portrait of Unauthorized Immigrants into the United States," Pew Hispanic Center, Washington, D.C., April 14, 2009, 2.

51. "Immigration," *Gallup.Com*.

52. Robert Pear, "'86 Law Looms Over Immigration Fight," *New York Times*, June 12, 2007.

Bibliography

Archival Sources

AD Council Historical File, 1942–1997, University of Illinois Archives, Urbana.

American Jewish Committee (AJC) Records, Blaustein Library, American Jewish Committee Headquarters, New York.

Center for Migration Studies of New York, CMA Archive, Staten Island, New York.

Century of Progress World Exposition Collection, Yale Library, Yale University, New Haven, Connecticut.

George Meany Memorial Archives, National Labor College, Silver Spring, Maryland. Museum of Television and Radio (MTR), New York.

National Conference of Christians and Jews (NCCJ) Collection, Social Welfare History Archives (SWHA), Elmer L. Andersen Library, University of Minnesota, Minneapolis.

Papers of the NAACP, Library of Congress (LOC), Manuscript Reading Room, Washington, D.C.

Papers of the NAACP, microfilm, Rhode Island College, Providence.

Papers of President Kennedy, Pre-Presidential Papers, John F. Kennedy Library, Boston.

Records of the Office of Education (ROE), RG 12; National Archives, College Park, Maryland (NACP).

Records of the Office of Government Reports (ROGP), RG 44, NACP.

Records of the Immigration and Naturalization Service (INS), RG 85; National Archives Building (NAB), Washington, D.C.

Theodore E. Sorensen Papers, John F. Kennedy Library, Boston.

Universal Newsreels, RG 200, NACP.

YIVO Institute for Jewish Research, American Jewish Historical Society (AJHS), New York.

Serials

American Jewish Committee Reporter
Anti-Defamation League Bulletin
Atlantic Monthly

Chicago Daily Tribune
Chicago Defender
The Century
Common Ground
Commentary
Commonweal
Fortune
Harper's Weekly
Human Events
Life
Look
The Nation
Newsweek
New Republic
New York Times
Saturday Evening Post
Time
Washington Times
Watson's Magazine

Films

Blackboard Jungle. Directed by Richard Brooks. MGM, 1955.

Crossfire. Directed by Ed Dmytryk. RKO, 1947.

Exodus. Directed by Otto Preminger. MGM, 1960.

Gentlemen's Agreement. Directed by Elia Kazan. Fox, 1947.

The Godfather. Directed by Francis Ford Coppola. Paramount, 1972.

The Godfather: Part II. Directed by Francis Ford Coppola. Paramount, 1974.

Go for Broke! Directed by Robert Pirosh. MGM, 1951.

Guadalcanal Diary. Directed by Lewis Seller. Fox, 1943.

Gung Ho. Directed by Ray Enright. Republic, 1943.

The House I Live In. Directed by Mervyn LeRoy. RKO, 1945.

The Life of Hank Greenberg. Directed by Aviva Kempner. Fox, 1999.

The Pawnbroker. Directed by Sidney Lumet. Republic, 1965.

Pride of the Marines. Directed by Delmer Daves. Warner Brothers, 1945.

Sands of Iwo Jima. Directed by Allan Dwan. Republic, 1949.

School House Rock: Special Thirtieth Anniversary Edition. Directed by Tom Warburton.
    Buena Vista Home Entertainment, 2002.

Steel Helmet. Directed by Sam Fuller. Lippert, 1951.

Why We Fight. Directed by Frank Capra. Special Service Division, Army Service Forces.
    episode 7.

Published References

Adamic, Louis. *A Nation of Nations*. New York, 1944.

———. "No 'Hyphens' This Time." *New York Times Magazine*, November 1, 1942.

———. "The St. Paul Festival of Nations." *Common Ground* 1, 4 (Summer 1941): 103–10.

———. "Thirty Million New Americans." *Harper's Weekly*, November 1934, 184–94.

Altschuler, Glenn C., and Stuart Blumin. *The G.I. Bill: A New Deal for Veterans*. Oxford, 2009.

Ambrose, Stephen. *Nixon: The Education of a Politician, 1913–1962*. New York, 1987.

Arnessen, Eric. "Whiteness and the Historians' Imagination." *International Labor and Working-Class History* 60 (Fall 2001): 3–32.

Bayor, Ronald. *Neighbors in Conflict: The Irish, Germans, Jews, and Italians of New York City, 1929–1941*. Baltimore, 1978.

Bayor, Ronald H. "Another Look at 'Whiteness': The Persistence of Ethnicity in American Life." *Journal of American Ethnic History* 29, 1 (Fall 2009): 13–30.

Bell, Daniel. *The End of Ideology: On the Exhaustion of Political Ideas in the Fifties*. Glencoe, Ill., 1960.

Bennett, David. *Party of Fear: From Nativist Movements to the New Right in American History*. New York, 1995.

Berlin, Ira. *The Making of African America: The Four Great Migrations*. New York, 2010.

Blum, John. *V Was for Victory: Politics and American Culture During World War II*. New York, 1976.

Bon Tempo, Carl J. *Americans at the Gate: The United States and Refugees During the Cold War*. Princeton, N.J., 2008.

Borjas, George. *Friends or Strangers: The Impact of Immigrants on the U.S. Economy*. New York, 1990.

Bortelsmann, Thomas. *The Cold War and the Color Line: American Race Relations in the Global Arena*. Cambridge, Mass., 2001.

Bourne. Randolph. *History of a Literary Radical and Other Essays*. New York, 1969 ed.

Brinkley, Alan. "The Illusion of Unity in Cold War Culture." In *Rethinking Cold War Culture*, ed. Peter Kuznick and James Gilbert. Washington, D.C., 2001.

———. *Voices of Protest: Huey Long, Father Coughlin, and the Great Depression*. New York, 1982.

Cannato, Vincent. *American Passage: The History of Ellis Island*. New York, 2009.

Carmichael, Stokely, and Charles Hamilton. *Black Power: The Politics of Liberation in America*. New York, 1967.

Carty, Thomas. *A Catholic in the White House? Religion, Politics, and John F. Kennedy's Presidential Campaign*. New York, 2004.

Caute, David. *The Great Fear: The Anti-Communist Purge Under Truman and Eisenhower*. New York, 1979.

Chen, Anthony. *The Fifth Freedom: Jobs, Politics, and Civil Rights in the United States, 1941–1972*. Princeton, N.J., 2009.

Cohen, George. *The Jews in the Making of America*. Boston, 1924.

Converse, Philip E., Angus Campbell, Warren E. Miller, and Donald E. Stokes. "Stability and Change in 1960: A Reinstating Election." *American Political Science Review* 55, 2 (June 1961): 269–80.

Crevecoeur, J. Hector St. John de. *Letters from an American Farmer*. New York, 1981 ed.

Dallek, Robert. *An Unfinished Life: John F. Kennedy, 1917–1963*. Boston, 2003.

Daniels, Roger. *Asian America: The Chinese and Japanese in the United States Since 1850*. Seattle, 1988.

———. *Coming to America: A History of Immigration and Ethnicity in American Life*. New York, 2002.

———. *Guarding the Golden Door: American Immigration Policy and Immigrants Since 1882*. New York, 2004.

Daniels, Roger, and Otis L. Graham, eds. *Debating American Immigration, 1882– Present*. Lanham, Md., 2001

Denning, Michael. *The Cultural Front: The Laboring of American Culture in the Twentieth Century*. London, 1996.

Diner, Hasia R. *We Remember with Reverence and Love: American Jews and the Myth of Silence After the Holocaust, 1945–1962*. New York, 2009.

Dinnerstein, Leonard. *America and the Survivors of the Holocaust*. New York, 1982.

———. *Anti-Semitism in America*. New York, 1994.

Divine, Robert. *American Immigration Policy, 1924–1952*. New Haven, Conn., 1957.

Doherty, Thomas. *Projections of War: Hollywood, American Culture, and World War II*. New York, 1999.

Dower, John. *War Without Mercy: Race and Power in the Pacific War*. New York, 1986.

Du Bois, W. E. B. "The Negro Mind Reaches Out." In *The New Negro: An Interpretation*, ed. Alain Locke. New York, 1925.

Dudziak, Mary L. *Cold War Civil Rights: Race and the Image of American Democracy*. Princeton, N.J., 2000.

Filene, Peter "'Cold War Culture' Doesn't Say It All." In *Rethinking Cold War Culture*, ed. Peter Kuznick and James Gilbert. Washington, D.C., 2001.

Finan, Christopher. *Alfred E. Smith: The Happy Warrior*. New York, 2002.

Fitzgerald, Frances. *America Revised: History Textbooks in the Twentieth Century*. Boston, 1979.

Foner, Eric. *Story of American Freedom*. New York, 1998.

Fuchs, Lawrence. *American Kaleidoscope: Race, Class, and Civic Culture*. Hanover, N.H., 1990.

———. "The Reactions of Black Americans to Immigration" In *Immigration Reconsidered: History, Sociology, and Politics*, ed. Virginia Yans-McLaughlin. New York, 1990.

The Gallup Poll: Public Opinion 1935–1971. Vols. 1 and 2. New York, 1972.

Garcia, Juan Ramon. *Operation Wetback: The Mass Deportation of Mexican Undocumented Workers in 1954.* Westport, Conn., 1980.

Gerstle, Gary. *American Crucible: Race and Nation in the Twentieth Century.* Princeton, N.J., 2001.

Gillon, Steven. *"That's Not What We Meant to Do": Reform and Its Unintended Consequences in Twentieth-Century America.* New York, 2000.

Glazer, Nathan. "The Integration of American Immigrants." *Law and Contemporary Problems* 21, 2 (Spring 1956): 256–69.

———. *We Are All Multiculturalists Now.* New York, 1997.

Glazer, Nathan, and Daniel Patrick Moynihan, *Beyond the Melting Pot: The Negroes, Puerto Ricans, Jews, Italians, and Irish of New York City.* Cambridge, Mass., 1963.

Gleason, Philip. *Speaking of Diversity: Language and Ethnicity in Twentieth-Century America.* Baltimore, 1992.

Goodwin, Doris Kearns. *No Ordinary Time: Franklin and Eleanor Roosevelt: The Home Front in World War Two.* New York, 1994.

Goudsouzian, Aram. *Sidney Poitier: Man, Actor, Icon.* Chapel Hill, N.C., 2004.

Graham, Otis. "Regulating Immigration in the National Interest." In *Debating American Immigration, 1882–Present,* ed. Roger Daniels and Otis L. Graham. Lanham, Md., 2001.

Grant, Madison. *The Passing of the Great Race.* New York, 1916.

Greeley, Andrew. *The Catholic Revolution: New Wine, Old Wineskins, and the Second Vatican Council.* Berkeley, Calif., 2004.

Greenberg, Cheryl. *Troubling the Waters: Black-Jewish Relations in the American Century.* Princeton, N.J., 2006.

Gregory, James. *The Southern Diaspora: How the Great Migrations of Black and White Southerners Transformed America.* Chapel Hill, N.C., 2005.

Guerrin-Gonzales, Camille. *Mexican Workers, American Dreams: Immigration, Repatriation, and California Farm Labor, 1900–1939.* New Brunswick, N.J., 1994.

Guterl, Matt. *The Color of Race in America, 1900–1940.* Cambridge, Mass., 2001.

Hadley, Eleanor A. "A Critical Analysis of the Wetback Problem." *Law and Contemporary Problems* 21, 2 (Spring 1956): 334–57.

Handlin, Oscar. *The Uprooted.* New York, 1951.

Hansen, Marcus Lee. *The Atlantic Migration, 1607–1860.* Cambridge, Mass., 1940.

———. *The Immigrant in American History.* New York, 1940.

Harris, Mark. *Pictures at a Revolution: Five Movies and the Birth of the New Hollywood.* New York, 2008.

Hartz, Louis. *The Liberal Tradition in America: An Interpretation of American Political Thought Since the Revolution.* New York, 1955.

Hattam, Victoria. *In The Shadow of Race: Jews, Latinos, and Immigrant Politics in the United States.* Chicago, 2007.

Herberg, Will. *Protestant, Catholic, Jew: An Essay in American Religious Sociology*. Garden City, N.Y., 1955.

Hertzberg, Arthur. *The Jews in America: Four Centuries of an Uneasy Encounter: A History*. New York, 1989.

Higham, John. *Strangers in the Land: Patterns of American Nativism*. New Brunswick, N.J., 1955.

———. "The Transformation of the Statue of Liberty." In Higham, *Send These to Me: Immigrants in Urban America*, 71–80. Baltimore, 1975.

Hirsch, Arnold. *The Making of the Second Ghetto: Race and Housing in Chicago, 1940–1960*. New York, 1983.

Hollinger, David. *Postethnic America: Beyond Multiculturalism*. New York, 1995.

Huntington, Samuel P. *Who Are We? The Challenges to American Identity*. New York, 2004.

Hutchinson, E. P. *Legislative History of American Immigration Policy*. Philadelphia, 1981.

Huthmacher, J. Joseph. *Senator Robert F. Wagner and the Rise of Urban Liberalism*. New York, 1968.

Hyatt, Marshall. *Franz Boas, Social Activist: The Dynamics of Ethnicity*. New York, 1990.

Jacobson, Matthew Frye. *Roots Too: White Ethnic Revival in Post-Civil Rights America*. Cambridge, Mass., 2006.

———. *Whiteness of a Different Color: European Immigrants and the Alchemy of Race*. Cambridge, Mass., 1998.

Jaffe, Louis L. "The Philosophy of Our Immigration Law." *Law and Contemporary Problems* 21, 2 (Spring 1956): 358–75.

Jones, Maldwyn Allen. *American Immigration*. Chicago, 1960.

Kanstrom, Daniel K. *Deportation Nation: Outsiders in American History*. Cambridge, Mass., 2007.

Kennedy, David. *Freedom from Fear: The American People in Depression and War*. New York, 1999.

———. *Over Here: The First World War and American Society*. New York, 1980.

Kennedy, John F. *A Nation of Immigrants*. New York, 1958; 2nd ed. 1964.

King, Desmond. *Making Americans: Immigration, Race, and the Origins of the Diverse Democracy*. Cambridge, 2000.

Kraut, Alan. *Huddled Masses*. Arlington Heights, Va., 1982.

Lawson, Steve. *Running for Freedom: Civil Rights and Black Politics in America Since 1941*. New York, 1991.

Lind, Michael. *The Next American Nation: The New Nationalism and the Next American Revolution*. New York, 1995.

Lipstadt, Deborah. *Beyond Belief: The American Press and the Coming of the Holocaust, 1933–1945*. New York, 1986.

Loescher, Gil, and Scanlan John. *Calculated Kindness: Refugees and America's Half-Open Door, 1945 to the Present*. New York, 1986.

Lubell, Samuel. *The Future of American Politics*. New York, 1952.

Martin, Susan. *A Nation of Immigrants*. Cambridge, Mass., 2011.

Marzio, Peter C., ed. *A Nation of Nations: The People Who Came to America as Seen Through Objects and Documents Exhibited at the Smithsonian Institution*. New York, 1976.

McCullough, David. *Truman*. New York, 1992.

McSweeney, Edward F. "Racial Contributions to America." Knights of Columbus, *www.kofcmuseum.org/en/resources/racial_contributions_b.pdf.*

Mettler, Suzanne. *Soldiers to Citizens: The G.I. Bill and the Making of the Greatest Generation*. Oxford, 2005.

Mirel, Jeffrey. *Patriotic Pluralism: Americanization Education and European Immigrants*. Cambridge, Mass., 2010.

Moore, Deborah Dash. *At Home in America: Second-Generation New York Jews*. New York, 1991.

———. *GI Jews: How World War II Changed a Generation*. Cambridge, Mass., 2004.

Morgan, Chester M. *Redneck Liberal: Theodore G. Bilbo and the New Deal*. Baton Rouge, La., 1985.

Murrow, Edward R. *In Search of Light: The Broadcasts of Edward R. Murrow, 1938–1961*. New York, 1967.

Myrdal, Gunnar. *An American Dilemma: The Negro Problem and Modern Democracy*. New York, 1944.

National Park Service. *A Study Report on Ellis Island*. Washington, D.C., 1964.

Natural Resources Committee. *The Problems of a Changing Population*. Washington, D.C., 1938.

Ngai, Mae. *Impossible Subjects: Illegal Aliens and the Making of Modern America*. Princeton, N.J., 2004.

Noll, Mark. *American Evangelical Christianity: An Introduction*. Malden, Mass., 2001.

Novak, Michael. *The Rise of the Unmeltable Ethnics: Politics and Culture in the Seventies*. New York, 1971.

Novick, Peter. *The Holocaust in American Life*. Boston, 1999.

Passel, Jeffrey. "The Size and Characteristics of the Unauthorized Migrant Population in the U.S." Research Report, Pew Hispanic Center. Washington, D.C., March 7, 2006.

Passel, Jeffrey, and D'Vera Cohn. "A Portrait of Unauthorized Immigrants in the United States." Pew Hispanic Center, Washington, D.C., April 14, 2009.

Patterson, James. *Grand Expectations: The United States, 1945–1974*. New York, 1996.

Petigny, Alan. *The Permissive Society, America, 1941–65*. Cambridge, Mass., 2010.

Pitt, James. *Adventures in Brotherhood*. New York, 1955.

Polenberg, Richard. *One Nation Divisible: Class, Race, and Ethnicity in the United States Since 1938*. New York, 1980.

Pool, Ithiel Sola, Robert P. Abelson, and Samuel L. Popkin. *Candidate, Issues, and Strategies: A Computer Simulation of the 1960 Presidential Election*. Cambridge, Mass., 1964.

The Public Papers of the Presidents of the United States: Harry S. Truman: . . . *1945–1952/3.* Washington, D.C., 1961–66.

———. *Dwight D. Eisenhower:* . . . *1953-[1960–61].* Washington, D.C., 1958–61.

———. *John F. Kennedy:* . . . *1961–1963.* Washington, D.C., 1962–64.

———. *Gerald R. Ford:* . . . *August 9, 1974, to January 20, 1977.* Washington, D.C., 1975–79.

———. *Ronald Reagan: 1981–1988–89.* Washington, D.C., 1982–91.

Reimers, David. *Still the Golden Door: The Third World Comes to America.* New York, 1985.

———. *Unwelcome Strangers: American Identity and the Turn Against Immigration.* New York, 1998.

Ribuffo, Leo. *The Old Christian Right: The Protestant Far Right from the Great Depression to the Cold War.* Philadelphia, 1983.

Roediger David. *Wages of Whiteness: Race and the Making of the American Working Class.* London, 1991.

———. *Working Toward Whiteness: How America's Immigrants Became White.* Cambridge, Mass., 2005.

Rohrbaugh, W.J. *The Real Making of the President: Kennedy, Nixon, and the 1960 Election.* Lawrence, Kan., 2009.

Roosevelt, Franklin D. *Nothing to Fear: The Selected Addresses of Franklin Roosevelt, 1932–1945.* Boston, 1946.

—. *The Public Papers and Addresses of Franklin Roosevelt.* 13 vols. Comp. Samuel I. Rosenman. New York, 1938–[c1950].

Roosevelt, Theodore. *The Works of Teddy Roosevelt.* Vol. 13. New York, 1926.

Rosenfield, Harry N. "The Prospects for Immigration Amendments." *Law and Contemporary Problems* 21, 2 (Spring 1956): 401–26.

Rydell, Robert. *World of Fairs: The Century- of- Progress Expositions.* Chicago, 1993.

Schlesinger, Arthur, Jr. *The Disuniting of America: Reflections on a Multicultural Society.* New York, 1998.

Schrecker, Ellen. *Many Are the Crimes: McCarthyism in America.* Boston, 1998.

Schultz, Kevin. *Tri-Faith America: How Catholics and Jews Held Postwar America to Its Protestant Promise.* New York, 2011.

Selig, Diana. *Americans All: The Cultural Gifts Movement.* Cambridge, Mass., 2008.

Shankman, Arnold. *Ambivalent Friends: Afro-Americans View the Immigrant.* Westport, Conn., 1983.

Short, K. R. M. "Hollywood Fights Anti-Semitism." In *Feature Films as History,* ed. K. R. M. Short. Knoxville, Tenn., 1981. 157–89.

Silk, Mark. *Spiritual Politics: Religion and America Since World War II.* New York, 1988.

Sollors, Werner. *Beyond Ethnicity: Consent and Descent in American Culture.* New York, 1986.

Steele, Richard. "The War Against Intolerance: The Reformulation of American Nationalism." *Journal of American Ethnic History* 9 (Fall 1989): 9–35.

Stember, Charles Herbert. *Jews in the Mind of America*. New York, 1966.

Stephenson, George. *A History of American Immigration, 1820–1924*. Boston, 1926.

Stoddard, Lothrop. *Re-Forging America: The Story of Our Nationhood*. New York, 1927.

Stouffer, Samuel, Edward A Suchman, Leland C. Devinney, Shirley A. Star, and Robin M. Williams, Jr. *The American Soldier: Adjustment During Army Life*. Vol. 1. New York, 1949.

Sugrue, Thomas. *The Origins of the Urban Crisis: Race and Inequality in Postwar Detroit*. Princeton, N.J., 1996.

Svonkin, Stuart. *Jews Against Prejudice: American Jews and the Fight for Civil Liberties*. New York, 1997.

Terkel, Studs. *"The Good War": An Oral History of World War Two*. New York, 1984.

Tichenor, Daniel. *Dividing Lines: The Politics of Immigration Control*. Princeton, N.J., 2002.

Ueda, Reed. "The Changing Path to Citizenship: Ethnicity and Naturalization During World War II." In *The War and American Culture*, ed. Lewis Erenberg and Susan Hirsch. Chicago, 1996.

U.S. Department of Commerce, Bureau of the Census. "Educational Attainment of the Population 25 Years Old and Over in the United States: 1940." April 25, 1942.

———. "The Foreign-Born Population in the United States: 2010." May 2012.

———. *Historical Statistics of the United States: Colonial Times to 1970, Part 1*. Washington, D.C., 1976.

———. "Profile of the Foreign-Born Population in the United States: 2000." December 2001.

U.S. Department of Homeland Security, Office of Immigration Statistics. *2003 Yearbook of Immigration Statistics*. Washington, D.C., 2004.

U.S. Department of Justice, Immigration and Naturalization Service. *1996 Statistical Yearbook of the Immigration and Naturalization Service*. Washington, D.C., 1997.

U.S. House Committee on Immigration and Naturalization. 76th Cong., 1st Sess., *Admission of German Refugee Children*. Washington, D.C., 1939.

———. 71st Cong., 2nd Sess., March 13, 1930. *Immigration from Countries of the Western Hemisphere*. Washington, D.C., 1930.

U.S. Senate Committee on the Judiciary, 81st Cong., 2nd Sess. *The Immigration Systems of the United States*. 1950. Senate Report 1515.

———. Subcommittees on Immigration and Naturalization of the Committee on the Judiciary. 89th Cong., 1st Sess. Washington, D.C., 1965.

U.S. Senate and House. Subcommittee of the Committee on Immigration, Senate and Subcommittee of the Committee on Immigration and Naturalization, House. 76th Cong., 1st Sess. *Admission of German Refugee Children*. Washington, D.C., 1939.

Wagner, Stephen Thomas. "The Lingering Death of the National Origins Quota System: A Political History of United States Immigration Policy, 1952–1965." Ph.D. dissertation, Harvard University, 1986.

Wall, Wendy. *Inventing the "American Way": The Politics of Consensus from the New Deal to the Civil Rights Movement.* Oxford, 2008.

Weiss, Richard. "Ethnicity and Reform: Minorities and the Ambience of the Depression Years." *Journal of American History* 66 (December 1979): 566–85.

White, Theodore. *The Making of the President 1960.* New York, 1961.

Whitfield, Stephen J. *The Culture of the Cold War.* Baltimore, 1991.

Whom Shall We Welcome: Report of the President's Commission on Immigration and Naturalization. Washington, D.C., 1953.

Wilson, Woodrow. *The Public Papers of Woodrow Wilson, the New Democracy: Presidential Messages, Addresses and Other Papers.* Vol. 1. Ed. Ray Standard Baker and William E. Dodd. New York, 1926.

Winkler, Allan M. *The Politics of Propaganda: The Office of War Information, 1942–1945.* New Haven, Conn., 1978.

Wittke, Carl. *We Who Built America: The Saga of the Immigrant.* New York, 1939.

Wolfe, Alan. *One Nation After All: What Middle-Class Americans Really Think About: God, Country, Family, Racism, Welfare, Immigration, Homosexuality, Work, the Right, the Left, and Each Other.* New York, 1998.

Wong, K. Scott. *Americans First: Chinese Americans and the Second World War.* Cambridge, Mass., 2005.

Ybarra, Michael. *Washington Gone Crazy: Senator Pat McCarran and the Great American Communist Hunt.* Hanover, N.H., 2004.

Zangwill, Israel. *The Melting Pot: Drama in Four Acts.* New York, 1975 ed.

Zeitz, Joshua Michael. *White Ethnic New York: Jews and Catholics and the Shaping of Postwar Politics.* Chapel Hill, N.C., 2007.

Zimmerman, Jonathan. *Whose America? Culture Wars in the Public Schools.* Cambridge, Mass., 2002.

Zohlberg, Aristide. *A Nation by Design: Immigration Policy and the Fashioning of America.* Cambridge, Mass., 2006.

Textbooks

Augspurger, Everett, and Richard McLemore. *Our Nation's Story.* Chicago, 1954.

Barker, Eugene C., and Henry Steele Commager. *Our Nation.* Evanston, Ill., 1941.

Barker, Eugene C., William E. Dodd, and Henry Steele Commager. *Our Nation's Development.* Evanston, Ill., 1934.

Beard, Charles, and William C. Bagley. *History of the American People.* New York, 1928.

Beard, Charles, and Mary Beard. *History of the United States.* New York, 1925.

Bourne, Henry Eldridge, and Elbert Jay Benton. *A History of the United States.* Boston, 1925.

Bragdon, Henry, and Samuel McCutchen. *History of a Free People.* New York, 1954.

Canfield, Leon H., Howard B. Wilder, Frederic L. Paxson, Ellis Merton Coulter, and Nelson P. Mead. *The United States in the Making.* Boston, 1937; 2nd ed. 1946.

Caughey, John W., John Hope Franklin, and Ernest May. *Land of the Free: A History of the United States.* New York, 1966.

Faulkner, Harold Underwood, Tyler Kepner, and Edward H. Merrill. *History of the American Way.* New York, 1950.

Fish, Carl Russell. *History of America.* New York, 1925.

Freeland, George, and James Thurlow Adams. *America and the New Frontier.* New York, 1936.

————. *America's Progress in Civilization.* New York, 1949.

Harlow, Ralph Volney. *Story of America.* New York, 1937; 2nd ed. 1947; 3rd ed. 1953.

Latane, John Holladay. *The History of the American People.* Boston, 1938; 2nd ed., 1948.

Moon, Glenn. *Story of Our Land and People.* New York, 1949.

Moon, Glenn, and Don C. Cline. *Story of Our Land and People.* New York, 1964.

Schwartz, Melvin, and John O'Connor, *Exploring America's History.* New York, 1966

Tryon, Rolla M., and Charles Lingley. *The American People and Nation.* Boston, 1927.

Wilder, Howard, Robert P. Ludlum, and Harriet McCune Brown. *This Is America's Story.* Boston, 1960.

Index

Acknowledgments

To list everyone I need to acknowledge will be extremely difficult, but there is no doubt my immediate family deserves to be listed first. My parents, Bruce and Ruth Fleegler, provided considerable moral and financial support throughout the whole process, from the first to the last draft of the book. Furthermore, my sister Melissa also offered tremendous support, including copyediting the entire manuscript, providing an invaluable service.

James Paterson was an excellent primary reader, getting back chapters unbelievably quickly. While I might have seemed frustrated by his input at times, his comments dramatically improved the manuscript. Matthew Frye Jacobson at Yale took on a student from another institution and gave tremendous help in shaping the direction of the project. Howard Chudacoff offered important assistance, while Elliott Gorn and Mike Vorenberg also provided key comments. In particular, Mike Vorenberg gave key advice throughout my career and has continued to do so since I left Brown for the University of Mississippi.

I also benefited from help from a considerable number of Brown colleagues. In particular, Andrew Huebner read every chapter (in some cases more than once), and our daily lunches clearly shaped the focus of the book. Josh Zeitz also gave key comments on each chapter. A number of other friends read parts of the book and offered comments, including Alan Petigny, James Sparrow, Daniel Williams, and Morgan Grefe. Several other friends provided important assistance, including Chris Brick, Mark Robbins, Erik Andersen, Gabe Rosenberg, and Paige Meltzer.

Once I arrived at the University of Mississippi in 2006, I received help from several colleagues. Charles Eagles and Jeff Watt helped me navigate the publication process. Jeff also reviewed a copy of the all-important prospectus, as did Mindy Rice. As my only colleague at the Southaven campus since 2008, Mindy offered help in any number of other ways. My department chair at Ole Miss, Joe Ward, pushed for me to receive travel assistance so that I could finish the research necessary to make the changes required by Penn's outside readers.

A number of others offered assistance throughout the writing of the book. Alan Brinkley read the prospectus and gave me a research job when I was working on the manuscript in New York City. Mary Helen Dupree provided key help in bringing the project to fruition. Don Critchlow read the entire book and has offered help throughout my career. Sarah Potter read each chapter and provided essential assistance in getting the manuscript ready to be examined by academic presses.

Finally, I want to particularly thank my editor at Penn Press, Robert Lockhart, for expeditiously pushing the manuscript and getting it under contract. He has offered help at every turn and been incredibly responsive.